Consumption and Social Welfare

The most widely cited social welfare statistics in the United States are based on tabulations of family income. The picture that emerges is cause for concern; real median family income has hardly changed since the early 1970s, while inequality has increased and poverty has remained persistently high. Yet consumption-based statistics as employed in this work yield rigorous and quite different estimates of individual and social welfare. Closely linked to economic theory, Professor Slesnick's examination of standards of living, inequality, and poverty reveals that the U.S. standard of living has grown significantly while poverty has decreased to relatively low levels. Inequality does not show the classic U-turn that is widely reported. Slesnick's assessment is drawn from extended period data in order to chart long-run trends. The work will be of interest to economists, sociologists, economic historians, political scientists, and other readerships in the social and policy sciences. Designed to be accessible to non-economists, it relegates technical details to appendixes.

Daniel T. Slesnick is Rex G. Baker, Jr. Professor of Political Economy at the University of Texas, Austin. His published research on applied microeconomics and related topics has appeared in eminent journals such as the *Journal of Political Economy*, the *Review of Economic Studies*, the *Economic Journal*, the *Review of Economics and Statistics*, and *The Journal of Econometrics*.

Consumption and Social Welfare

Living standards and their distribution in the
United States

DANIEL T. SLESNICK
University of Texas, Austin

CAMBRIDGE
UNIVERSITY PRESS

PUBLISHED BY THE PRESS SYNDICATE OF THE UNIVERSITY OF CAMBRIDGE
The Pitt Building, Trumpington Street, Cambridge, United Kingdom

CAMBRIDGE UNIVERSITY PRESS
The Edinburgh Building, Cambridge CB2 2RU, UK
40 West 20th Street, New York, NY 10011-4211, USA
10 Stamford Road, Oakleigh, VIC 3166, Australia
Ruiz de Alarcón 13, 28014 Madrid, Spain
Dock House, The Waterfront, Cape Town 8001, South Africa

http://www.cambridge.org

First published 2001

Printed in the United States of America

Typeface Times Roman 10.5/13 pt.   *System* QuarkXPress [BTS]

A catalog record for this book is available from the British Library.

Library of Congress Cataloging in Publication Data
Slesnick, Daniel T.
    Consumption and social welfare: living standards and their distribution in
    the United States / Daniel T. Slesnick.
        p.   cm.
    Includes bibliographical references and index.
    ISBN 0-521-49720-5
    1. Income distribution – United States.   2. Cost and standard of living –
    United States.   3. Consumption (Economics) – United States.   4. United
    States – Economic conditions – 1945–   I. Title.
    HC110.I5 S616   2000
    339.4'7'097309049 – dc21

                                                                                99–047766

        ISBN   0 521 49720 5   hardback

Contents

Acknowledgments

A number of people have played important roles in this project. I have a tremendous intellectual debt to Dale Jorgenson, who has served as a mentor and role model over the last two decades. My hope is that I can be as helpful and generous to my students as he has been to me. Many friends and colleagues have commented on various aspects of this work and have helped shape the manuscript in a number of ways. While it is impossible to list all contributors, special thanks go to Doug Dacy, Price Fishback, Dan Hamermesh, Mun Ho, Henk Houthakker, Marvin Kosters, Arthur Lewbel, Pete Wilcoxen, and Frank Wolak. Many of the results presented here are extensions of joint research with Dale Jorgenson.

The professionals at Cambridge University Press have been enormously helpful in seeing this project through to completion. I'd like to thank Scott Parris for proposing that I undertake this task and helping me achieve closure. Janis Bolster's editorial assistance greatly improved the manuscript, and she showed infinite patience as I missed one deadline after another. Betsy Hardinger provided expert copyediting, and Shirley Kessel helped with the index.

Most important, Kathy provided unwavering love, understanding, and support. Tyson, Nolan, and Lara reminded me over and over again of the power of unconditional love. Donna and Irwin made all of this possible as dedicated, patient, and loving parents.

1 Introduction

Are you better off now than you were four years ago? This question is posed incessantly by politicians and reveals the key role of the standard of living and its distribution in the political economy of the United States. Even without the obfuscation induced by political rhetoric, an answer is far from straightforward. Should one's judgment be based exclusively on the change in material well-being, and if so, how should it be measured? How do changes in personal circumstances, such as the birth of a child, influence welfare? Should the crime rate or the level of pollution affect our assessment of living standards? How should welfare be compared across families and over time?

Despite the inherent complexity of the exercise, there is surprisingly little variation in the methods used to measure the standard of living in the United States. The foundation for most statistics is the level of family income, and with this as the basis, there is near unanimity of opinion as to what has happened to living standards since World War II. At the risk of oversimplification, the prevailing view can be summarized by three sets of statistics produced by the Bureau of the Census.[1]

---

1. The Gini coefficient of family income was obtained from the Bureau of the Census website. Median family income and the official poverty rate were obtained from various issues of the *Current Population Reports, Series P-60*. Median family income was adjusted for inflation using the Consumer Price Index for urban households (CPI-U). Unless otherwise noted, all future references to the CPI are to this index produced by the Bureau of Labor Statistics.

1

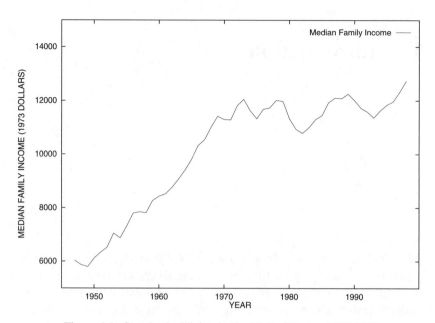

Figure 1.1. Standard of living in the United States, 1947–1998

Real median family income, shown in Figure 1.1, is often used to measure the average standard of living. This index shows substantial growth until the early 1970s (more than 2.5 percent per year) but little net change thereafter. For some analysts, this slowdown is evidence that, for the first time since the Great Depression, younger generations are at risk of having standards of living that are below those of their parents.

Not only is the size of the pie fixed, but the pie itself has become more unequally distributed. Much has been made of the infamous U-turn in income inequality. The Gini coefficient of family income, presented in Figure 1.2, shows that inequality decreased through the late 1960s and then, in 1998, reached its highest level since World War II. This precipitated a number of ominous articles over the last decade in the popular press about economic polarization in the United States and the disappearance of the middle class.[2]

2. As just two of many examples, see Andrew Hacker, "Meet the Median Family," *Time*, January 29, 1996, and Don L. Boroughs, "Winter of Discontent: With Wages Frozen, American Workers Find Themselves Out in the Cold," *U.S. News and World Report*, January 22, 1996.

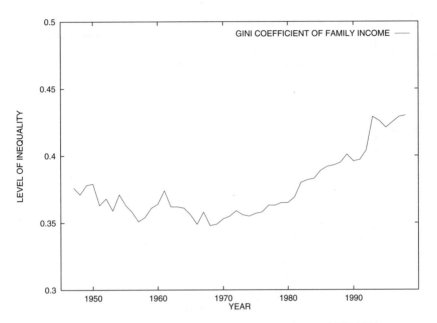

Figure 1.2. Income inequality in the United States, 1947–1998

The official poverty statistics have added fuel to the fire. The poverty rate (Figure 1.3) exhibited a trend that approximated the mirror image of median family income: it fell through the early 1970s and then increased in the 1980s. As late as 1993, 15.1 percent of the population was below the poverty line, a level that exceeded the poverty rate in 1966. The unhappy conclusion is that the gains in alleviating poverty in the first half of the postwar era were followed by a conspicuous lack of progress despite a concerted and expensive government initiative that began with President Johnson's War on Poverty.

I will present evidence to show that this pessimistic view of the standard of living in the United States is unwarranted and arises primarily from the inappropriate use of family income as a measure of well-being. Consumption provides a more accurate indicator of welfare, and its substitution for income leads to dramatically different conclusions. Consumption-based estimates of the standard of living show substantial growth, rather than stagnation, since 1970. Inequality and poverty rates based on households' consumption

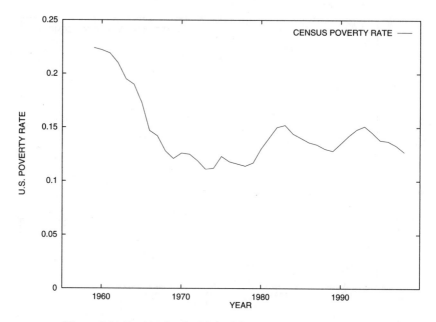

Figure 1.3. Poverty in the United States, 1959–1998

levels are substantially lower than those reported by the Bureau of the Census. The long-run trends of inequality and poverty in the United States differ markedly from those obtained using income as a measure of household welfare.

Why do consumption-based social welfare statistics present such a different picture? Differences in dispersion between the income and consumption distributions have behavioral explanations related to households' tendencies to smooth consumption over time in order to maintain their standard of living. When income is temporarily low, because the individual is young or has experienced a transitory reduction in income, consumption levels are preserved either by drawing down the savings account or by borrowing. The reverse occurs when income is temporarily high. The result is that income-based statistics overstate the extent of inequality and poverty relative to those calculated using consumption levels.

In Chapter 2 I present a conceptual framework for the use of consumption as a measure of welfare. An individual's material well-being is a function of the goods consumed rather than the income received.

This not only provides a more accurate "snapshot" view of welfare but also yields a better approximation of lifetime well-being. The choice of the appropriate "income" variable, however, is only one component of a measure of the standard of living. A price deflator is needed to convert nominal expenditures into real equivalents, and, as important, a method of comparing the welfare of different types of households must be developed.

The measurement of welfare at the micro level is an essential first step, but analysts are primarily concerned with the welfare of groups of households. In many applications, the aggregation problem is treated superficially. Median family income is a reasonable index of social welfare only if the family in the middle of the distribution is representative of the entire population. This need not be the case, and in fact, I'll show that this method of aggregation distorts the estimate of the average standard of living. Of course, any method of weighing the gains to some against the losses to others involves subjective judgments. My goal in this chapter is not to make a case for the perfect social welfare measure but rather to state explicitly the normative bases for various approaches and to assess the sensitivity of conclusions to these assumptions.

No matter how sound the conceptual framework, measures of welfare are only as good as the data used to calculate them. The first step is to describe what is included in consumption. It is common practice, for example, to measure consumption using the current level of spending. This ignores the fact that many items have an element of durability and are purchased infrequently. The measure of consumption should reflect the fact that the services received from a car extend beyond the year in which it was purchased. Some items, such as publicly provided goods or the leisure enjoyed by individuals, are not purchased but have a significant effect on the well-being of the population. Is it possible to include such items in a consumption-based measure of living standards?

Data availability is the primary obstacle to the measurement of a broadly defined concept of consumption. Aggregate estimates of many of the components of consumption are presented in the National Income and Product Accounts (NIPA) at annual and higher frequencies. Although these data can be used to examine national spending patterns and measure the average standard of living, they do not shed light on changes in the distribution of welfare. Distributional issues can be addressed only by using disaggregated information obtained from household survey data. Before 1980, surveys of household expenditures in the United States were administered approximately every decade. After 1980, comprehensive information on household spending became available on a quarterly basis. The differences in the methods of collecting the data and the length of time separating the surveys cause a number of problems that are difficult to resolve. Are the data sets comparable over time? Are the consumption data credible? How do they compare with estimates from the national accounts? Is there a sensible way to interpolate the consumption distribution between survey years? These issues and others are examined in Chapter 3.

An important input to the measurement of social welfare is an estimate of the cost of living. Comparisons over time must account for the fact that prices of goods and services have changed. A dollar today will not buy the same quantity of goods as a dollar ten years ago. Over the years, the CPI (Consumer Price Index) has served as the workhorse for converting nominal variables into real equivalents even though, as a price index, it is widely acknowledged to be flawed. Its treatment of owner-occupied housing, for example, resulted in an overestimate of the inflation rate in the late 1970s and early 1980s. It is overly aggregated and, therefore, unlikely to provide an accurate measure of the cost of living for households whose tastes and spending patterns differ markedly from the average. Moreover, there is no conceptual basis for using the CPI to compare living standards as prices change. In Chapter 4 I describe alternative price indexes at different levels of aggregation that are more suitable for this purpose.

Practical issues related to welfare comparisons of different types of households are examined in Chapter 5, where I implement a consumption-based index of the standard of living for the United States. The conclusions drawn from this index are at odds with the stylized facts. I find that social welfare has increased throughout the postwar period, and there is no indication of stagnation. On the contrary, recent growth rates are approximately equal to the historical average, and this finding of sustained growth is robust across alternative methods of measuring social welfare. In fact, among all indicators, median family income is unique in its depiction of a constant standard of living after the early 1970s.

For some analysts, growth is all that matters. For others, it's not the size of the pie but how it is divided. In Chapter 6 I show that consumption-based estimates of welfare indicate lower levels of inequality and greater progress in reducing inequality over time than do comparable estimates based on the income distribution. Income-inequality estimates (such as those shown in Figure 1.2) are misleading both because of the use of family income as a welfare measure and because of the failure to account for heterogeneity among families.

Some would argue that social policy should be judged on the basis of its ability to provide aid to our poorest citizens. With the Great Society initiative, a statistical program was developed to measure the gains in the War on Poverty. Unlike other social welfare statistics, poverty was defined on the basis of individuals' consumption levels. Annual income was used as a proxy for consumption because only income data were available at the required frequency.

In Chapter 7 I demonstrate that income is an inaccurate approximation for consumption among the poor. Consumption-based poverty rates are lower than comparable estimates computed using income. Replicating the method used by the Census Bureau to measure poverty but substituting consumption for income reduces the poverty rate by roughly 50 percent. Unlike the official estimates, my estimate of poverty decreases over time, although the magnitude of the reduction is sensitive to the method of accounting for differences in the consumption requirements of households.

What are the policy implications of these findings? The consumption-based social welfare statistics present a more optimistic picture of living standards in the United States. The standard of living is growing, and inequality and poverty are lower than previously thought. These empirical results suggest a number of questions to be answered by future research. Has the War on Poverty been won? Are taxes and transfers successful in reducing disparities among households? What accounts for the periods of high growth? A summary and some final thoughts are provided in the concluding chapter.

2 The measurement of economic welfare

2.1. INDIVIDUAL WELFARE

How should the standard of living be measured? Although welfare measurement is a fundamental element of economic analysis, it is also an undertaking fraught with peril. Well-being is influenced by a number of factors related not only to an individual's economic position but also to his or her social, political, physical, emotional, and psychological status. Measuring an inherently multidimensional concept by a single statistic almost certainly ignores relevant information.

The definition of welfare presented in this chapter is based exclusively on material well-being. This is obviously a narrow perspective, and there are compelling arguments for using information other than economic status. There are also many serious obstacles that have yet to be overcome. Rather than tackle these issues, I acknowledge at the outset that I am looking at only one of many possible dimensions of the standard of living. The development of a more comprehensive concept of individual and social welfare will be left for future investigation.

The key assumption of the traditional approach to welfare economics is that well-being is derived from the consumption of goods and services. The standard theoretical paradigm describes consumers as "rational" agents who choose the combination of goods that maximizes welfare (i.e., utility) subject to the constraint of limited financial resources. Well-being is a function of the quantities consumed so that, in this framework, it is at least theoretically possible to infer the level of welfare from the observed quantities of the goods consumed.

The earliest, and still the most popular, method of translating observed consumption into a measure of well-being is consumer's surplus. It is the amount, net of the actual expenditure, that an individual would be willing to pay for the right to purchase goods and services at market prices.[1] The concept is made operational by assuming that the marginal willingness to pay is represented by the demand curve so that the difference between the area under the demand curve (the total willingness to pay) and the amount actually spent provides an estimate of welfare.

Consumer's surplus is easy to compute since knowledge of the relationship between prices and the quantity demanded is all that is required. The inherent simplicity undoubtedly explains its widespread use, but the key question is whether it provides an accurate measure of welfare. In general, the answer is no. Only under empirically untenable conditions does the area under the demand curve represent the individual's utility level.[2] Although it is flawed, the use of consumer's surplus established a long tradition of welfare measurement that is appropriately based on individuals' consumption levels.

Alternative methods have been developed which do not have the same limitations. In the context of policy-induced price changes, Hicks's (1942) equivalent variation is the income an individual would be willing to sacrifice (before the price change) to attain the post-reform welfare level.[3] This is an "exact" measure of the change in well-being in the sense that it is positive if and only if the individual is better off before the reform. Although this resolved the conceptual problem of welfare measurement, Hicks's approach did little to help practitioners because his measures require knowledge of the compensated demands that (it was originally thought) are unobservable.

Willig (1976) made the first attempt to tackle this empirical problem by demonstrating that, in the case of a single price change, it is

1. This method originated with Dupuit (1844) but is largely associated with Marshall (1920).
2. A summary of the arguments against the use of consumer's surplus as a measure of welfare was provided by Samuelson (1947). See also Chipman and Moore (1976, 1980) and Slesnick (1998b).
3. The compensating variation is the amount the individual must be compensated at post-reform prices to attain the pre-reform level of welfare.

possible to use (observable) estimates of consumer's surplus to approximate the equivalent or compensating variations.[4] He gave a number of examples illustrating the accuracy of his approach, although it was only a matter of time before counterexamples (usually involving goods with large income effects) began to appear.[5] More damaging is the fact that, with multiple price and income changes, consumer's surplus is not single-valued and is of no use in providing an approximation to the Hicksian surplus measures.[6]

If consumer's surplus cannot be used as an approximation, is there any hope of obtaining a welfare measure that is ordinally equivalent to the utility function? Immediately following the publication of Willig's paper, empirical procedures were developed that had the same data requirements as consumer's surplus without the conceptual problems.[7] Each method requires the statistical estimation of demand functions that can be used to recover the underlying utility and expenditure functions.[8] The recovery procedure involves "integrating backwards" from the demands; in practice, this can be difficult if the functions are at all complicated. A monetary measure of individual welfare is the minimum income needed to attain this utility level and, unlike consumer's surplus, is ordinally equivalent to the utility function.

The measure of welfare used in subsequent empirical work is in this tradition. To describe it explicitly I assume that households, which are taken to be the basic economic units, consume N goods and have J characteristics which influence demand patterns. For household k, the quantity consumed of the ith good is x_{ik} and all households are

4. Since the equivalent and compensating variations provide upper and lower bounds for consumer's surplus, the accuracy of the approximation depends on the size of the income effect of the price change. This is a function of the magnitude of the price change, the importance of the good in the budget, and the income elasticity of demand.
5. For example, Hausman (1981) considered the problem of labor-leisure choice and found Willig's method to be inaccurate. Although his basic point was correct, Hausman's calculation of the error was overstated because of an arithmetic error. See Haveman, Gabay, and Andreoni (1987).
6. This point was illustrated by McKenzie (1979).
7. See Hausman (1981), Jorgenson, Lau, and Stoker (1980, 1981), McKenzie and Pearce (1976), Muellbauer (1974), Rosen (1978), and Vartia (1983). Other examples of this general approach are presented by Banks, Blundell, and Lewbel (1993) and Hausman and Newey (1995).
8. Specifically, the utility function is derived as a solution to a system of partial differential equations. The viability of this approach depends on the consistency of the estimated demands with the integrability conditions implied by utility maximization. See Hurwicz and Uzawa (1971) for further details and the summary by Jorgenson (1990).

assumed to face the same prices for goods and services given by the vector $\mathbf{p} = (p_1, p_2, \ldots, p_N)$. Total expenditure, the nominal value of consumption, is $M_k = \sum_{n=1}^{N} p_n x_{nk}$. Using this notation, I represent the welfare function of the kth household as[9]

$$W_k = \frac{M_k}{P_k(\mathbf{p}, \mathbf{p}_0, V_k) m_0(\mathbf{p}_0, V_k, \mathbf{A}_k)} \tag{2.1}$$

W_k can be interpreted as the level of consumption per household equivalent member. Nominal expenditure M_k is deflated by a household-specific price index $P_k(\mathbf{p}, \mathbf{p}_0, V_k)$ where $\mathbf{p}_0$ is the vector of prices in the initial or base period. V_k is the utility of the household that has total expenditure M_k and faces prices $\mathbf{p}$. Differences in the consumption requirements of households are accounted for by deflating total expenditure by $m_0(\mathbf{p}, V_k, \mathbf{A}_k)$ where $\mathbf{A}_k = (A_{1k}, A_{2k}, \ldots, A_{Jk})$ is a vector of household attributes such as family size, age, gender, and so on.

How does this welfare measure differ from real family income, the index most often used to measure the standard of living? First and foremost, the "income" concept is expenditure rather than before-tax income. This aspect of the index turns out to be particularly important in explaining differences between my estimates of the standard of living and those based on more traditional approaches. Moreover, whereas measures of welfare based on family income usually ignore heterogeneity, it is accounted for in (2.1) by deflating total expenditure by an equivalence scale. The differential impacts of relative price changes are incorporated using the indexes P_k, which vary across households. I consider the potential importance of each of these differences in turn.

2.2. THE "INCOME" CONCEPT

What "income" variable should be used to measure material well-being? To a large extent, the answer depends on the time horizon over which welfare is evaluated. For a single period, total expenditure is the right variable. If we want to measure welfare over the indi-

---

9. The ordinal equivalence of this index with the underlying utility function is demonstrated in the technical appendix to this chapter.

vidual's entire life, the appropriate summary variable is either the flow of "permanent" income or the stock of wealth.[10]

Clearly, an intertemporal measure of well-being is preferred. At a practical level, measuring the lifetime income as the annuity value of wealth requires enormous inputs of data that are difficult to obtain. Nonhuman wealth must be computed using inventories of physical and financial assets along with projected rates of return. This is a difficult but tractable exercise since there exist (infrequent) surveys of household wealth such as the *Survey of Consumer Finances* administered by the Federal Reserve Board.[11]

Nonhuman wealth, however, is only a fraction of the total wealth of most individuals. A typical medical student has few financial assets but high lifetime income embodied in the future return on education and training.[12] An accurate assessment of lifetime income must therefore include the expected return to a changing stock of human capital. At a micro level this is an onerous task because of the stringent data requirements and the assumptions needed for empirical implementation. If one yields to pragmatic considerations of tractability and restricts attention to either consumption or income, the question is, which variable provides a better approximation to lifetime income?

Friedman's (1957) permanent income hypothesis suggests that, on average, consumption should provide a more accurate proxy for welfare over an extended time horizon. If equal increments in consumption yield decreasing increments in utility (as seems reasonable), it follows that an individual will spread consumption over time rather than concentrate it in a single period.[13] Any deficit between

10. Some may view this indicator as excessively narrow as well. If individuals care not only about their own lifetime consumption but also about that of all future generations, then it is the consumption of the infinitely lived "dynasty" that is relevant to welfare measurement. The incorporation of this type of intergenerational altruism was introduced by Barro (1974) to analyze the impact of fiscal policy on economic behavior. Altonji, Hayashi, and Kotlikoff (1992) and Hayashi (1995), among others, test this hypothesis. Jorgenson, Slesnick, and Wilcoxen (1992) use a dynasty model to evaluate the welfare impacts of carbon taxes.
11. See, for example, Wolff (1994). Hurst, Luoh, and Stafford (1996) also examine the evolution of the wealth distribution using the Panel Study on Income Dynamics (PSID).
12. Empirical estimates indicate that human wealth is, by far, the largest component of most individuals' wealth holdings. Jorgenson and Fraumeni (1989), for example, show that human wealth is approximately 84 percent of aggregate wealth in the United States.
13. Although Friedman explicitly considered the issue of consumption smoothing over time, recent studies have considered the stronger proposition that individuals' con-

consumption and the realization of income is accommodated through dissaving, or borrowing. If income is unexpectedly high, the windfall is saved for a rainy day. Friedman postulated that consumption decisions are based on permanent income and that transitory changes in income have no influence on spending.[14]

If one accepts this description of spending behavior, it is clear that consumption likely provides a better approximation to lifetime welfare than does current income. The income of the medical student is temporarily low, but she has a high level of human wealth. Her consumption reflects her permanent income, and the consumption-to-income ratio is high. Because of this smoothing behavior, consumption more accurately reflects her lifetime well-being.[15]

More generally, consider the relationship between consumption and income for individuals at all points of the income distribution. Figure 2.1 shows the incomes of groups of individuals along the horizontal axis and their corresponding consumption levels on the vertical axis. Consumption decisions are based on permanent income, and the relationship is shown by the straight line emanating from the origin.[16] For individuals who have current incomes equal to the mean $\overline{Y}$, the transitory component is, on average, zero, and current income is equal to permanent income. The consumption for these individuals is $\overline{C}$.

sumption streams are insured against such events as unemployment, changes in health status, and the like. See, for example, Cochrane (1991), Nelson (1994), Mace (1991), Ravallion and Chaudhuri (1997), and Townsend (1994).

14. In the absence of owned financial assets, individuals must be able to borrow in order to smooth consumption over time. Evidence of the extent to which capital markets are imperfect and individuals are liquidity constrained is presented by Hall and Mishkin (1982), Mariger (1987), and Zeldes (1989). For a survey of the theoretical and empirical research describing the intertemporal allocation of consumption, see Deaton (1992).

15. Additional arguments for the use of consumption as a proxy for lifetime welfare in the United States are provided by Poterba (1989, 1991). Note, however, that consumption is a proxy for permanent income and can itself be a noisy measure of welfare. Indeed, Chaudhuri and Ravallion (1994) find that, in some cases, consumption gives a very inaccurate representation of lifetime well-being in village India. Moreover, Blundell and Preston (1998) note that consumption will provide a better indication of welfare for comparisons within age cohorts rather than between cohorts. There is no denying that consumption only approximates lifetime welfare. My contention is only that it is likely to be a more accurate indicator of lifetime welfare than is current income.

16. This reflects the empirical observation, originally attributed to Kuznets (1946), that, in the long run, the aggregate average propensity to consume in the United States is constant.

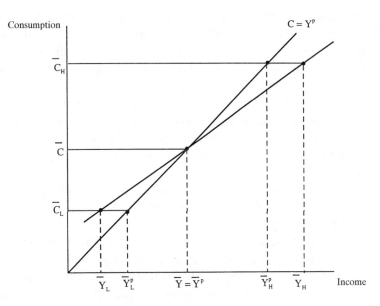

Figure 2.1. The relationship between consumption and income

For individuals whose incomes are less than the mean, the average transitory component of their income is negative so that current income $\overline{Y}_L$ is less than permanent income $\overline{Y}_L^P$. Since consumption decisions are based on the level of permanent income, their consumption is $\overline{C}_L$ and they have a high ratio of consumption to income. The reverse is true for high-income individuals whose current income $\overline{Y}_H$ exceeds their permanent income; their consumption is $\overline{C}_H$ and the consumption-to-income ratio is low.

The correspondence between consumption and income shown in Figure 2.1 illustrates why consumption outperforms income as a proxy for permanent income. For individuals who have current incomes less than the mean, permanent income is equal to consumption but is understated by current income.[17] The opposite holds for those who have higher than average incomes. In both cases, consumption is equal to permanent income and provides a more accurate reflection of lifetime welfare.

17. This assumes that the slope of the line going through the origin is 1. The qualitative feature of the argument is unaffected by a more realistic choice of the long-run average propensity to consume.

Because of consumption smoothing alone, income- and consumption-based welfare measures are likely to tell two different stories about living standards. However, there are other reasons why the two estimates might differ. Individuals pay taxes that vary systematically with their reported income. An index based on before-tax income can misrepresent the movement in both the level and the distribution of well-being as tax rates change.[18]

In the 1980s, approximately 60 percent of all households in the United States lived in their own home.[19] If the home is owned outright, little or no payment is made for housing services which contribute to the overall level of welfare. A similar issue arises with durable goods such as cars, major appliances, and so on. A comprehensive consumption-based index of the standard of living includes the services received from housing and durables, whereas a typical income-based estimate does not.

The magnitudes of each of these components could be large. Differences in the *levels* of income- versus consumption-based social welfare statistics can arise from changes in tax payments, homeownership, and the propensity to borrow and save. The *distributions* are also different because, with a progressive tax structure, households with low incomes pay less tax than the rich. If owner-occupied housing and consumer durables are luxuries, wealthier households receive more of these services than the poor. Systematic differences in saving patterns between the rich and the poor also cause differences between the income and consumption distributions.

2.3. PRICES AND ECONOMIC WELFARE

Consumption data in the United States (and most other countries) are reported as the expenditures of households. To compare welfare, it is therefore necessary to account for differences in the prices faced by households; an increase in total expenditure need not imply an increase in the quantities consumed. A natural question is whether

---

18. The degree of progression in the U.S. tax code and its impact on the income distribution have been the objects of substantial study. See Pechman (1985) and Fullerton and Rogers (1993), among others.
19. This estimate is based on tabulations using the Bureau of Labor Statistics' *Consumer Expenditure Surveys*.

the common practice of deflating expenditures by a national price index such as the CPI is appropriate for comparisons of the standard of living over time.

In any given year, the prices of virtually all goods and services change, with some increasing and others decreasing. A price index is designed to estimate the average magnitude of these changes from one period to the next. The CPI is a Laspeyres index that measures the cost of living as a weighted average of the changes of a large number of prices, using as weights the (fixed) proportions of total expenditure allocated to each commodity. Changes in the prices of goods that are important in the budget are, therefore, most influential in determining the cost of living.

Although widely used, the CPI is flawed as a measure of inflation for a variety of reasons. The spending on goods and services is assumed to be unchanged when, in fact, households adjust their spending patterns when relative prices change. If the price of beef increases, households substitute chicken for beef in their diets, thereby partially mitigating the effect of the price increase. This type of substitution is not accounted for in the CPI, and the inflation rate is overstated.[20]

A potentially more serious problem is the level of aggregation at which the CPI is applied. An individual living in Boston who commutes to work using public transportation does not allocate a large share of his budget to gasoline, oil, and vehicle maintenance. For somebody living in suburban Los Angeles who commutes 100 miles per day, transportation expenses are a larger fraction of total spending. Even if nominal prices are the same in Boston and Los Angeles, the impact of an increase in the relative price of gasoline leads to a larger increase in the cost of living for the person living in Los Angeles. A national price index cannot capture this effect.

More than a half century ago, disaggregated cost-of-living indexes were developed to measure the expenditure necessary to maintain one's standard of living as prices change.[21] These household-specific price indexes were defined as the ratio of the (minimum) expendi-

20. The price increase will be overestimated if the weights are the shares in the base period. Inflation is underestimated if the current period shares are used as in a Paasche index.
21. See, for example, Konus (1939). Modern developments in the theory of index numbers are summarized by Deaton and Muellbauer (1980) and in the collection of papers in Diewert (1990).

ture needed to attain a given level of utility at current prices to that required to attain the same welfare at base prices. Let $M(\mathbf{p}, V_k, \mathbf{A_k})$ be the expenditure function representing the minimum cost of attaining utility level V_k for a household with attributes $\mathbf{A_k}$ facing prices $\mathbf{p}$. The household's cost of living index for a change in prices from $\mathbf{p_0}$ to $\mathbf{p}$ is

$$P_k(\mathbf{p}, \mathbf{p_0}, V_k) = \frac{M(\mathbf{p}, V_k, \mathbf{A_k})}{M(\mathbf{p_0}, V_k, \mathbf{A_k})} \tag{2.2}$$

This index allows for the possibility that price changes affect households differently and accounts for substitution between goods as relative prices change. Perhaps more important, it is designed to address welfare economic questions. For a fixed level of total expenditure, a change in prices that causes P_k to increase necessarily implies that individual welfare has decreased.

To illustrate this approach to the measurement of the cost of living, assume for simplicity that a household consumes only food and clothing. The combinations of the two goods that yield the same utility are represented by the indifference contour U^0 in Figure 2.2. At the initial prices, the household's chosen combination of the two goods is rep-

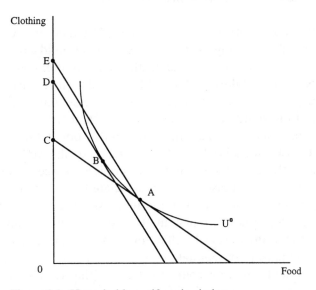

Figure 2.2. Household-specific price index

resented by point A, and total expenditure (deflated by the price of clothing) is given by point C. If the price of food increases while the price of clothing remains unchanged, the (optimal) market basket which yields the same utility is represented by point B. The total expenditure required to attain this welfare level at the new prices is given by point D, and the household price index is the ratio of the distance OD to OC.

Figure 2.2 illustrates the influence of households' spending habits on the cost-of-living index. The extent to which consumption patterns differ between the rich and the poor, those living in urban versus rural areas, or between males and females dictates the magnitudes of the differences between the price indexes. This is true even if all households face the same nominal prices for goods and services. Note, also, that the household adjusted its spending from market basket A to market basket B when prices changed. A fixed-weight index is calculated under the assumption that the quantities of food and clothing consumed remain unchanged. The total cost of this fixed market basket at the new prices is represented by point E, and the price index is the ratio of OE to OC, which overestimates the true inflation rate.

2.4. NEEDS AND ECONOMIC WELFARE

Perhaps the most controversial aspect of welfare measurement is the comparison of well-being of heterogeneous households. If a household of two adults has the same expenditure as another composed of two adults and two children, what can be said of their relative welfare levels? An answer to this simple question is essential to the measurement of the standard of living, inequality, and poverty.

The set of responses spans the spectrum of possibilities. At one extreme, the two households can be viewed as equally well off. If fertility is perfectly controllable and family size is a "choice" rather than a "constraint," the increase in utility associated with a larger family exactly compensates for the increase in consumption requirements. This is the assumption implicit in the use of real median family income as a measure of social welfare or the Gini coefficient of family income as a measure of inequality.

This argument fails to account for the fact that fertility decisions are made over the course of a lifetime in an environment of uncertainty. One's *ex ante* assessment of welfare may not coincide with *ex post* reality, and, unlike other goods, children cannot be discarded to obtain the "optimal" consumption bundle. Furthermore, there is the presumption that only the parents' preferences matter. The parents may be equally well off with the arrival of an additional child, but what of the other children, who must share a fixed level of resources with more people?[22]

At the opposite end of the spectrum is the assumption that households' needs increase linearly and identically with each additional member. This is the "per capita" adjustment and implies that a household with two adults and two children attains a standard of living equal to one-half that of two adults with the same expenditure. Although this adjustment is common, it relies on the dubious assumption that the needs of a child are the same as those of an adult. A per capita estimate also ignores potential economies of scale in consumption. We are all familiar with the old adage that two can live as cheaply as one. The extent to which this is true is ultimately an empirical question.

If one rejects these two types of adjustments, how should one compare the needs of heterogeneous households? A somewhat more sophisticated method of head-counting involves estimating the number of "equivalent adults" in the household. Suppose, for example, that children are equivalent to half an adult in terms of their needs. A couple with two children forms a household with three adult equivalents, has 50 percent greater consumption requirements, and has two-thirds the welfare of a childless couple with the same expenditure.[23]

In a survey of the literature, Deaton and Muellbauer (1980, p. 192) describe three methods that have been used to estimate the number of adult equivalent members in households. Perhaps the most widely used set of estimates is based on the nutritional requirements of each member. This appears to be an objective approach founded on firm scientific evidence of the intake necessary to avoid malnutrition, although there is far from a consensus among nutritionists as to what the nutritional standard should be.[24] Furthermore, man does not live

---

22. See Nelson (1993) for further elaboration of this point.
23. With economies of scale in consumption, the number of adult equivalents in the household would be even lower.
24. See Dasgupta and Ray (1990) for an overview of this debate.

by food alone, and comparisons of needs and welfare should reflect the fact that households consume goods other than food.

An alternative method that has been used in a number of applications is to convene a panel of experts for the purpose of assessing differences in needs. Adoption of this approach implicitly assumes that external third parties (the experts) are better informed than the households themselves (as revealed through their expenditure decisions) as to their consumption requirements. An inherent danger with this approach is that the "estimates" can change for reasons that have little to do with objective evidence related to the determinants of material well-being. In the United States, for example, poverty thresholds were initially set on the basis of the nutritional requirements of households distinguished by their size, age, gender, and farm versus nonfarm residence. In 1981, the differences across gender and type of residence were eliminated by an expert panel not because of new scientific evidence on nutritional standards but because of threatened litigation.[25]

A third approach, which will be utilized in subsequent chapters, is to use data on consumption patterns to estimate "household equivalence scales." These indexes are defined to be the expenditure required, relative to a reference household, to attain a specific standard of living at fixed prices. If a household composed of two adults requires $15,000 to attain the same welfare as a single adult with $10,000, the equivalence scale is 1.5 and the couple is "equivalent" to one and one-half adults. This implies that a couple with expenditures of $30,000 is better off than a single adult with $18,000 because its expenditure per equivalent member is higher.[26]

The equivalence scales used in the welfare function (2.1) can be defined in terms of the expenditure function

$$m_0(\mathbf{p}, V_k, \mathbf{A}_k) = \frac{M(\mathbf{p}, V_k, \mathbf{A}_k)}{M(\mathbf{p}, V_k, \mathbf{A}_R)} \qquad (2.3)$$

where $\mathbf{A}_R$ is the vector of characteristics of a reference household. Note that (2.3) is analogous to the price index (2.2). Price indexes measure the relative cost of attaining a given level of utility as prices

25. This is reported by Ruggles (1990), p. 87.
26. An implicit assumption in this example is that the equivalence scale does not change with the welfare level.

change, whereas equivalence scales measure the same thing as the household characteristics change. Just as expenditure patterns influence inflation rates, they also affect the estimated equivalence scales. As a result, the scales will vary not only over household size but also over any characteristics which influence spending patterns.[27]

Consider the two identical individuals who live in Boston and Los Angeles. Their equivalence scales represent the relative costs of attaining a common level of utility, which differ because of differences in commuting expenses. If, for example, the price of gasoline is high compared to that of public transportation, it costs the Californian more to attain the same standard of living and his equivalence scale exceeds that of his counterpart in Boston. This is true even though both people face the same nominal prices for gasoline and public transportation.

I illustrate this method of estimating equivalence scales in Figure 2.3. Assume there are only two goods – food and gasoline – and let U^B denote the indifference contour of the Bostonian. The indifference contour representing the same utility for the individual from Los Angeles is U^{LA}. Both individuals face the same prices, so the optimal consumption bundles are given by points A and B. The minimum expenditure (deflated by the price of gasoline) needed for the Bostonian to attain this welfare is represented by point C, whereas the corresponding expenditure for the individual from Los Angeles is given by point D. If the Bostonian is the reference household, the equivalence scale of his counterpart is the ratio of OD to OC.

This illustrates why equivalence scales vary over any characteristics which influence consumption patterns. In this case, the only difference between the two individuals is their region of residence. Note also that the scales depend on the prices at which they are evaluated; in this example an increase in the price of food would decrease the

---

27. Empirical estimates of household equivalence scales for the United States are presented by van der Gaag and Smolensky (1982), Jorgenson and Slesnick (1987), Lazear and Michael (1980, 1988), Johnson (1994), and Nelson (1988). Estimates of equivalence scales for other countries are presented by Blundell and Lewbel (1991), Deaton and Muellbauer (1986), Pashardes (1995), and Ray (1983), among many others. Pashardes (1991) and Banks, Blundell, and Preston (1994) have extended this general approach by considering the costs of children in an intertemporal context. Surveys of the various methods of estimating equivalence scales are presented by Deaton and Muellbauer (1980) and Browning (1992).

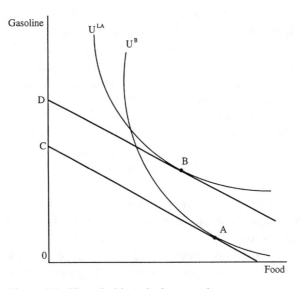

Figure 2.3. Household equivalence scales

equivalence scale. Figure 2.3 also shows that equivalence scales generally depend on the welfare level chosen for the comparison.[28]

Although equivalence scales are similar to price indexes, there is an important distinction. Price indexes compare the relative costs of attaining a given level of utility for the *same* household as prices change. Equivalence scales, on the other hand, require interpersonal comparisons of welfare across *different* households, and that necessarily introduces a normative element into the analysis.[29] Interpersonal comparability has, in the past, been dismissed by economists as being "meaningless" because it cannot be inferred from observable behavior. This critique has been universally ignored by policy makers because comparisons of well-being are the essence of virtually every

28. However, for my empirical work, I will use equivalence scales which are restricted to be independent of the welfare level at which they are evaluated. This property is referred to as "equivalence scale exactness" by Blackorby and Donaldson (1988b). See Lewbel (1989) as well.
29. See Blackorby and Donaldson (1988b) and Lewbel (1989) for a formal statement of the degree of comparability required to assess the needs of households using household equivalence scales.

issue of practical concern. Assessments of this type are needed to adjust the poverty line across different types of households, index transfer payments such as Social Security and Aid to Families with Dependent Children (AFDC), and evaluate the costs of children for various purposes.

With the assumption of interpersonal comparability come objections. The most eloquent critique of the use of household equivalence scales for welfare comparisons was presented by Pollak and Wales (1979). Their argument is that expenditure patterns provide information only on the household's well-being conditional on its demographic characteristics. Welfare, however, must be based on the household's unconditional preferences. The two assessments can differ because conditional estimates do not take into account how the household feels about the observed characteristics.[30]

Suppose that the attribute of interest is family size and we consider a couple that has been trying to have children for years and is finally successful. With no change in total expenditure, the conditional preferences will indicate a decrease in utility because of the increase in consumption requirements. The measured welfare effect of this demographic change does not take into account how the couple feels about having children. If the unconditional utility function could be identified, it would (appropriately) indicate an increase in well-being.

The prospects for resolving this problem are not good. It has been suggested that the solution is to model the choice of the characteristics that are endogenous. For example, we can measure how couples feel about having children by explicitly analyzing their (presumably) rational choice of family size. Although this identifies the unconditional welfare effect of additional children, it does not solve the identification problem for characteristics which are exogenous, such as age, race, or gender. For these characteristics, one might identify the welfare effect by asking individuals how they feel about being a particular age or race. Although this approach is possible, it is not practical since such information is not readily available.[31]

---

30. Additional discussion of this issue is presented in Chapter 5. For additional elaboration, see Fisher (1987), Gronau (1988), and the discussion by Pollak (1991).
31. An alternative approach is to impose "identification restrictions" on the form of the equivalence scale. See Blundell and Lewbel (1991), Lewbel (1997), and Lewbel and Weckstein (1995) for further elaboration.

2.5. THE MEASUREMENT OF SOCIAL WELFARE

Although the measurement of welfare at the micro level is an important first step, analysts are primarily concerned with the impacts of policies on groups of households. Changes in public policy result in both winners and losers, so for welfare economics to be useful to practitioners, a method of aggregating these effects is essential. This requires an elaboration of the ethical basis by which the benefits to some are balanced against the losses to others. What is the best way to do this? I begin with a brief examination of the evolution of economists' thinking on this issue.

Although utility was initially considered to be both measurable and comparable, by the end of the 1930s economists began to reject welfare judgments founded on interpersonal comparisons of utility.[32] The focus of attention returned to the use of the Pareto principle as the foundation for policy prescriptions. If everyone is better off under policy A than under B, then it is also socially preferred, and normative judgments concerning the trade-offs in welfare are unnecessary. Unfortunately, such unanimity is the exception rather than the rule.

In an effort to obtain a complete ranking of outcomes, the Pareto principle was used in conjunction with hypothetical compensation schemes. It was suggested, for example, that policy A be judged preferred to B if it is possible to distribute goods in A to yield an allocation that is Pareto superior to B. Although this criterion, and others like it, has been used extensively, it introduces both conceptual and practical problems. It is possible to obtain what Blackorby and Donaldson (1990) refer to as "Scitovsky reversals" in which one policy is judged to be an improvement over another and vice versa. Even if one excludes from consideration allocations for which these reversals can occur, Gorman (1955) has shown that orderings of policies need not be transitive. As a method of ranking social states, the Scitovsky compensation criterion falls short.

The Kaldor-Hicks-Samuelson criterion provides a more stringent rule for comparing outcomes. Policy B is preferred to policy A if, for

32. Robbins's (1932, 1938) critique of this approach to welfare economics has been taken to be the watershed event that shifted the focus from the prevalent use of utilitarianism to an exclusive reliance on the Pareto principle founded on ordinally noncomparable utility. Cooter and Rappoport (1984) provide an historical review of the debate of the appropriate conceptual basis for welfare economics.

any allocation of aggregate goods under A, it is possible to find an allocation under B that is Pareto superior to it. Chipman and Moore (1971) have shown that this compensation principle does not suffer from the preference reversals and intransitivities that plague other compensation criteria. However, the stringency of the requirement for a welfare improvement results in an ordering of social states that is often incomplete.

Ignoring this problem, the practical issue is how to make this particular compensation principle operational. Clearly, it is infeasible to examine all possible distributions of goods across the population under each scenario. Efforts have focused on aggregate income as an indicator of the change in "potential welfare." The problem is that increases in income reveal increases in potential welfare only under restrictive conditions.[33]

Despite these problems, compensation principles remained the method of choice among welfare economists due, in part, to the parallel development of Arrow's (1951) impossibility theorem. This famous result demonstrated that under a set of "reasonable" conditions, the only social welfare function that ranks outcomes consistently is a dictatorship. This starkly negative finding became a major stumbling block to the empirical implementation of an aggregate measure of the standard of living. How can we develop benevolent public policy if the only way to rank alternatives consistently is to use the preferences of a single person?

The Arrow impossibility theorem spawned a subfield of economic theory which focused on its robustness. Theorem after theorem demonstrated that modest changes to the axiomatic framework left the dictatorial result intact.[34] The inescapable conclusion was that if one precludes interpersonal comparisons of welfare, the *only* logically consistent foundation for welfare analysis is the Pareto principle. For economic theorists, welfare economics became completely summarized by the two Fundamental Theorems of Welfare Economics relating competitive equilibria to Pareto optimality.

Of course, this was bad news for practitioners. The Pareto principle can only rarely be applied in practice, and most people would

---

33. Chipman and Moore (1973) have shown that a rise in income is only a necessary condition for an increase in potential welfare. It is sufficient if and only if preferences are identical and homothetic.
34. See Sen (1995) for a synthesis and review of the axiomatic basis for Arrow's theorem.

agree that a dictatorship is an inappropriate foundation for the evaluation of public policy. This left a gap between what theorists felt was a suitable framework for applied welfare economics and what policy analysts needed to provide a complete and consistent ranking of policies.[35]

What additional information is required? While theorists published literally hundreds of papers focusing on impossibility, this fundamental question remained unanswered. The breakthrough occurred with a series of seminal books and papers by Sen (1970, 1973, 1977), who approached the problem of collective choice in a less nihilistic light. He viewed the Arrovian axioms as restrictive since they rule out by assumption the ability of the analyst to weigh the gains to some against the losses to others. Sen showed that once the measurability and comparability of welfare levels are allowed, it is possible to accommodate a wide variety of social welfare functions.[36]

Sen's results suggest that practical application of welfare economics requires information based on the analyst's assessment of the impacts of policies on different households. The greater the ability to measure and compare welfare, the wider the set of feasible social welfare functions. If welfare is ordinal but levels are comparable across households, the ordering of outcomes depends on what happens to the worst-off household.[37] This approach is consistent with Rawls's (1971) Difference Principle and places a premium on equity as reflected by the welfare of the poorest household.

If the analyst is unable to rank welfare levels but can make the judgment that a change in policy hurts household A twice as much as household B, then social welfare is evaluated on the basis of the sum or weighted sum of the welfare of all members of the group.[38]

35. It should be noted that while most of the profession rejected the feasibility of social welfare functions, Bergson (1938) and Samuelson (1947) maintained the position that explicit social welfare functions were an appropriate basis for policy analysis.
36. It is possible to have a nondictatorial social welfare function without interpersonal comparability if other axioms are relaxed. However, the possibilities remain quite limited. For example, if preferences are single-peaked (i.e., unrestricted domain is relaxed) the social welfare function is majority rule and aggregate preferences are those of the median voter. Thus, a dictatorial social welfare function is replaced by a "positional" dictatorship in which the median voter is decisive.
37. Hammond (1976), Roberts (1980c), and Sen (1977) refer to this degree of comparability as ordinal-level comparability and demonstrate the axiomatic basis for "leximin" social welfare functions in Arrow's framework.
38. This is the assumption of cardinal unit comparability in which welfare is cardinally measurable and differences in welfare across outcomes are comparable. For further details, see Maskin (1978) and Roberts (1980c).

In contrast with Rawls's framework, this utilitarian social welfare function places the least emphasis on equity. An allocation in which one household has all the resources and the others have nothing yields the same level of social welfare as occurs when resources are divided equally among all members of society.

These are two of many possible ways to measure social welfare consistently. There are no objective means of choosing between them because the choice ultimately depends on the analyst's assessment of the relative importance of efficiency and equity. "Possibility" results were synthesized and extended in a series of papers by Roberts (1980b, c, d), and, by the early 1980s, theoretical results demonstrating the existence of logically consistent, nondictatorial social welfare functions had been established.

The early 1980s also marked the beginning of a series of efforts to link policy analysis with an explicit social welfare function founded on the possibility theorems developed by Sen, Roberts, and others. The idea was to recover utility functions from household demands in the manner described in section 2.1. These welfare functions were used as arguments of an explicit social welfare function that formed the basis for the measurement of the standard of living and its distribution.[39]

The standard of living index used in subsequent chapters is developed within this social choice theoretic framework.[40] To describe it formally, let V_G be a distribution-free measure of social welfare attained at current prices $\mathbf{p}$ and aggregate expenditure level $M = \sum_{k=1}^{K} M_k$. The social standard of living is represented as

$$W_G = \frac{M}{P(\mathbf{p}, \mathbf{p}_0, V_G) \sum_{k=1}^{K} m_0(\mathbf{p}_0, V_k, \mathbf{A}_k)} \tag{2.4}$$

The function W_G is best interpreted as an indicator of efficiency since it is independent of the distribution of welfare across households. That is, a transfer of resources from a rich household to a poor house-

---

39. The earliest example of this type of applied welfare analysis can be traced to Muellbauer (1974). Other examples include Deaton (1977), Deaton and Muellbauer (1980), Jorgenson and Slesnick (1983, 1984), and King (1983).
40. Details of the framework used to measure social welfare are provided in the technical appendix to this Chapter.

hold leaves W_G unchanged. I choose this particular form not because I view distributional considerations to be unimportant but to maintain comparability with commonly used measures of the standard of living, such as per capita income or real median family income.

Index (2.4) can be interpreted as the average level of per equivalent consumption. The cost-of-living index $P(\mathbf{p}, \mathbf{p}_0, V_G)$ is the ratio of the (minimum) expenditure needed to attain welfare contour V_G at prices $\mathbf{p}$ to that required to attain the same welfare at reference prices $\mathbf{p}_0$.[41] The total number of household equivalent members $\Sigma m_0(\mathbf{p}_0, V_k, \mathbf{A}_k)$ measures the aggregate consumption requirements of society.

It is worth reiterating that many of the commonly used indicators of the standard of living are special cases of (2.4). Real per capita income replaces total expenditure with income, typically uses the CPI as a price deflator, and measures the aggregate consumption requirements using the total number of people. Real family income is identical except that aggregate need is represented by the number of families. Real gross domestic product (GDP), which is also frequently cited as an indicator of social welfare, replaces aggregate expenditure with GDP and makes no adjustment for the consumption requirements of the population.

2.6. QUALIFICATIONS AND ALTERNATIVE APPROACHES

I have described a model of welfare measurement that is founded on households' material well-being. Although this framework will be used in subsequent empirical work, it is important to note its limitations and discuss qualifications that must accompany conclusions.

"Welfarist" versus "nonwelfarist" welfare measurement

Welfare is a multidimensional concept that is a function not only of material well-being but also of such things as an individual's life expectancy, health status, personal liberty, and the like. It has been

---

41. The group cost-of-living index was developed by Pollak (1981).

suggested that consumption is best viewed as an input to the production of well-being and should be considered a means to an end
rather than an end itself.[42]

Sen (1984a, 1985, 1987, 1992) developed a theoretical framework
in which the utility derived from consumption ("welfarism") is
replaced by a function of individual "capabilities." Commodities are
consumed for the characteristics they provide, which, in turn, are
inputs to the production of individuals' capabilities. Food is consumed to provide the characteristic related to nutrition which gives
the capability of living in the absence of malnutrition. The health
care characteristic provides the capability of living a long life, and
the transportation characteristic provides the capability of physical
mobility.[43]

Sen's approach provides a conceptual link between the purchases
of goods and the capabilities that provide utility. The mapping
between goods and capabilities is complex so that using this approach
to measure the standard of living is difficult. The link between food
purchases and the nutritional capability is probably the most straightforward of those mentioned, and even this remains the subject of
heated debate. One can only imagine the complexity associated with
the mapping between the purchases of food, health care and leisure
consumption, and an individual's life expectancy.

Without these mappings, the empirical implementation of the
capabilities approach to welfare measurement is very difficult.[44] The
problem is that there is no objective way to assess how individuals
trade off material well-being with other capabilities such as life
expectancy. If we take away $100,000 in wealth but provide an addi-
tional year of life, is the individual better off? This can be answered
only in an arbitrary way. One possible solution is simply to ask
her, although it is one thing to answer a hypothetical question,

42. For further elaboration of this point, see Anand and Ravallion (1993). An implication
    is that access to goods may improve the well-being of individuals but need not do so.
    Behrman and Deolalikar (1987), for example, find that the income elasticity of nutri-
    ents is zero in India.
43. Atkinson (1991) presents an argument that income (as opposed to consumption) facil-
    itates individuals' capability of participating in society. If this is true (and this capabil-
    ity is of central concern), a case could be made for income as the preferred basis for
    the measurement of welfare.
44. There have been attempts to derive "quality of life" indicators. See, for example, Morris
    (1979). Mayer and Jencks (1989) also attempt to quantify "material hardship" and to
    expand welfare measurement beyond pecuniary measures of the standard of living.

but another issue altogether to reveal one's preferences through behavior.

Although there are obstacles to the empirical implementation of a single, comprehensive nonwelfarist measure of the standard of living, it is certainly possible to examine individual capabilities or quality-of-life indicators separately. By way of illustration, consider infant mortality and life expectancy in the United States. As with measures of material welfare, aggregate statistics on capabilities reveal only limited information since distributional considerations are also important. Nevertheless, Table 2.1 shows that living standards have generally improved along some of these dimensions. Infant mortality has decreased by more than one-half between 1970 and 1990. Life expectancy at birth has increased since 1950, and, as with infant mortality, most of the change occurred between 1970 and 1990.

Another indicator that is often used to assess the quality of life is the ambient air quality. The estimates in Table 2.2 are based on the weights of the pollutants and, for those considered, show a significant reduction after 1970. Carbon monoxide increased between 1950 and 1970 but subsequently fell by 1990. Lead pollutants decreased after 1970, as did the level of particulate matter in the atmosphere. The amounts of other pollutants, such as sulfur oxides and volatile organic compounds (which are not shown), also fell after 1970. As with infant mortality and life expectancy, substantial improvement in the average air quality occurred over this period.

The level of educational attainment and the crime rates are presented in Table 2.3. The former characteristic is represented by the

Table 2.1. *Infant mortality and life expectancy*

Year	Infant mortality[a] (per 1000 live births)	Change (%)	Life expectancy[b] at birth (years)	Change (%)
1950	29.2	—	68.2	—
1960	26.0	−11.6	69.7	2.2
1970	20.0	−26.2	70.8	1.6
1980	12.6	−46.2	73.7	4.0
1990	9.2	−31.4	75.4	2.3

[a] *Source*: Bureau of the Census (1994), Table 90.
[b] *Source*: Bureau of the Census (1975a), Table B-107, and Bureau of the Census (1994), Table 118.

Table 2.2. *Air pollution in the United States*

Year	Carbon monoxide (millions)	Change (%)	Lead (thousands)	Change (%)	Particulate matter (millions)	Change (%)
					Metric tons	
1950	87.6	—	NA	—	24.9	—
1960	89.7	2.4	NA	—	21.6	−14.2
1970	101.4	12.3	203.8	—	18.5	−15.5
1980	79.6	−24.2	70.6	−106.0	8.5	−77.8
1990	60.1	−28.1	7.1	−229.7	7.5	−12.5

Source: Bureau of the Census (1992), Table 353.

Table 2.3. *Education and crime rate*

Year	Education[a] Percent not HS grad (persons 25 and over)	Change (%)	Crime rate[b] Total number of crimes (per 100,000 persons)	Change (%)
1950	65.7	—	NA	—
1960	58.9	−10.9	1,876	—
1970	47.7	−21.1	3,985	75.3
1980	33.5	−35.5	5,950	40.1
1990	22.4	−40.2	5,820	−2.2

[a] *Source*: Bureau of the Census (1990), Table 215, and Bureau of the Census (1992), Table 222.
[b] *Source*: Bureau of the Census (1975b), Table 248; Bureau of the Census (1980), Table 302; and Bureau of the Census (1992), Table 287.

fraction of the population, age twenty-five and over, that has not graduated from high school. By this standard, there has been a rise in educational attainment that has accelerated since 1970. Whereas 65.7 percent of all persons over twenty-five did not have a high school diploma in 1950, the proportion in 1990 was only 22.4 percent. The trend in the crime rate runs counter to all the other quality-of-life indicators and increased markedly between 1960 and 1990.

Along these dimensions, the quality of life in the United States has generally improved since 1950. Tables 2.1–2.3 also illustrate, however, the many problems associated with expanding the domain over which welfare is measured. A natural question is whether, in the aggregate, the increase in life expectancy compensates sufficiently for the increase in the crime rate. Furthermore, each aggregate indicator provides an excessively narrow view of the entire picture. The measures of air pollution ignore other, possibly more toxic, types of pollutants. Counting the total number of crimes obscures the fact that not all crimes are the same. As in the case of material well-being, aggregate indexes fail to take distributional considerations into account. Although the proportion of individuals graduating from high schools has increased, some segments of the population may not have enjoyed the same progress, or the quality of a high school diploma may have diminished over time. Pollution in general has decreased, but some urban areas may have experienced increases.

Intrahousehold allocation

The ultimate concern is the impact of policies on individuals rather than families or households. In practice, though, the data largely dictate the units of observation. If expenditure data are used, spending is aggregated over individuals who share resources and welfare is calculated for the household. With this in mind, most empirical models treat households rather than individuals as the basic decision units.

There are at least two ways to justify this assumption. Samuelson's (1956) consensus model of the household assumes that all members pool their resources and work in concert to maximize a common utility function.[45] Becker's (1981) altruist model assumes the existence of a benevolent dictator who allocates goods optimally within the household. Each model assumes a different relationship among household members, but both of them imply that households can be treated as rational agents who maximize utility subject to a budget constraint.

If there are wide disparities among individuals within households, treating the household as a "representative consumer" can lead to erroneous inferences concerning the standard of living and its distri-

---

45. This terminology and classification of household models is due to Lundberg and Pollak (1993, 1996).

bution.[46] What is the empirical evidence on this issue? A definitive assessment is difficult because data on within-household transactions are rare. There is, however, evidence against certain representations of the household model. Apps and Savage (1989) and Lundberg (1988) show that labor supply behavior cannot be modeled as a joint household decision. Other studies show that the division of resources within the household influences observed outcomes, which suggests that treatment of the household as a representative agent is inappropriate. Using Brazilian data, for example, Thomas (1990, 1994) has found that the share of income contributed by the mother or father influences the expenditures made on behalf of children as well as their health. Browning, Bourguignon, Chiappori, and Lechene (1994) find that the relative share of income provided by women influences the share of expenditures on goods consumed exclusively by them. Sen (1984b) and Haddad and Kanbur (1990) use data on food consumption to show that estimates of both poverty and inequality are distorted if the intrahousehold allocation of resources is ignored.

Alternatives to the traditional household model have focused on conceptual models of bargaining over resources by the adult members. Bourguignon and Chiappori (1994), Chiappori (1988, 1992), Manser and Brown (1980), McElroy and Horney (1981), and Lundberg and Pollak (1993) formulate game-theoretic models to describe how resources might be divided among individuals within the household. Assessing the consistency of these models with data requires information on the distribution of goods across members. For some goods, such as leisure, this is feasible since data on hours of work are typically provided for all members of the household. For other goods, within-household consumption levels are unavailable in the United States.[47] This implies that the intrahousehold distribution must be inferred, and it is difficult to assess the consistency of the estimated distribution with the actual distribution. Even if it were known, welfare measurement requires an assessment of individuals' valuations of the goods. For private goods, this could be done in the usual way. However, many household goods are public, so welfare

46. Nelson (1993) examines the policy implications of parents who do not benevolently allocate resources to their children.
47. Nelson (1989) looks at the within-household consumption of clothing. Browning et al. (1994), Lazear and Michael (1988), and Thomas (1990) infer the consumption patterns of individuals based on the expenditures of households with different compositions.

measurement requires knowledge of each individual's willingness to pay, which is difficult to assess. It is undoubtedly the case, moreover, that members of a family or household have interdependent preferences, and that adds an additional complication to the welfare calculations.

Subjective measures of well-being

In the framework outlined in this chapter, household welfare is inferred from observations of consumption patterns. An alternative approach is to measure well-being using polling data in which individuals are asked how they feel about different levels of income. This method was pioneered by van Praag (1971) and is best illustrated by one of the survey questions:

Please try to indicate what you consider to be an appropriate amount for each of the following cases? Under my (our) conditions I would call a net household income per week/month/year of

> *about (   ) – very bad*
> *about (   ) – bad*
> *about (   ) – insufficient*
> *about (   ) – sufficient*
> *about (   ) – good*
> *about (   ) – very good*

Please enter an answer on each line and underline the period you refer to.[48]

The incomes reported in the six classifications are mapped into a cardinal representation of welfare.[49]

van Praag and his associates have provided an interesting alternative approach to welfare measurement. This method has been extended to obtain subjective measures of poverty by examining households' estimates of the minimum income required to "make ends meet." Variation in the responses across households provides information that can be used to determine subjective poverty lines, the corresponding poverty rate, and household equivalence scales.[50]

Although one could make the argument that what matters most is the perception of well-being, there are several impediments to

48. This is taken from van Praag (1994), p. 92.
49. A general survey of this approach is presented by van Praag (1994).
50. Examples of this general approach to poverty measurement are provided by Kilpatrick (1973), Goedhart et al. (1977), Danziger et al. (1984), and Hagenaars (1986), among others.

using this approach. First and foremost, there are few data of this type in the United States.[51] Second, the perception of well-being can vary substantially with short-run circumstances, so responses to the questions can change from one day to the next. There is no way of knowing whether the observed response on the day of the survey is representative of the individual's welfare. Finally, when all is said and done, actions speak louder than words. I would expect well-being to be more accurately revealed by the purchases of goods and services than by the answers to hypothetical questions.

TECHNICAL APPENDIX

Measuring household welfare

To describe the theoretical basis for welfare measures described in this chapter, I begin with the theory of consumer behavior. Households are assumed to maximize utility subject to a budget constraint:[52]

$$\max_x U(x_{1k}, x_{2k}, \ldots, x_{Nk}, \mathbf{A_k}) \tag{A2.1}$$

subject to

$$\sum_{i=1}^{N} p_i x_{ik} = M_k$$

where U is the utility function, x_{ik} is the quantity consumed of the ith good by household k, p_i is the price of the ith good, M_k is the level of total expenditure, and $\mathbf{A_k}$ is the vector of attributes.

The solution to this problem yields demands as functions of prices, total expenditure, and the vector of attributes of the household.

$$x_{ik} = x_{ik}(\mathbf{p}, M_k, \mathbf{A_k}) \tag{A2.2}$$

---

51. A similar question is posed in the Gallup survey and was used by Kilpatrick (1973) to estimate a subjective poverty line. Other questions have been asked infrequently in ongoing surveys such as the *Income Survey Development Program* and the *Consumer Expenditure Surveys*, but they are not comprehensive nor frequent enough to facilitate overall welfare measurement.
52. The theory of consumer behavior is described by Varian (1992), Chapters 7–9, and Deaton and Muellbauer (1980). I present a survey of applied welfare economics in Slesnick (1998b).

These demand functions enable us to define the indirect utility function as the maximum utility attainable for a household facing prices $\mathbf{p}$ with attributes $\mathbf{A}_k$ and total expenditure M_k:

$$V(\mathbf{p}, M_k, \mathbf{A}_k) = \max U$$
$$= U(x_{1k}(\mathbf{p}, M_k, \mathbf{A}_k), x_{2k}(\mathbf{p}, M_k, \mathbf{A}_k), \ldots, x_{Nk}(\mathbf{p}, M_k, \mathbf{A}_k))$$

$$(A2.3)$$

The inverse of the indirect utility function is the expenditure function, $M(\mathbf{p}, V_k, \mathbf{A}_k)$, which is the minimum total expenditure required to attain a given level of utility at fixed prices:

$$M(\mathbf{p}, V, \mathbf{A}_k) = \min_x \sum_{n=1}^{N} p_n x_{nk} \qquad (A2.4)$$

subject to

$$U(x_{1k}, x_{2k}, \ldots, x_{Nk}, \mathbf{A}_k) \geq V$$

The expenditure function provides a means of translating utility levels into monetary equivalents. If $V_k = V(\mathbf{p}, M_k, \mathbf{A}_k)$ is the utility attained by the household, the (indirect) money metric utility function is[53]

$$\mu(\mathbf{p}_0, \mathbf{A}_r; \mathbf{p}, M_k, \mathbf{A}_k) = M(\mathbf{p}_0, V(\mathbf{p}, M_k, \mathbf{A}_k), \mathbf{A}_r) \qquad (A2.5)$$

where $\mathbf{p}_0$ is a vector of reference prices, and $\mathbf{A}_r$ is a vector of reference characteristics. The money metric utility function is ordinally equivalent to the household's indirect utility function and provides a monetary measure of well-being.

The welfare function introduced in (2.1) is of the form

$$W_k = \frac{M_k}{P_k(\mathbf{p}, \mathbf{p}_0, V_k) m_0(\mathbf{p}_0, V_k, \mathbf{A}_k)}$$

Substituting (2.2) for the household-specific price index and (2.3) for the equivalence scale yields

$$W_k = M(\mathbf{p}_0, V_k, \mathbf{A}_r)$$
$$= \mu(\mathbf{p}_0, \mathbf{A}_r; \mathbf{p}, M_k, \mathbf{A}_k)$$

---

53. This concept was originally developed by McKenzie (1956–57), and the terminology is due to Samuelson (1974).

The welfare function (2.1) is therefore a money metric utility function and provides an exact representation of the underlying level of utility.

In empirical applications, this method of welfare measurement usually begins with the specification of a parametric representation of the demand functions (A2.2).[54] Since the maintained hypothesis is utility maximization, the demand system is estimated subject to the integrability conditions implied by static utility maximization. Specifically, the demand functions must be homogeneous of degree zero in prices and total expenditure and must be nonnegative and summable, and the matrix of compensated price effects must be symmetric and negative semidefinite.[55] Given estimates of the unknown parameters of the demand functions, it is possible to recover the indirect utility function and the expenditure function.

To illustrate, consider the following demand system introduced by Jorgenson, Lau, and Stoker (1982):

$$\mathbf{w}_k = \frac{1}{D(\mathbf{p})}(\alpha_p + B_{pp}\ln\mathbf{p} - \iota B_{pp}\ln M_k + B_{pA}\mathbf{A}_k) \qquad (A2.6)$$

where $D(\mathbf{p}) = -1 + \iota'B_{pp}\ln\mathbf{p}$ and $\mathbf{w}_k$ is the vector of budget shares of all goods consumed by the kth household. The unknown parameters α_p, B_{pp}, and B_{pA} can be estimated by fitting the system of share equations to data on consumer expenditures.

Given estimates of these parameters, integration yields a household indirect utility function of the form

$$\ln V(\mathbf{p}, M_k, \mathbf{A}_k) = C(\mathbf{A}_k) + \alpha_p'\ln\mathbf{p} + 1/2\ln\mathbf{p}'B_{pp}\ln\mathbf{p}$$
$$- D(\mathbf{p})\ln M_k + \ln\mathbf{p}'B_{pA}\mathbf{A}_k \qquad (A2.7)$$

Solving (A2.7) for total expenditure as a function of utility yields the expenditure function

$$\ln M(\mathbf{p}, V_k, \mathbf{A}_k) = \frac{1}{D(\mathbf{p})}(C(\mathbf{A}_k) + \alpha_p'\ln\mathbf{p} + 1/2\ln\mathbf{p}'B_{pp}\ln\mathbf{p}$$
$$+ \ln\mathbf{p}'B_{pA}\mathbf{A}_k - \ln V_k) \qquad (A2.8)$$

54. Hausman and Newey (1995) have estimated welfare changes using nonparametric kernel regression. Afriat (1967) and Varian (1982) have used index number methods to measure welfare without specifying a particular functional form for the demand function. See Slesnick (1998b) for additional details.

55. See Jorgenson (1990) for further details.

With prices, total expenditure, and the attributes of the household, one has all the components needed to derive a household welfare measure of the type (2.1).

Measuring social welfare

To this point I have described welfare measurement at the micro level. To obtain group welfare functions, I extend the framework to incorporate the fundamental principles of social choice. The first step is to choose the appropriate arguments for the social welfare function. Given the preceding discussion, it would seem reasonable to define social welfare to be a function of money metric utility functions (A2.5). However, Blackorby and Donaldson (1985, 1988a), Roberts (1980a), and Slesnick (1991a) have all given arguments against this type of specification.

Instead, I define social welfare over the vector of indirect utility functions for every household. Let

$$\mathbf{u} = (V_1, V_2, \ldots, V_K)$$

where V_k is the indirect utility function (A2.3) for household k. To describe the choice-theoretic basis for the social welfare function, I define R to be the set of complete, reflexive, and transitive orderings over the set of social states X.[56] A social welfare functional f is a mapping from the set of household welfare functions to the set of social orderings so that $f(\mathbf{u}) = f(\mathbf{u}')$ implies $R = R'$. Let L_k be the set of admissible welfare functions for the kth household and define L to be the Cartesian product of all such sets. Finally, define Λ to be the partition of L such that all elements of Λ yield the same social ordering. Using this notation, the Arrovian axioms are described as follows.

> *Unrestricted Domain*: The social welfare functional f is defined for all possible vectors of household welfare functions **u**.
> *Independence of Irrelevant Alternatives*: For any subset A contained in X, if $\mathbf{u}(\mathbf{x}) = \mathbf{u}'(\mathbf{x})$ for all x in A, then $R:A = R':A$, where $R = f(\mathbf{u})$ and $R' = f(\mathbf{u}')$ and $R:A$ is the social ordering over the subset A.

---

56. This formulation follows the framework developed by Sen (1977) and Roberts (1980b, c, d).

Weak Pareto Principle: For any x, y in X, if $V_i(x) > V_i(y)$ for all households i, then xPy.

Ordinal Noncomparability: The set of household welfare functions, Λ, that yield the same social ordering is defined by

$$\Lambda = \{u': V_k' = \phi_k(V_k)\}$$

where ϕ_k is increasing and $f(u) = f(u')$ for all u in Λ.

The axiom of unrestricted domain is self-explanatory. Independence of irrelevant alternatives requires the social ranking of any two social states to be independent of a third state. The Pareto principle implies that a social state is socially preferred if every household (strictly) prefers it, and the axiom of ordinal noncomparability requires the social welfare functional to be invariant to monotonic transformations of the welfare functions that vary across households. Arrow (1951) proved that under these conditions, the only social welfare function satisfying these axioms is a dictatorship.

A nondictatorial social welfare function requires information that is based, either implicitly or explicitly, on the analyst's assessment of the relative impacts of policies on different households. The greater the (assumed) ability to measure and compare welfare levels, the wider the set of possible social welfare functions. Suppose, for example, that policy makers are able to rank households' welfare levels but cannot measure the magnitudes of the differences. In this instance, preferences are ordinally comparable.

Ordinal Comparability: The set of household welfare functions, Λ, that yields the same social ordering is defined by

$$\Lambda = \{u': V_k' = \phi(V_k)\}$$

where ϕ is an increasing function and $f(u) = f(u')$ for all u in Λ.

This degree of comparability (given the other axioms) yields Rawls's leximin ordering as the social welfare function:

$$W(u, x) = \min_k V_k$$

As another example, assume that the assumptions of unlimited domain and of independence of irrelevant alternatives and the weak Pareto principle are retained but that ordinal noncomparability is replaced with the assumption that *both* levels and differences in welfare across social states are meaningfully compared across households. More formally:

> *Cardinal Full Comparability*: The set of household welfare functions Λ that yield the same social ordering is defined by
>
> $$\Lambda = \{\mathbf{u}': V_k' = \alpha + \beta(V_k)\}$$
>
> where $\beta > 0$ and $f(\mathbf{u}) = f(\mathbf{u}')$ for all $\mathbf{u}$ in Λ.

Roberts (1980c) showed that, under these conditions, the real-valued representation of the social ordering must be of the form

$$W(\mathbf{u}, x) = \overline{V}(x) + g(V_1 - \overline{V}, V_2 - \overline{V}, \ldots, V_K - \overline{V})$$

where

$$\overline{V} = \sum_{k=1}^{K} a_k V_k$$

and g( ) is a linearly homogeneous function.

Note that this social welfare function is a function of the distribution of household welfare. If W is assumed to be concave in the household welfare functions, then progressive transfers increase social welfare, and the maximum level of social welfare – say, W_{max} (for a fixed level of aggregate expenditure $M = \Sigma M_k$) – is attained at the perfectly egalitarian distribution of welfare. This is the potential level of social welfare and can be interpreted as a measure of efficiency.

Social welfare can be converted into monetary equivalents using the social expenditure function introduced by Pollak (1981). Exactly analogous to the individual expenditure function, it is defined as the minimum level of aggregate expenditure required to attain a specific social welfare contour at fixed prices:

$$M(\mathbf{p}, W) = \min\{M: W(\mathbf{u}, x) \geq W, \Sigma M_k = M\}$$

The social expenditure function can be used to define an aggregate cost of living index as the ratio of the minimum level of aggregate expenditure required to attain social welfare W at prices $\mathbf{p}$ to the expenditure required to attain the same level of social welfare at base period prices $\mathbf{p}_0$:

$$P(\mathbf{p}, \mathbf{p}_0, W) = \frac{M(\mathbf{p}, W)}{M(\mathbf{p}_0, W)}$$

Using the social expenditure function, the group welfare function (2.4) is defined as

$$W = \frac{M}{P(\mathbf{p}, \mathbf{p}_0, W_{max}) \sum_{k=1}^{K} m_0(\mathbf{p}_0, V_k, \mathbf{A}_k)}$$

$$= \frac{M(\mathbf{p}_0, W_{max})}{\sum_{k=1}^{K} m_0(\mathbf{p}_0, V_k, \mathbf{A}_k)}$$

For a given population, this index is ordinally equivalent to the level of potential welfare W_{max} and provides an exact representation of the level of social welfare.

3 Measuring consumption: An initial look at the data

As is usually the case, obstacles related to the nature, quality, and availability of critical data must be overcome in order to move from the theoretical development to the empirical implementation. This is particularly true of issues related to consumption. In this chapter I propose a definition of consumption that can be used to measure the standard of living, and I examine the extent to which it can be implemented using existing data sources.

3.1. WHAT IS CONSUMPTION?

The Haig-Simons definition of consumption is frequently used as a starting point in many empirical studies. Consumption is defined as the difference between income and the change in net worth. Given the variety of ways income can be measured, this does not provide much practical guidance as to how to proceed. As an alternative, I define consumption to be the flow of goods and services to the household that influence well-being over a specific time period. For many items, this is reasonably approximated by the purchases of the household. Overall spending, however, is an inaccurate estimate of total consumption because some goods are consumed without a transaction.[1]

---

1. Some authors (Cutler and Katz 1991) distinguish between "expenditure" and "consumption." Expenditure is simply the household's total spending, whereas consumption includes the services from inventories of goods for which there are no recorded pur-

Leisure is probably the most important example of such a commodity. An individual who works eighteen hours per day is not as well off as someone who has the same expenditure but works only eight hours. Excluding leisure from consumption, therefore, could have important consequences for the measurement of the standard of living. It has been argued, for example, that the increase in labor force participation by women and the concomitant increase in the number of two-earner households is an important source of growth in living standards in the United States. Since women are working more, a welfare measure based on nominal expenditures that excludes leisure may overstate the increase in social welfare and mismeasure movements in the distribution.[2]

Public goods, such as police and fire protection, education, and the construction and maintenance of roads and highways, are also consumed without being purchased. These goods provide services that both raise the standard of living and change its distribution. Families with children, for example, value public education differently from others, and its provision not only increases their well-being but also changes their relative position in the distribution.[3]

The spending on owner-occupied housing and consumer durables does not accurately reflect the level of consumption of these goods for many households. An elderly woman who lives in her own home and pays insurance and property taxes, but makes no mortgage payments, has expenditures that understate the housing services received. Also, using expenditures to measure durables consumption erroneously indicates high levels when a purchase is made and no consumption at other times. Services are actually received over the good's lifetime, and this feature should be incorporated in the consumption estimate.

The same is true of recipients' valuations of in-kind transfers, which have become increasingly important sources of support for the poor since the 1960s.[4] Inclusion of these items in a comprehensive measure

---

chases (e.g., owner-occupied housing and durables). I make no such distinction here and define expenditure as the nominal value of consumption. Real expenditure (i.e., expenditure adjusted for inflation) is what I refer to as consumption.

2. Of course, it may be that women have simply substituted nonmarket labor for market labor, so leisure, correctly measured, has not changed.
3. A similar argument can be made for the inclusion of externalities in the consumption measure. See Nordhaus and Tobin (1972) for a discussion.
4. The growth of in-kind transfers is documented by Sawhill (1988).

of consumption is problematical because food stamps, school lunch programs, housing subsidies, and health care services are valued at less than (or equal to) their market values. Manser (1987), for example, finds that food stamps are valued at par but that health care benefits are valued at substantially less than their cash equivalent.[5] Schwab (1985) reports that public housing is also valued at substantially less than the nominal value of the subsidy.

To what extent can existing data sources accommodate a comprehensive definition that incorporates these components of consumption? Nondurables and services (food, clothing, travel expenses, etc.) can be measured using recorded purchases in household budget surveys. As we shall see, it is also possible to estimate the services received from housing and durables at both the aggregate and the micro level. The inclusion of other items is more difficult. Since no decisions are made to purchase public goods, there are no market-based measures of the values of these goods to consumers. One must rely on their stated "willingness to pay," which, under ordinary circumstances, need not be revealed truthfully.[6]

The successful integration of leisure into a consumption measure requires that a number of confounding issues be resolved. How should we define leisure? Is it the time not spent working? If so, how should we account for parents staying at home with their children or students investing in human capital? The price of leisure is the individual's wage, so an imputation is required for those who do not work.[7] The most serious obstacle is the lack of disaggregated data on both leisure and consumption in the United States. Only the *Consumer Expenditure Surveys* in the 1980s and 1990s provide such information, and since the goal is to provide a measure of the standard of living over a longer time period, I narrow the focus and leave the analysis of the impact of leisure on living standards for future

---

5. For additional discussion of this issue, see Moffitt (1989) and Murray (1994). Smeeding (1982) developed an ad hoc procedure to estimate the recipient value of in-kind transfers, and this has been used by the Bureau of the Census to estimate poverty rates using an income measure augmented by the consumption value of in-kind transfers. See, for example, the *Current Population Reports, Series P-60*, No. 186RD. This mixes apples (income) with oranges (consumption). The appropriate procedure would be to use total expenditure, rather than income, in conjunction with the estimates of the consumption value of the in-kind transfers. For further discussion, see Slesnick (1996).
6. The preference revelation problem is summarized in Chapter 23 of Varian (1992).
7. In spite of such problems, Nordhaus and Tobin (1972) develop an aggregate measure of the standard of living that incorporates leisure consumption.

research. Similar considerations require that in-kind transfers also be ignored.

Even with public goods, leisure, and in-kind transfers omitted, there are only two comprehensive sources of consumption data in the United States. Aggregate expenditures on more than 100 different types of goods and services are reported as personal consumption expenditures (PCE) in the National Income and Product Accounts. The PCE are measured using information from a number of sources and provide estimates of the expenditures of the household sector of the economy. These series cover the period from 1946 to the present at monthly, quarterly, and annual frequencies but reveal nothing about the distribution of expenditure across subgroups of the population.

An alternative source of expenditure data is the *Consumer Expenditure Surveys* (CEX). These surveys record the purchases of hundreds of items by a representative sample of households and are the only sources of information on expenditures at a disaggregated level. In the next section I describe both the PCE and the CEX. The reader uninterested in the details of the consumption definition, method of estimation, and population coverage of the two data sets can skip this section without loss of continuity.

3.2. AGGREGATE CONSUMPTION IN THE UNITED STATES

Personal consumption expenditures in NIPA

The PCE are the most widely used source of aggregate expenditure data in the United States. These data include the spending of the civilian noninstitutionalized population, military families, U.S. citizens traveling overseas, U.S. citizens living abroad, foreign citizens in the United States, and nonprofit institutions. The coverage generally conforms to what is needed to measure welfare using the model developed in Chapter 2 except for the inclusion of nonprofit institutions.[8]

---

8. These include, among other things, private hospitals, private educational institutions, and religious and welfare agencies. The share of aggregate expenditures in the PCE attributable to nonprofit institutions has grown substantially over the postwar period. See Slesnick (1998a).

In the "benchmark" years (those ending in 2 or 7), detailed information from the decennial and quinquennial censuses is used to estimate the PCE. Expenditures on durable and nondurable items are
estimated using an input-output technique in which shipments of
goods from manufacturers are classified according to their NIPA
commodity definitions, net imports are added, and increases in inventories, business purchases, and government purchases are subtracted.[9]
Taxes, trade, and transportation margins are added to yield the spending attributable to final demand by households. In nonbenchmark
years, less information is available and the levels are adjusted using
an extrapolation procedure based on monthly retail sales surveys.[10]

Services are estimated using original source data. Housing services
are calculated using aggregate housing stocks along with an average
rental rate tabulated from a survey of residential finance. Brokerage,
bank, and transportation services are estimated using the administrative records of government agencies. For other categories of services, the PCE estimates are based on the quinquennial censuses of
the service industries in the benchmark years and the Service Annual
Survey in the other years.

The PCE are designed to measure the spending of the household
sector and differ markedly from the "out-of-pocket" concept used in
most household expenditure surveys. This difference is particularly
important for medical care, which, in the PCE, includes the payments
made on behalf of households by Medicaid, Medicare, insurance companies, and employers. Insurance "expenditure" is represented by the
difference between the premiums and the benefits paid by private
insurance companies. There is no distinction between the purchases
of gifts and expenditures made for personal use. The rental equivalent of owner-occupied housing is (appropriately) included in the
PCE, but the service flows from consumer durables are not.

To maintain consistency with the treatment of housing, I adjust the
PCE by deleting the purchases of new durable goods from aggregate
expenditure and replacing them with the estimated service flows from
the stocks of durables. This adjustment is made for eleven categories:
furniture, appliances, china and glassware, other household furnish-

---

9. For a complete description of the method used to estimate personal consumption
   expenditures, see Carson (1987). See also the discussion by Wilcox (1992).
10. Motor vehicle sales and sales of gasoline and oil are based on original source data and
    are not computed in the same way as other durable and nondurable goods.

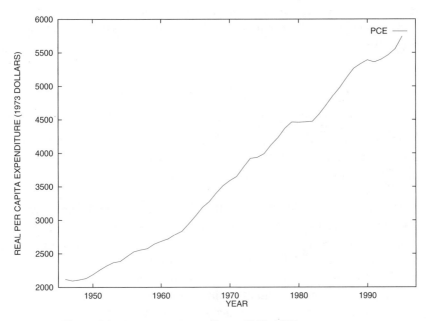

Figure 3.1. Aggregate expenditure, 1946–1995

ings, radios and televisions, jewelry, ophthalmic products, books, durable toys and sports equipment, automobiles, and other motor vehicles.[11]

Figure 3.1 presents the resulting estimates of per capita consumption over the period 1946 to 1995.[12] It is evident that average consumption grew significantly over the postwar period. The greatest growth occurred in the 1960s, but even in the 1980s and 1990s the increase was considerable. If per capita consumption approximates the average standard of living, Figure 3.1 provides the first indication that social welfare increased significantly in the United States

11. The method used for this adjustment is outlined in the technical appendix to this chapter. Tires, tubes, and other auto parts are treated as consumer goods, with nominal consumption assumed to be equal to the expenditure level. As it turns out, replacing purchases with estimates of the services received from the stock of durables has little effect on the aggregate estimate of the PCE (Slesnick 1992).
12. Consumption (i.e., real expenditure) is obtained by deflating the PCE (adjusted to include durable services) by a price index that is a function of the PCE implicit price deflators. The prices of durables reported by the Bureau of Economic Analysis (BEA) are replaced by implicit price deflators for durable services. The per capita adjustment is made by dividing real expenditures by an estimate of the population reported by the Bureau of the Census (1991, 1994, 1996).

throughout the postwar era. There is no evidence of persistent stagnation as is found when real median family income is used to measure social welfare.

The Consumer Expenditure Surveys

Alternative estimates of aggregate consumption can be obtained from the CEX, which also provide disaggregated information on household spending. They differ from the PCE in terms of their population coverage, the expenditure definition, and the methods used to collect the data.

There are surveys for 1960–61, 1972, 1973, and 1980 through 1995.[13] The basic observational unit is called a "consumer unit," which is either a financially independent unrelated individual or a group of individuals who pool their resources. After 1980 the definition was extended to include all members of a household who are related by blood or legal arrangement. The population coverage changed slightly over the years but primarily consists of the civilian noninstitutionalized population. Military personnel living off base were included in the sample, whereas those living on post were excluded. Travel expenditures abroad were part of the reported totals, but spending by U.S. citizens stationed overseas was not. In the 1961, 1972, and 1973 surveys, college students were treated as members of their parents' consumer unit, but after 1980 they were included in the sample as independent households.

The survey methods used in the earlier years differed from those used after 1980 in a number of ways. Expenditures in the 1961 survey were estimated using a single interview, whereas in 1972 and 1973 the consumer unit was interviewed over five quarters.[14] In each of the three surveys, only the annual expenditures for each household were reported. The sample size in the 1961 survey was approximately

13. Earlier surveys were administered, but the records are no longer available. The surveys in 1982 and 1983 restricted the sample to urban households. In these years the levels of expenditure of the rural population were interpolated using the 1981 and 1984 surveys as end points. The method of interpolation had little effect on the aggregate totals. Note also that there is a significant lag in the release of the CEX. At the time this manuscript was completed, the most recent survey covered expenditures for 1995.
14. The survey in 1960–61 represents the entire population only when both years are combined. I inflated the income and expenditure in 1960 to 1961 levels to preserve comparability.

13,000 consumer units and was around 9,500 units in the 1972 and 1973 surveys.

Beginning in 1980, the surveys changed to a rotating panel format in which each consumer unit was interviewed over five quarters.[15] Twenty percent of the households were dropped each quarter and replaced by a new group. The sample sizes were smaller than in the earlier surveys, ranging from 4,000 to 6,000 consumer units. The first interview collected demographic information and a partial inventory of consumer durables. In the remaining four interviews, detailed expenditure information was collected and reported on a quarterly basis. Questions related to income were asked in the second and fifth interviews, with a twelve-month recall.

To preserve comparability over time, it is necessary to obtain annual estimates from the quarterly expenditures reported in the surveys after 1980. Under ideal circumstances this could be done by following the households over four quarters and simply adding up their expenditures. Unfortunately, there was a high rate of attrition in the sample, and that reduced the number of complete observations in each year to an unacceptably low level. To maintain an adequate sample size, I use the second quarter of each year and multiply the reported expenditures by 4. This procedure distorts the estimates of total spending (relative to tabulations based on annual data) in several ways. The concentration of observations in the first half of the year undoubtedly understates expenditure levels due to price increases over the course of the year. Reliance on data from a single quarter also amplifies the variation in expenditures across consumers, whereas seasonality in spending decisions likely influences both the level and the distribution of consumption.[16]

The data reported in the CEX were the consumer units' out-of-pocket expenditures. The Bureau of Labor Statistics (BLS) included gifts and cash contributions to persons outside the household as part of total expenditure in the 1980s and 1990s. Spending on owner-occupied housing and durables was included instead of the imputed rental equivalents. In the later surveys, contributions to pensions, retirement funds, and Social Security were added to total expenditure, whereas most in-kind transfers were not. Food stamps and meals

---

15. For a more detailed description of the CEX data in the 1980s, see Bureau of Labor Statistics (1989).
16. For further discussion of these issues, see Johnson and Shipp (1997).

and rent received as pay were included in total expenditure to the extent that they were reported accurately.

As I did with the PCE, I modify the BLS expenditure definition to conform as closely as possible to the model developed in Chapter 2. Gifts and cash contributions are deleted because altruism requires a conceptual framework that is different from most analyses of individual and social welfare. Pensions, retirement contributions, and Social Security payments are also removed because they represent components of saving rather than consumption. Spending on owner-occupied housing and consumer durables is replaced by the appropriate rental equivalents. This is a straightforward exercise for housing because the estimated rental value of the home is reported in all but three of the surveys.[17] The service flows from consumer durables are calculated using a method described in the technical appendix to this chapter.

Even after these adjustments, the CEX and PCE differ in terms of whose expenditures are covered and what is classified as consumption. In Figure 3.2 I compare estimates of per capita consumption from each source, and, relative to the PCE, there was substantially less growth in the CEX.[18] Between 1961 and 1995, the PCE levels were higher than those reported in the CEX and grew faster; the average growth rate was 2.2 percent per year compared to 0.7 percent per year for the CEX. The expanded definition of expenditure and the larger population universe in the PCE can account for some of the difference, although the divergence of the two series is puzzling. The ratio of per capita consumption in the CEX to the PCE estimate was 0.94 in 1961, 0.80 in 1973, 0.68 in 1980, 0.61 in 1990, and 0.56 in 1995. The absolute difference between the CEX and PCE

17. Rental equivalents in 1960–61 are estimated using a hedonic regression estimated using the 1973 CEX. The variables employed in the regression include the market value of the home, the before-tax income of the consumer unit, and various demographic characteristics, such as the region of residence, urban versus rural residence, and so on. In the other years for which rental equivalences are unavailable (1980 and 1981), a hedonic regression is estimated using the 1984 survey and much more detailed information on the characteristics of the home.

18. The PCE series is identical to that presented in Figure 3.1. The CEX series is based on tabulations from the Consumer Expenditure Surveys and are linearly interpolated between survey years. The same price index (based on the PCE implicit price deflators) is used to convert nominal expenditures in each survey to constant 1973 dollars.

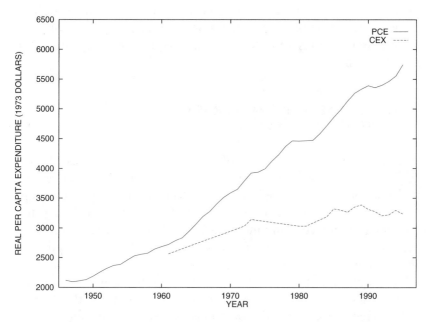

Figure 3.2. CEX versus PCE aggregate expenditure, 1946–1995

reached $2,180 billion in 1995.[19] As a frame of reference, total (durables adjusted) PCE in 1995 was $4,996 billion.[20]

Why are these two estimates so different? The CEX represent the out-of-pocket expenditures of consumer units, whereas the PCE are based on the receipts of businesses. The rapid growth of expenditures on health care, without a commensurate increase in out-of-pocket spending, can account for some of the differences between the two series. The PCE include a category called "services furnished without payment by financial intermediaries," which has no counterpart in the CEX. This "commodity" increased from 1.3 percent of total expenditure in 1961 to 3.0 percent in 1995. The services component of the PCE also includes the expenditures of private religious and welfare agencies, which, again, has no counterpart in the CEX. In

19. This assumes that both samples represent 263.0 million persons.
20. To identify the sources of the differences, I have compared the two data sources at a lower level of commodity aggregation over the same period (Slesnick 1992). See also Branch (1994), Gieseman (1978, 1987), and Houthakker and Taylor (1970).

previous work (Slesnick 1992) I find that only one-half of the discrepancy can be explained by definitional differences. The source of the remaining gap is a mystery that can be resolved only by further investigation.[21]

3.3. EXPENDITURE PATTERNS IN THE UNITED STATES

Are Americans spending more of their resources on the basic necessities of life such as food, housing, and health care, or are they able to spend more on luxuries? Whereas information on total consumption is essential for an assessment of the standard of living, the growing importance of in-kind transfers and tax expenditures reflects the accompanying concern of policy makers for the consumption of specific items.

The information in the PCE enables us to examine how the average spending patterns have changed over time in the United States. Aggregate demands for goods and services depend on the level and distribution of income, the demographic structure of the population, and prices. Disentangling the effects of these variables is a central element of the analysis of demand that has preoccupied researchers for decades.[22] Rather than digress and provide an explanation for the observed expenditure patterns, I present a purely descriptive analysis of the allocation of total expenditure across seven broad categories of goods and services:

> *Food*: food at home, food at restaurants, tobacco, and alcohol.
> *Housing*: owner-occupied and rental housing.
> *Medical Care*: health insurance, drugs, physician services, dental services, and hospital and nursing home care.

21. Under-reporting in the CEX undoubtedly explains some of the differences, and Branch (1987) provides corroborative evidence of under-reporting in her comparison of medical care expenditures in the CEX to the National Health Accounts. Branch (1994) and Gieseman (1987) find that food expenditures in the CEX are closer than are the PCE to alternative, independent estimates of spending on food.
22. Modern econometric analysis of demand arguably began with the seminal work of Prais and Houthakker (1955) and Stone (1954). Surveys of the literature are presented by Deaton and Muellbauer (1980) and Blundell (1988). An assessment of the extent to which aggregate demands respond to changes in prices, aggregate income and the joint distribution of income, and the demographic characteristics has been considered by Jorgenson, Lau, and Stoker (1982) and more recently by Blundell, Pashardes, and Weber (1993).

Consumer Durables: service flows from automobiles, other motor vehicles, appliances, home furnishings, books, and other durable goods.

Energy: gasoline, electricity, natural gas, fuel oil, and coal.

Other Consumer Services: transportation, recreation, education, and personal business and other services.

Consumer Goods: clothing, sport and garden supplies, reading material, and other nondurable items.

It has long been hypothesized that expenditure patterns provide information on both the levels and the trends of well-being. Engel's Law, for example, asserts the existence of an inverse relationship between the standard of living and the proportion of total spending devoted to food. This empirical regularity is typically found to hold for rich and poor countries as well as for individual households with different levels of resources. If Engel's Law can be applied at an aggregate level, an increase in social welfare will be reflected by a concomitant decrease in the average share of spending on food. Figure 3.3 shows such a secular decline in the fraction of total spending on food in the United States from 1946 through 1995.[23] Food accounted for 36.1 percent of aggregate expenditure in 1946 but only 15.9 percent in 1995. Although far from conclusive (there are many alternative explanations for a decrease in the food share), the observed trend is consistent with a rise in the standard of living over this period.[24]

The share of spending on housing, in contrast, has been relatively stable. Between 1946 and 1958, housing expenditures increased from 10.1 percent of total expenditure to 14.0 percent. Since 1958, however, there has been surprisingly little change. This runs counter to the popular perception that, over time, housing has become less affordable and an increasing fraction of households' total spending. It is important to keep in mind, however, that these expenditures represent national averages. There is substantial variation in housing values and rents across the country, which suggests that regional differences are likely to be important. One would expect spending on

23. Data presented in Figure 3.3 and Figure 3.4 are based on the author's calculations using the PCE over this period.

24. The aggregate food share depends not only on the level of real income but also on relative prices, the demographic composition of the population, and the distribution of income. It would be easy to construct examples in which the food share falls over time even though the standard of living is unchanged.

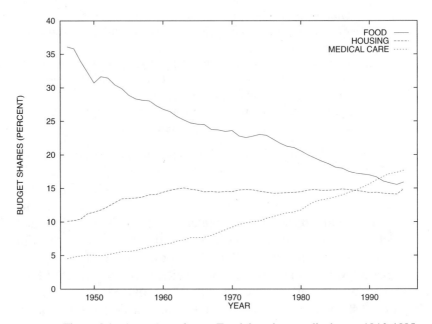

Figure 3.3. Aggregate shares: Food, housing, medical care, 1946–1995

housing to be more important for somebody living in urban California than for someone living in rural Nebraska. Although the average share has remained between 14 percent and 15 percent over the past forty years, the variation in expenditures across regions or between urban and rural areas could be pronounced.

Spending on health care is another focal point of policy makers. The concern is that households are spending a larger and larger fraction of their resources on health maintenance and, as a result, have less to allocate to other goods that improve their overall standard of living. Figure 3.3 shows that such concerns are not easily dismissed. Since 1946 there has been a fourfold increase in the share of spending on medical care from 4.5 percent to 17.7 percent by 1995; spending on health care currently exceeds the amount spent on both housing and food. Note, however, that these estimates are somewhat misleading because they represent not only households' out-of-pocket expenditures but also the spending made on their behalf by private third parties. It is true that, as a nation, we are spending proportionately more on health care than we were, but the actual

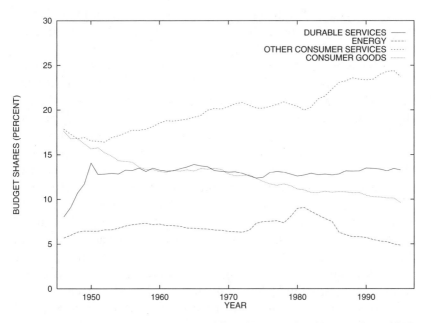

Figure 3.4. Aggregate shares: Durables, nondurables, services, 1946–1995

incidence of these expenditures and their impact on living standards cannot easily be discerned from a graph such as Figure 3.3.[25]

Access to consumer durables is almost certainly correlated with a rise in the standard of living, and even the most casual observation suggests that items such as televisions, computers, and motor vehicles have become increasingly important in the spending habits of households. Figure 3.4 shows that this general perception is accurate but that the most significant change occurred in the years immediately following World War II. The share of services from durables jumped from 8.0 percent in 1946 to approximately 12.9 percent in 1953 due, largely, to an increase in car ownership. As with housing, there has been little net change after this initial increase, with the share fluctuating between 12 percent and 14 percent of total spending. This stability is somewhat surprising, although there is greater uncertainty in these estimates than with other items. This arises both because of the imputations required to calculate the services received from the

25. For a discussion of issues related to the demand for health care, see the survey by Pauly (1986).

aggregate stocks of consumer durables and because of the difficulty in incorporating the dramatic changes in the general quality of these goods that occurred over this period.

Much has been made of the increased importance of services in the U.S. economy. Even with exclusion of housing and medical care, the fraction of spending on consumer services in 1995 was the highest of all commodity groups considered. The share rose from 17.9 percent in 1946 to 23.7 percent in 1995 due, in part, to an increase in spending on personal business items such as legal services, financial services, insurance, and the like. Expenditures on consumer goods (a group composed primarily of clothing and accessories) fell from 17.7 percent of the total in 1946 to 9.6 percent in 1995. The energy share, which includes utilities and gasoline, was between 6 percent and 8 percent until the 1970s, when the oil price shocks had the effect of ratcheting spending upward. By 1981, the fraction of total spending on these products reached a high of 9.1 percent and, as consumers began to conserve (and prices fell), decreased to 4.9 percent in 1995.

Cross-sectional variation of consumption patterns can be a critical input to the decision of how best to help our least fortunate citizens. Figures 3.5 and 3.6 show tabulations from the 1995 CEX of the average shares for groups of households distinguished by their per capita expenditure.[26] This variable is positively correlated with the standard of living so that each graph describes differences in spending between rich and poor households. Most conspicuously, Figure 3.5 shows that the food share falls with per capita expenditure, which, again, is consistent with Engel's Law. The energy share also decreases with per capita consumption, although the decline is more attenuated. Perhaps more surprising is the fact that the housing share of the poorest households is actually lower than that of the wealthiest, whereas the fraction of total expenditure allocated to consumer durables hardly varies across households with different welfare levels. The share of consumer services increases with per capita consumption, which generally accords with expectations.[27] The overall conclusion is that the poor devote a larger fraction of their resources to food and, to a lesser extent, energy than those who are better off.

26. Specifically, the tabulations are averages across groups that correspond to, roughly, the deciles of the per capita expenditure distribution. To conserve space I combine medical care spending and other services into a category called consumer services.
27. The cross-sectional pattern in earlier years is qualitatively similar.

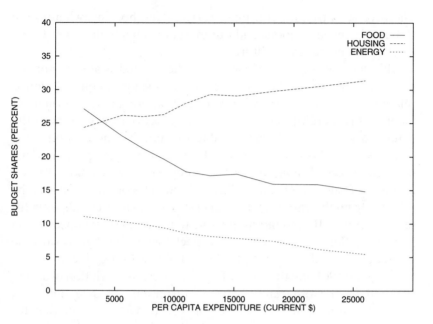

Figure 3.5. 1995 CEX shares: Food, housing, energy

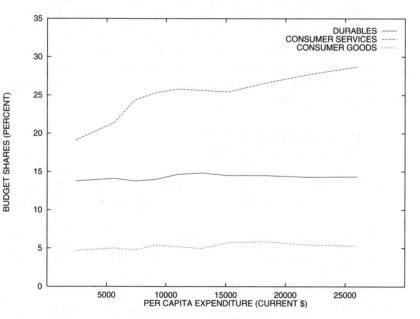

Figure 3.6. 1995 CEX shares: Durables, services, nondurables

The reverse is true for consumer services and housing, whereas the shares of consumer goods and durables are roughly invariant to the level of per capita expenditure.

Although an analysis of saving in the United States is not my primary focus, the ability of households to smooth consumption is related to the accuracy with which it approximates permanent income. It is, therefore, appropriate to digress briefly and examine the extent to which households are able to smooth consumption when incomes vary. This phenomenon is best examined using longitudinal data that record households' consumption and income. In the absence of such data, the ability to smooth consumption can be inferred from the variation in saving rates across households with different incomes. If households are able to maintain their consumption as income fluctuates, one would expect low saving by low-income households and the opposite for households with high incomes.

Using the 1961 and the 1995 CEX, I examine the variation of saving (defined as the difference between disposable income and total outlays) across income classes.[28] Figures 3.7 and 3.8 illustrate that, for two cross sections separated by more than thirty years, the relationship between disposable income and the saving rate is generally consistent with consumption smoothing behavior. There is substantial dissaving for low-income households and saving for those who are richer. In 1961 the poorest households had an average saving rate of −22.1 percent, whereas households with the highest incomes saved 27.8 percent of their disposable income. The same general relationship was found in 1995.[29]

3.4. DEMOGRAPHIC CHANGE IN THE UNITED STATES

Because the welfare measure (2.1) is a function of the demographic characteristics of the household, the composition of the population

28. Disposable income is defined to be personal income plus the services received from owner-occupied housing and consumer durables minus taxes. Measuring saving as a residual is plagued by the problem that both income and consumption are measured with error. This, coupled with the inaccuracies in reported tax liabilities in the CEX (reported by Bosworth, Burtless, and Sabelhaus 1991), suggests that caution is in order in using the CEX to analyze saving behavior.
29. Tabulations for the intervening years reveal essentially the same relationship between saving and the level of disposable income. Although the pattern of saving is replicated in each year, the extreme levels of saving and dissaving for households in the tails of the income distribution undoubtedly reflect the measurement error referred to in footnote 28.

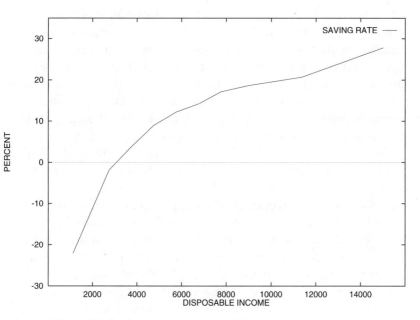

Figure 3.7. Saving rate by income, 1961

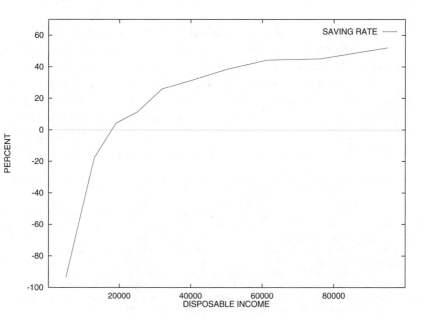

Figure 3.8. Saving rate by income, 1995

will influence both the level and the distribution of household welfare. If female-headed households are substantially worse off than their male-headed counterparts, for example, an increase in their representation will (all other things being equal) dampen the growth rate of social welfare and increase inequality. A decrease in average household size reduces the average need of the population and increases the standard of living for a fixed level of aggregate consumption. In this section I make a cursory examination of changes in the demographic composition of the population in the United States using data reported in the *Current Population Reports, Series P-60*.[30]

Among the most prominent demographic changes since World War II has been the decrease in average household size from 3.2 persons per household in 1947 to 2.4 in 1995.[31] The fraction of households of different sizes, depicted in Figure 3.9, shows that the average size fell, primarily, because of an increase in the relative number of single-member households and a decrease in the fraction of large households. Between 1947 and 1992, the proportion of households with a single member increased from 18 percent to 35 percent, whereas those of size five or more decreased from 19 percent to 9 percent. Changes in the representation of other household types were more attenuated.

The composition of households distinguished by the age of the head is presented in Figure 3.10. The fraction of elderly households (age 65 and over) increased from 15 percent in 1947 to 20 percent in 1992. The youngest households (those with a head age 16–24) constitute a relatively small fraction of all households, although, taken together, the representation of households in the early and late stages of the life cycle increased from 21 percent to 27 percent between 1947 and 1992. These households are at greater risk of having low incomes

---

30. I also use the Bureau of the Census (1967) for the period 1947–1964. These tabulations are over the combined population of families and unrelated individuals. For ease of exposition I will refer to the population of families and unrelated individuals (as well as consumer units in the CEX) as "households." Note that this concept of a household is distinct from the Bureau of the Census's definition, which classifies a household as a group of individuals who live in the same residence. I use families and unrelated individuals as the basic observation in this context because they are more comparable to a consumer unit in the CEX. The two populations will differ to the extent that unrelated individuals live together, share expenses, and form a consumer unit.

31. The number of persons is obtained from the Bureau of the Census (1991, 1994, 1996). The number of households (i.e., families and unrelated individuals) is obtained from various issues of the *Current Population Reports, Series P-60*.

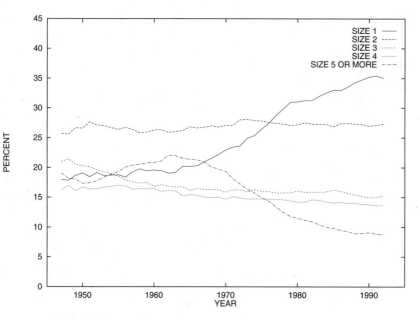

Figure 3.9. Proportion of households by size, 1947–1992

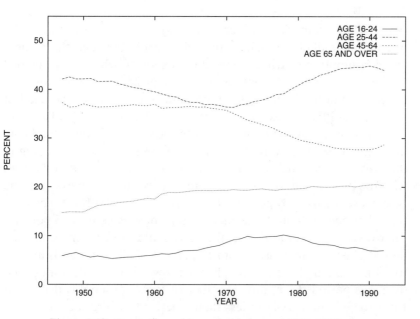

Figure 3.10. Proportion of households by age, 1947–1992

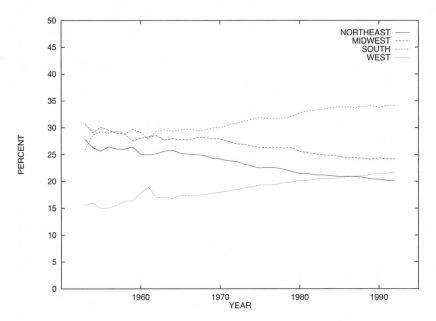

Figure 3.11. Proportion of households by region, 1953–1992

(and high consumption-to-income ratios), so a change in their relative numbers likely influences the relationship between the income and consumption distributions and the extent to which they diverge.

The proportions of households distinguished by region of residence, race of the head of the household, and gender of the head of the household are presented in Figures 3.11 through 3.13. The fraction of households living in the South increased between 1953 (the first year these data were available) and 1992, as did those living in the West. The Northeast and the Midwest shared equally in the loss, with the proportions decreasing from 28 percent to 20 percent in the Northeast and from 31 percent to 24 percent in the Midwest. The fraction of nonwhite households increased from 9 percent to 15 percent. There was a dramatic rise in the representation of female-headed households; they increased from 18 percent of all households in 1947 to 30 percent in 1992. Although not shown, it is worth noting that over this period the relative number of farm households decreased from 16 percent in 1947 to less than 2 percent toward the end of the sample period.

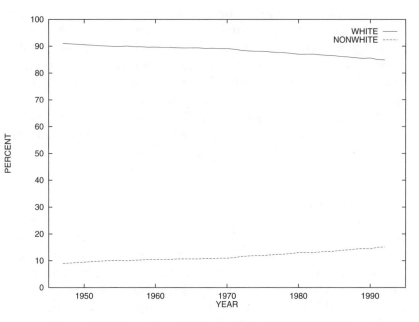

Figure 3.12. Proportion of households by race, 1947–1992

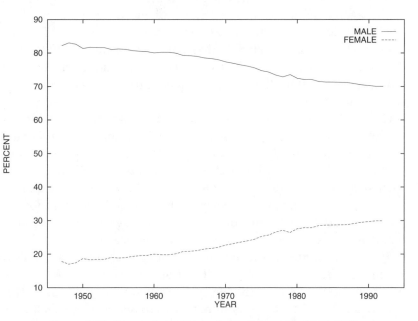

Figure 3.13. Proportion of households by gender, 1947–1992

These data show major changes in the composition of the population over the past five decades. Average household size has fallen,
primarily because of an increase in the fraction of single-member
households and a decrease in the relative number of large families.
Farm households have virtually disappeared, more households live in
the Sun Belt, and the composition of the population by age, gender,
and race has changed significantly. The extent to which these compositional changes have influenced the level and distribution of well-
being will be examined in subsequent chapters.

3.5. SUMMARY

This brief examination of U.S. consumption data provides a preview
of results to be presented more formally in later chapters. First and
foremost, the growth of per capita consumption is suggestive of a
rising standard of living. Spending patterns have also changed significantly over this period; the shares of consumer services and health
care have increased, while the fraction of total expenditure devoted
to food has decreased. To the extent that Engel's Law can be applied
in the aggregate, the downward trend of the food share provides
ancillary evidence of a sustained increase in the standard of living.
Cross-sectional variation in spending patterns indicates that the poor
devote a larger fraction of their budgets to food and energy than do
those who are better off and spend smaller proportions on consumer
services and housing.

One of the reasons that the income- and consumption-based social
welfare statistics might differ is because of consumption smoothing
behavior by households. Tabulations from the CEX are generally consistent with the ability of households to even out their consumption
when incomes fluctuate. Households with low incomes have expenditure levels exceeding income, whereas the reverse is true for those at
the upper end of the income distribution. This suggests the possibility
that the income and expenditure distributions are quite different.

The composition of the population of households has changed
significantly since World War II. The fractions of households at the
beginning and the end of the life cycle have grown significantly. This
feature alone could substantially influence cross-sectional estimates of
inequality and poverty. All other things being equal, the decrease in

average household size has the effect of increasing the overall level of welfare.

TECHNICAL APPENDIX: COMPUTING THE SERVICE FLOWS FROM CONSUMER DURABLES

I briefly describe the method used to estimate the service flows from the stock of consumer durables in the PCE as well as in the CEX.

Adjusting the PCE for durable service flows

Following Christensen and Jorgenson (1969, 1973) and Diewert (1974), the service flow at time t, say S_t, derived from a particular durable good is computed as:

$$S_t = r_t p_t + (p_t - p_{t+1})$$

where r_t is the after-tax rate of return on the asset in period t, and p_t is the corresponding value of the capital stock. This estimate is founded on the assumption that the purchase price of an asset is equal to the present discounted value of the services it provides over its life.

As part of this calculation, it is necessary to determine the size of the capital stock. This is done using the perpetual inventory method, in which the capital stock in period t is equal to the current level of investment plus the non-depreciated portion of last period's capital stock:

$$K_t = I_t + (1 - \delta)K_{t-1}$$

where K_t is the capital stock in period t, I_t is the level of investment, and durables are assumed to depreciate at a constant geometric rate δ.[32] The investment data for each durable category are produced by the BEA.[33]

---

32. Hulten and Wykoff (1981a, 1981b) have shown that geometric depreciation provides a reasonable approximation to the observed depreciation of capital stocks in the United States. It should be noted, however, that this assumption is not without its critics. The estimated depreciation rates are furniture, 0.1268, appliances, 0.1570, radios and televisions, 0.1749, books, 0.1855, durable toys and sports equipment, 0.1649, automobiles, 0.255, other motor vehicles, 0.1996, china and glassware, 0.1943, jewelry, 0.1540, and ophthalmic products, 0.3027.
33. See Musgrave (1979) for a description of the method employed to compute the capital stocks by BEA.

Durable service flows in the CEX

Computing the service flows from consumer durables in the CEX is plagued by the problem that the inventory of the stock of durables is either absent or incomplete in virtually all of the surveys. The notable exceptions are the 1972 and 1973 surveys, in which a comprehensive inventory is conducted for each consumer unit. If the durable depreciates at a constant geometric rate, the service flow from a good purchased s periods ago for a price of p_0 is

$$S_t = (r_t + \delta)(1 - \delta)^s p_0$$

Because the purchase price and age of the good are recorded in the 1972–1973 CEX, the services are easily calculated.

To estimate the services from durables in the other cross-section years, I appeal to the theory of two-stage budgeting. Households are differentiated according to six demographic characteristics: family size, age of the head of the household, region of residence, race of head of household, sex of head of household, and farm versus nonfarm residence. For each family type I assume that total expenditure is allocated across broad commodity groups, one of which is the sum of services from housing and consumer durables (capital services). Given the allocation of expenditure to capital services, I assume that the share of spending on housing and other consumer durables is constant for each household type. Given the shares of consumer durables out of total capital services in 1973 and the spending on housing in other years, I can estimate the service flows from durables in the other CEX.

4 The cost of living

Estimates of the cost of living are among the most important statistics produced by the federal government because of their widespread use in indexing government transfer payments. Social Security benefits are, by far, the largest of the federal outlays that are indexed, although Supplemental Security Income and a variety of other federal compensation and pension programs also contain provisions for indexing. Tax brackets are adjusted for inflation to avoid what is commonly known as "bracket creep," as is the personal exemption. It is clear that, taken together, relatively minor biases in the price indexes used for these adjustments can have an enormous impact on fiscal policy.

Cost-of-living indexes also play a critical role in the measurement of social welfare. They are used to adjust the poverty line over time and to account for inflation in comparisons of national income or expenditure. The standard-of-living index presented in Chapter 2, for example, requires the deflation of aggregate expenditures by an estimate of the cost of living. The key question is, which index should be used for this purpose?

Over the years, the CPI has been used extensively and virtually exclusively as the government's estimate of the cost of living despite increasing evidence of systematic biases.[1] A panel of experts con-

---

1. The BLS produces several consumer price indexes. It is worth reiterating that, unless otherwise stated, I am referring to the CPI-U. Note, though, that it is the CPI for Urban Wage Earners and Clerical Workers (CPI-W) that is used to adjust Social Security benefits.

vened to study the CPI concluded that the inflation bias is around 1.1 percent per year, with a "plausible" range of 0.8 percent to 1.6 percent.[2] This is in addition to permanent errors that were previously introduced in the BLS estimate of the price level. In the next section I summarize some of the problems with the CPI and assess their empirical importance.

If the CPI is flawed, what alternative index should be used to measure the cost of living? In section 4.2 I describe a price index that can be interpreted as the amount that expenditure must change in order to maintain the standard of living. By construction, it measures the impact of price movements on social welfare and can be meaningfully employed for cost-of-living adjustments. I find that estimates of inflation based on this index differ markedly from the CPI, and, in some years, have a substantial effect on the estimated rate of growth in the standard of living in the United States.

The effects of inflation can vary across groups of individuals if their spending patterns are different. If empirically significant, such variation is important not only for the measurement of the standard of living but also for issues related to indexing. If the cost of living of the elderly differs from that of the non-elderly, Social Security benefits should be adjusted using an index based exclusively on the spending patterns of recipients. In section 4.3 I examine differences in the cost of living across groups distinguished by age, race, and gender.

4.1. WHAT'S WRONG WITH THE CPI?

In most applications of cost-of-living indexes, the central issue is the amount that nominal wages, benefits, or expenditures must change in order to maintain a constant level of well-being. The CPI is ill suited for this exercise, and in recent years, the magnitudes of the biases have been large.[3]

Substitution biases

Some of the problems with the CPI have been described in Chapter 2. The CPI is calculated as a weighted average of changes in the prices

2. A summary of the final report is provided by Boskin et al. (1997).
3. See Moulton (1996) for a description of the methods used to calculate the CPI.

of individual commodities, where the weights are the fixed shares of expenditure allocated to each good. The assumption that weights are fixed induces an error because, as relative prices change, the composition of household expenditures changes and the impact of inflation is mitigated. The resulting bias is referred to as the "substitution bias."

Empirical studies have found the magnitude of this error to be relatively small. Braithwait (1980) estimated the average substitution bias as 0.1 percent per year over the period 1958 to 1973. Manser and McDonald (1988) found it to be 0.18 percent per year between 1959 and 1985. A more recent study by Aizcorbe and Jackman (1993) corroborated these findings using the raw inputs of the CPI, whereas Boskin et al. (1997) estimated the bias to be around 0.4 percent per year.

Although the existence of the substitution bias has been acknowledged for some time, recent research has shown that the fixed-weight assumption causes other errors that amplify the upward bias in the CPI. Until January 1997 the building blocks of the CPI were 9,108 disaggregated indexes that correspond to the prices of 207 categories of goods and services purchased in 44 urban areas. In each of these areas, the prices are obtained from a sample of retail outlets which are rotated at five-year intervals; 20 percent of the sample is dropped and replaced by new outlets each year. This method of sampling causes a problem because, as prices change, consumers search for the lowest price and purchase the good at the store that offers it. Since the CPI is computed using a sample of many of the same outlets, this "outlet substitution" is largely ignored and the resulting estimate of inflation is biased upward. Reinsdorf (1993) found this variant of the substitution bias to be particularly serious for certain food items and gasoline.[4]

Housing and consumer durables

The treatment of owner-occupied housing and consumer durables in the CPI introduces additional errors. Prior to 1983, the weight rep-

---

4. A further problem, described by Moulton (1993, 1996), lies in the method of linking and weighting the prices as outlets are rotated through the CPI sample. This has become known as the "formula bias," and changes in the method of calculating the CPI to account for it were implemented by the BLS in 1995. Diewert (1995) surveys these issues and provides estimates of the biases induced by each source.

resenting the budget share devoted to owner-occupied housing was based on the investment expenditures of the homeowner. The appropriate concept for owner-occupied housing is not the spending on taxes, insurance, and mortgage interest but rather the flow of services or the rental equivalent of the home. The high interest rates in the 1970s resulted in an overestimate of both the price of housing and its weight in the CPI.

The effect of this error was that inflation was overstated, and in some years the magnitude of the bias was large.[5] Although the treatment of housing in the CPI was modified after 1983, there was no historical revision of the index. Therefore, the post-1983 CPI is not comparable to the estimates made before 1983. The index was permanently biased upward, as were all the transfers whose automatic cost-of-living adjustments were tied to it.[6]

Consumer durables should be treated in the same way as owner-occupied housing, with the weights based on the rental equivalents of cars, furniture, and major appliances rather than the amounts spent at the time of purchase. As with the treatment of housing prior to 1983, BLS continues to use the investment expenditures on durables in measuring the cost of living. One would expect biases similar to those found with housing, although the magnitudes are undoubtedly smaller because of the smaller role played by durables in the spending of most households.

Quality changes

A cost-of-living index is designed to summarize changes in the prices of the same set of goods and services between two time periods. Although it is conceptually straightforward, complications arise from the fact that the characteristics of some goods change significantly. This requires identification of the fraction of a price increase that is purely inflationary and that due to an improvement in the quality of the product. If the price of a desktop computer increases by 20 percent between one year and the next, it would be inappropriate to ascribe the entire price increase to inflation if the new computer has

5. A more comprehensive discussion of the biases in the CPI attributable to the treatment of housing is presented by Gillingham and Lane (1982).
6. The adjustment to the CPI-W, which is used to index Social Security payments, was not made until 1985.

a faster processor and is bundled with the latest accessories and software. A method of distinguishing between "pure" price changes and those due to quality changes is necessary to accurately assess the true cost of living.[7]

BLS uses several methods to adjust the CPI for changes in quality.[8] In some cases, the good is modified by adding a specific item or piece of equipment. The portion of the price increase that is due to an improvement in quality is taken to be the cost of this item. Although easy to implement, this type of adjustment is not completely satisfactory because consumers' valuations of the product may not coincide with manufacturers' costs. If the added equipment is of no use to the consumer, there is effectively no change in quality and the price increase is purely inflationary. The direct measurement of the cost of changing the characteristics of the product will, in this case, overstate the quality-induced price change.

In the absence of a well-defined change in the product's characteristics, BLS uses a number of imputations to assess the effect of quality changes on prices. A method referred to as "linking" measures the pure price effect as the average change in the prices (within an urban area) of goods in the same general category. Any further change is attributed to variation in quality and is not incorporated in the inflation estimate.[9]

It's unlikely that either of these methods accurately accounts for changes in product quality. Are large biases introduced? To answer this question, a reasonable alternative must be proposed. A growing literature has developed around the idea of "hedonic pricing," in which the contribution of goods' characteristics to their final price is estimated. This information can be used to determine the fraction of a price change that is due to changes in the characteristics of the goods.[10] The evidence is thin, and final estimates of the magnitude of the quality bias in the CPI range from small (Fixler 1993, Moulton and Moses 1997) to large (Boskin et al. 1997).

---

7. A related issue is the "new goods" problem, in which prices must be imputed for goods that did not exist in the base period. See Fisher and Griliches (1995) for further discussion of this problem.
8. Kokoski (1993) and Moulton and Moses (1997) provide a more detailed description of these methods.
9. Moulton and Moses (1997) estimate the magnitude of these adjustments on the CPI.
10. See Liegey (1993) and Kokoski (1993) for application of hedonic techniques to the components of the CPI. See also the discussion by Pollak (1983b).

To assess the degree to which the CPI mismeasures inflation, I compare it to two alternative indexes. The first is an experimental index produced by BLS that treats owner-occupied housing consistently throughout the sample period.[11] Any difference between this index and the CPI is due to the inappropriate treatment of owner-occupied housing in the CPI. The second index is calculated using the implicit price deflators of the PCE. Owner-occupied housing is treated as the rental equivalent, and durable purchase prices are replaced by estimates of the prices of durable services. The substitution bias is partially mitigated using a chained Tornqvist (1936) index in which the average shares in the two periods, rather than the shares in the base period, are used as weights.[12] This index is described in greater detail in the appendix to this chapter and, for ease of exposition, will be referred to as the PCE price index.

Figure 4.1 shows the estimated inflation rates for the three indexes over the period 1948 through 1995. Each series exhibits the same qualitative pattern since World War II; prices fluctuated until the early 1960s and then increased steadily. Inflation accelerated in the 1970s – fueled, largely, by the oil price shocks – but subsequently decreased in the mid-1980s and early 1990s. Over the entire postwar period, the CPI increased at a rate of 4.0 percent per year compared to 3.8 percent for the other two indexes.

Although each index shows the same qualitative pattern of price movements, in some years the differences between the indexes were large. Between 1979 and 1980, for example, the CPI increased 12.7 percent compared to 10.6 percent for the CPI-X1. In an environment in which even the most minor error has important implications for government spending, a bias of this magnitude can (and did) have a large effect on fiscal policy.

Table 4.1 presents average inflation rates at five-year intervals (except at the end of the sample period) beginning in 1948. The

11. This index is referred to as the CPI-U-X1 (CPI-X1 for short) and is identical to the CPI after 1983.
12. The Tornqvist index is a discrete approximation to the Divisia index. Jorgenson and Griliches (1971) and Diewert (1976, 1981) discuss other attractive properties of this index. Since the PCE implicit price deflators use some of the same components as the CPI, the outlet substitution bias and the error induced by the treatment of quality remain. The PCE index in Figure 4.1 differs from the aggregate PCE deflator produced by BEA because of the different treatment of durables and different method of calculating the price index described earlier.

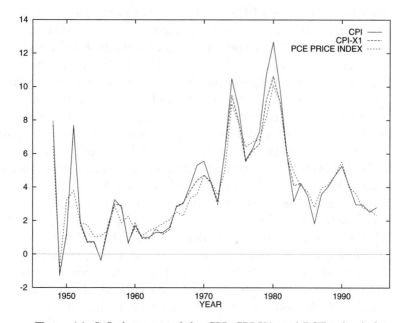

Figure 4.1. Inflation rates of the CPI, CPI-X1, and PCE price index, 1948–1995

Table 4.1. *Average inflation rate (%)*

Year	CPI	CPI-X1	PCE
1948–1952	3.5	3.5	2.9
1953–1957	1.2	1.1	1.6
1958–1962	1.4	1.5	1.6
1963–1967	2.0	2.0	2.1
1968–1972	4.5	4.0	3.9
1973–1977	7.4	7.1	7.0
1978–1982	9.3	8.3	8.1
1983–1987	3.3	3.5	3.9
1988–1992	4.2	4.2	4.4
1993–1995	2.8	2.8	2.6

Source: Author's calculations.

housing bias was small until the late 1960s, when the CPI and the CPI-X1 began to diverge. Over the fifteen-year period between 1968 and 1982, the largest component of the bias in the CPI resulted from the treatment of owner-occupied housing, and this error dwarfed the other biases. Between 1978 and 1982, for example, the CPI recorded an average inflation rate of 9.3 percent per year compared to 8.3 percent for the CPI-X1 and 8.1 percent for the PCE price index.

Differences between the CPI-X1 and the PCE price index suggest that the treatment of housing is not the only problem with the current estimates of inflation. Between 1983 and 1987, for example, the CPI-X1 increased 3.5 percent per year compared to 3.9 percent for the PCE price index. A bias of similar magnitude in the opposite direction occurred between 1948 and 1952. These differences can be attributed primarily to the treatment of durables and the fixed-weight assumption implicit in the CPI-X1. Although smaller than the housing bias, these differences are certainly large enough to warrant adjustment of the CPI.

What are the implications of these results? The CPI's overestimate of inflation in the 1970s and 1980s resulted in a permanent overinflation of the poverty thresholds, and the official poverty rate produced by the Census Bureau was biased upward. Standard-of-living indexes which used the CPI to deflate nominal income or expenditures were biased downward, and growth rates in the 1970s and 1980s were underestimated. Perhaps most important, all of the government's transfers and benefits which were indexed to the CPI over this period were overinflated, and that increased the deficit and resulted in the redistribution of billions of dollars. Duggan et al. (1995), for example, found that overinflation of Social Security benefits due to the housing bias alone had a cumulative effect on spending (with debt service) of hundreds of billions of dollars.[13]

4.2. THE SOCIAL COST-OF-LIVING INDEX

The CPI, the CPI-X1, and the PCE price index are statistical summaries of price changes developed in the tradition of Fisher (1922). Although widely used, these indexes provide a conceptual basis for welfare comparisons only under special circumstances. This presents a problem because it is precisely these types of applications that are

13. Boskin and Jorgenson (1997) also describe a CBO study of the effect of the upward bias in the CPI on future budget deficits. Correcting the CPI has the effect of increasing tax revenue, decreasing outlays, and decreasing deficits (or increasing surpluses) substantially.

of interest to policy makers. When wages or benefits are adjusted for inflation, we want to know the amount of additional income necessary to maintain recipients' standard of living. Given price variation over time and across states, what levels of AFDC benefits are necessary to preserve the welfare of the poor? These questions and others like them can be addressed only by using a cost-of-living index that has a clear welfare-theoretic foundation.

Konus (1939) developed such a framework by defining a cost-of-living index as the relative cost of attaining a given level of utility as prices change:

$$P_k(\mathbf{p}^1, \mathbf{p}^0, V) = \frac{M(\mathbf{p}^1, V, \mathbf{A}_k)}{M(\mathbf{p}^0, V, \mathbf{A}_k)} \tag{4.1}$$

where $M(\ )$ is the expenditure function, $\mathbf{p}^1$ is the vector of prices in the current period, $\mathbf{p}^0$ is the vector of prices in the base period, and V is the reference utility level. By construction, the index measures the amount that expenditure must change to maintain a stipulated standard of living.

Ideally, P_k would be estimated without assuming specific forms for either the expenditure or the utility functions. As a practical matter, however, this is often impossible, and the best one can do is to obtain upper and lower bounds that are valid for arbitrary representations of preferences. If the reference utility level is unspecified, for example, the minimum and the maximum commodity price ratios between the two periods provide bounds on the cost-of-living index.[14] If the base year utility level is chosen as the reference, a Laspeyres price index provides an upper bound, and the minimum price ratio is the lower bound.[15]

Since these bounds need not be tight, other methods have been proposed that retain the generality but yield more-precise estimates. Afriat (1967, 1977), Diewert (1973), and Varian (1982) advocate an approach in which repeated observations on prices and quantities are used to recover approximations to the expenditure function. The additional information on demands in the different price regimes results in less uncertainty as to the form of the expenditure function, and tighter bounds on the price index can be obtained. Although this

14. See Samuelson (1947).
15. See Pollak (1983a) for additional discussion and results.

approach has much appeal, the practical problem is that repeated observations on household demands are rare in general and, in fact, nonexistent in the United States.

Diewert (1976) derived price indexes that can be interpreted as Konus cost-of-living indexes for specific functional forms of the expenditure function and a unique reference utility level. His approach is attractive because no statistical estimation is necessary, although it does require repeated observations of demands. Balk (1990), Jorgenson and Slesnick (1983), and Kokoski (1987) assume a form for the expenditure function and estimate a household-level cost-of-living index econometrically. Although this approach is more difficult to implement, the cost of living can be estimated using readily available data sources.

The analytical framework for the cost of living that has been described to this point is appropriate for a single household. Cost-of-living measures designed for indexing government programs, however, refer to groups such as all Social Security beneficiaries or all taxpayers. This requires an extension of Konus's (1939) framework to measure the cost of living for a group of households.

The most common approach is to assume that market demands are generated by a representative consumer who maximizes utility subject to a budget constraint. Under this assumption, Konus's approach can be applied to aggregate data to yield a social cost-of-living index. The problem is that there is now a large body of evidence that suggests that the representative consumer assumption is inconsistent with aggregate demand patterns.[16]

In the absence of a representative consumer, how should household cost-of-living indexes be aggregated to yield estimates of the cost of living for groups? Prais (1959) proposed a "plutocratic" index as a weighted sum of household-specific price indexes in which the weights are the households' shares of aggregate expenditure.[17] This index was seen to have adverse ethical implications because the rich are more influential than the poor in determining the cost of living. To soften the normative basis, Prais also proposed a "democratic" index as the (unweighted) mean of the individual indexes. Although Prais emphasized the normative implications of his approach, the

16. See Kirman (1992) and Stoker (1993) for reviews.
17. The plutocratic index can be interpreted as the relative cost of attaining a utility possibility frontier under the two sets of prices.

welfare-theoretic foundation for these indexes is weak. Neither the plutocratic nor the democratic index addresses the question of the amount of additional income required to maintain a level of group welfare as prices change.

A solution to the conceptual problem of aggregation was provided by Pollak's (1981) social cost-of-living index (SCOLI). He defined the index as the ratio of the cost of attaining a given level of social welfare at current prices to that needed to attain the same welfare at base prices:

$$P(\mathbf{p}^1, \mathbf{p}^0, W) = \frac{M(\mathbf{p}^1, W)}{M(\mathbf{p}^0, W)} \tag{4.2}$$

where $M(\ )$ is a social expenditure function and W is the reference level of social welfare.[18] The normative basis of this index is made explicit through the choice of a social welfare function. Most important, it can be used to compare well-being across groups of individuals as prices change. If the index doubles between 1980 and 1990, the implication is that twice the expenditure is required to maintain a constant level of social welfare.

Bounds on unspecified forms of (4.2) can be obtained only if aggregate demands are consistent with the existence of a representative consumer, which is unlikely. It becomes necessary, therefore, to specify an explicit form of the social welfare function which adds a necessarily arbitrary element to the measurement of inflation. This is problematical because there is no reason to expect estimates to be invariant across different specifications.[19]

Does a social cost-of-living index of the type shown in (4.2) yield significantly different estimates of inflation in the United States? Using a model described in Appendix 1, I calculate an aggregate price index using the implicit price deflators that were used to calculate the PCE price index. Figure 4.2 shows that general conclusions concerning price movements are unchanged when I use a social cost-of-living index rather than the PCE price index. The SCOLI shows that inflation was initially low, averaging 2.2 percent per year between 1948

18. The social expenditure function is the minimum level of aggregate expenditure required to attain a level of social welfare at fixed prices. The formal definition is provided in the technical appendix to Chapter 2.
19. Previous empirical studies, however, suggest that the underlying social welfare function has little influence on the price index. See, for example, Slesnick (1991b).

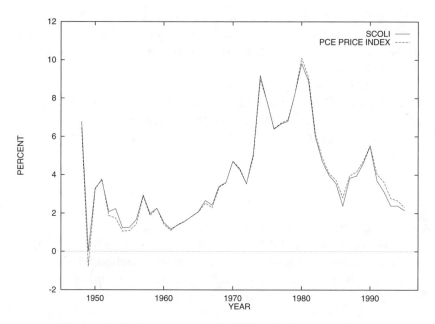

Figure 4.2. Inflation rates of the PCE price index and the social cost-of-living index, 1948–1995

and 1968. Prices rose sharply in the 1970s and early 1980s but subsequently showed much smaller increases through the mid-1990s. These estimates are very similar to those obtained using the PCE price index. In fact, over the entire sample period the average inflation rates are exactly the same. At five-year intervals, the PCE price index understates the average inflation rate by 0.1 to 0.2 percent per year between 1948 and 1962. There is an overestimate of roughly the same magnitude over the last fifteen years. The largest difference in any single year is less than 0.8 percent, which suggests that estimates of inflation are not very sensitive to the choice of either index.

4.3. GROUP COST-OF-LIVING INDEXES

The CPI, the PCE price index, and the social cost-of-living index summarize price changes at the highest level of aggregation. For many applications, though, it is important to know the impact of price

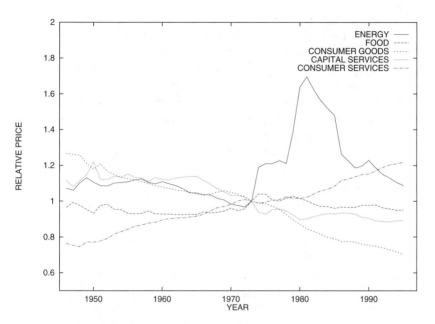

Figure 4.3. Real prices (1973 = 1.0), 1946–1995

movements on subgroups of the population. If the goal is to adjust Social Security payments to maintain the purchasing power of the elderly, it is necessary to use an index based on their spending patterns. Similarly, a cost-of-living index for poor, female-headed households is needed to assess the impact of inflation on welfare recipients.

Cost-of-living indexes may differ across groups if there are differences in their spending patterns and significant variation in relative prices. If the price of natural gas increases, households that use gas to heat their homes will experience an increase in their cost of living, whereas other households will be unaffected. An increase in the relative price of food will have a greater impact on the cost of living of households (such as the poor) who spend a larger fraction of their resources on food than others.

Figure 4.3 shows the relative prices of energy, food, consumer goods, capital services, and consumer services over the period 1946 through 1995. Each series is created by deflating the commodity group price by the PCE price index in each year.[20] Differences in expenditure patterns across demographic groups have a larger effect on the cost of living if there is substantial variation in relative prices over time. Figure 4.3 shows that the relative price of consumer services has increased steadily, reflecting the sharp rise in the prices of health care services. The price of consumer goods exhibited an equally precipitous decline from 1.3 in 1946 to 0.7 in 1995. The real price of food remained relatively stable, whereas the relative price of capital services (which includes housing) fell slightly. Most conspicuous is the sharp increase in the relative price of energy from 1973 through 1981.

This movement in relative prices suggests that differences in the cost of living across population subgroups are at least a theoretical possibility. Using a fixed-weight Laspeyres index tabulated from CEX data, Michael (1979) and Hagemann (1982) found substantial differences in the cost of living across households distinguished by a variety of demographic characteristics. Boskin and Hurd (1985) estimated price indexes for the elderly and non-elderly and found that differences were small. Econometric approaches to the measurement of the cost of living were developed by Balk (1990), Jorgenson and Slesnick (1983), and Kokoski (1987), with mixed conclusions concerning the variation across population subgroups.

Using an uninterrupted sequence of CEX cross sections from 1980 through 1995, I tabulate Tornqvist indexes for households distinguished by age, race, and gender of the head of the household.[21] Since rural households were not included in the 1982 and 1983 surveys, the indexes are tabulated only for those living in urban areas. The estimated inflation rates are reported in Table 4.2.

The differences between groups were large in some years. The inflation rates for the elderly in 1981 and 1982 averaged more than one-half of 1 percent higher than for the non-elderly. Differences in the other years were smaller, but the average difference over the fifteen years was one-tenth of 1 percent higher for the elderly. The

20. The price index for each commodity group is a Tornqvist index calculated using the PCE implicit price deflators of the items composing the group. Capital services represent housing and the service flows from consumer durables.
21. The average budget shares of each demographic group are used as weights for the commodity prices in calculating the index. Rather than using a chain index as with the PCE price index, 1973 is taken to be the fixed base. The price indexes described in footnote 20 are used as prices for each commodity group.

Table 4.2. *Tornquist-based inflation rates by demographic groups (%)*

Year	Age of head		Race of head		Gender of head	
	Non-elderly	Elderly	White	Nonwhite	Male	Female
1981	9.0	9.6	9.1	8.9	9.1	9.2
1982	5.8	6.2	5.9	5.7	5.8	6.2
1983	4.8	4.8	4.8	4.7	4.8	4.8
1984	4.0	4.2	4.0	4.0	4.0	4.2
1985	3.3	3.3	3.3	3.1	3.3	3.3
1986	2.0	2.3	2.1	2.1	2.1	2.2
1987	3.7	3.7	3.7	3.5	3.7	3.7
1988	3.9	4.0	3.9	3.9	3.9	3.9
1989	4.6	4.5	4.6	4.4	4.6	4.6
1990	5.5	5.6	5.5	5.5	5.5	5.4
1991	3.6	3.5	3.5	3.8	3.6	3.5
1992	3.3	3.4	3.3	3.1	3.3	3.3
1993	2.5	2.6	2.5	2.5	2.5	2.6
1994	2.6	2.7	2.6	2.7	2.6	2.7
1995	2.2	2.2	2.2	2.4	2.3	2.2
Avg.	4.1	4.2	4.1	4.0	4.1	4.1

Source: Author's calculations using the CEX and the PCE implicit price deflators.

cost-of-living differences between households distinguished by gender and race of the head of the household were similar. As a general rule, the differences in the cost of living for these groups were fairly small in spite of large changes in relative prices.

The Tornqvist index is subject to the same criticism as the PCE price index. It is a statistical index that relies on the dubious assumption of the existence of a representative consumer within each group. As an alternative approach, a group cost-of-living index can be defined by analogy with the social cost-of-living index; it is the ratio of spending required to attain a reference level of group welfare at current prices to the spending required at base prices. I calculate each index using the implicit price deflators of the PCE and assume that all members of the group face the same prices for goods and services.[22]

22. The specific forms of the group cost-of-living indexes are presented in Appendix 1.

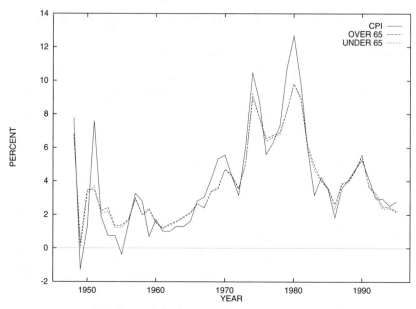

Figure 4.4. Group inflation rates by age, 1948–1995

Figure 4.4 presents differences between the cost of living for the elderly and for the non-elderly over the period 1948 through 1995. The reference welfare level is that attained in 1973, and, as with the Tornqvist index, I find the differences between the inflation rates to be relatively small over the entire sample period. In the 1980s and 1990s, however, the elderly faced higher inflation rates than the non-elderly. Figures 4.5 and 4.6 show a similar pattern of modest differences in the cost of living for households distinguished by race and gender of the household head.

There are, however, substantial differences between the cost of living for the elderly and the CPI.[23] The average annual inflation rate of the CPI is 2.1 percent in the 1950s, 2.7 percent in the 1960s, 7.5 percent in the 1970s, 4.6 percent in the 1980s, and 3.1 percent in the 1990s. The corresponding estimates for the elderly are 2.1 percent, 2.5 percent, 6.8 percent, 4.8 percent, and 2.8 percent. Group cost-of-living

23. The CPI-U is shown in Figure 4.4, whereas the CPI-W is used to adjust Social Security benefits. The qualitative differences between these indexes, however, are small except for the timing of the adjustment for owner-occupied housing.

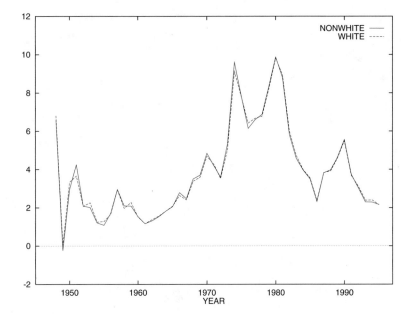

Figure 4.5. Group inflation rates by race, 1948–1995

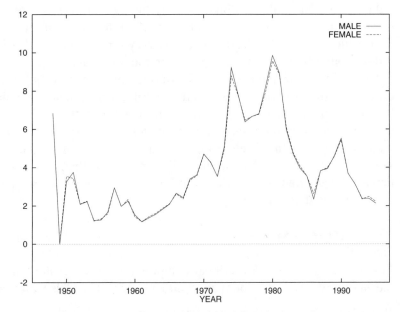

Figure 4.6. Group inflation rates by gender, 1948–1995

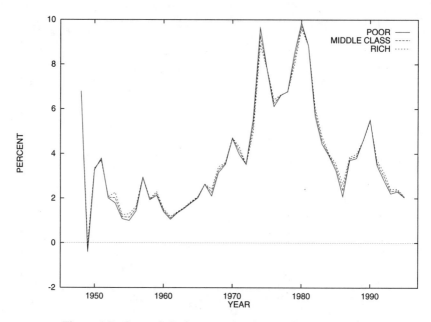

Figure 4.7. Group inflation rates by the standard of living, 1948–1995

indexes for households distinguished by the gender and race of the head of the household are also substantially different from the CPI.

How do measures of the cost of living vary across households with different standards of living? Increases in the prices of necessities relative to luxuries have the effect of increasing the cost of living for the poor more than the rich. To assess the distributional impacts of inflation, in Figure 4.7 I examine the inflation rates for groups of the population with low, moderate, and high standards of living.[24] The inflation rates for the three groups are, again, very similar. Over the sample period, the average annual inflation rate for the poor was 0.1 percent lower than for the rich. The largest difference in any single year was less than 1 percent.

4.4. CONCLUSIONS

Cost-of-living indexes are critical components for an evaluation of the standard of living, inequality, and poverty. They also play an

24. The household type is a family of four with a white, male head of household age 35–44, living in the urban Northeast. The reference utility level is that attained in 1973 at half the mean, the mean, and twice the mean expenditure level.

important role in fiscal policy because they are used to adjust government benefits and tax brackets as prices change. Over the years, the CPI has been used almost exclusively for this purpose despite a growing body of evidence which suggests that it mismeasures inflation.

Using a cost-of-living index with a well-defined welfare-theoretic foundation, I find that the most serious error in the CPI occurred over the period 1973–1983, when it incorporated a large upward bias in the price level. Although differences in the cost of living across different types of consumers are a theoretical possibility, I find that, over extended time periods, there is little variation in the price indexes defined over different types of consumers.

An implication of the results presented in this chapter is that substitution of alternative cost-of-living indexes for the CPI has the effect of increasing the growth rate of the standard of living over time, lowering the poverty thresholds and decreasing the poverty rate. The exact magnitude of these effects will be considered in the next couple of chapters. Perhaps more important, the upward bias in the CPI results in substantial overpayments to the beneficiaries of federal entitlement and mandatory spending programs. This bias also reduces federal revenues by overindexing the individual income tax. Correction of biases in the CPI designed to adjust benefits and taxes more accurately for changes in the cost of living could contribute importantly to reductions in future federal deficits (or increases in surpluses) and the national debt. These reductions can be attributed to higher revenues, lower outlays, and less debt service.

TECHNICAL APPENDIX

I describe the price indexes used to evaluate the cost of living using the following notation:

$\mathbf{p} = (p_1, p_2, \ldots, p_N)$ is the vector of prices of all commodities.

$\mathbf{x}_k = (x_{1k}, x_{2k}, \ldots, x_{Nk})$ is the vector of quantities consumed by the kth individual $(n = 1, 2, \ldots, N; k = 1, 2, \ldots, K)$.

$M_k = \sum_{n=1}^{N} p_n x_{nk}$ is the total expenditure of the kth individual $(k = 1, \ldots, K)$.

A_k is the vector of attributes of the kth individual (k = 1, 2, . . . , K).

Laspeyres price index

The CPI is a "modified" Laspeyres price index defined as the ratio of the expenditure required to purchase a market basket x_k at current prices p^1 to the expenditure needed to purchase the same market basket at base prices p^0:

$$P^{LA}(p^1, p^0, x^0) = \frac{\sum_{n=1}^{N}\sum_{k=1}^{K} p_n^1 x_{nk}}{\sum_{n=1}^{N}\sum_{k=1}^{K} p_n^0 x_{nk}} \tag{A4.1}$$

The Laspeyres index holds the quantities x_k fixed so that substitution by consumers is ignored. Pollak (1983a) has shown that the Laspeyres index is an exact cost-of-living index if the individual has Leontief preferences.

Tornqvist price index

The Tornqvist index provides alternative estimates of the cost of living that allow greater substitution possibilities:

$$\ln P^T(p^1, p^0, x_k^1, x_k^0) = \frac{1}{2}\sum_{n=1}^{N}(w_{nk}^0 + w_{nk}^1)\ln\frac{p_n^1}{p_n^0} \tag{A4.2}$$

where w_{nk}^0 is the share of the nth commodity in the base period, and w_{nk}^1 is the corresponding share in the current period. Diewert has shown that (A4.2) is a true cost-of-living index for a consumer with utility level $(V_k^0 V_k^1)^{1/2}$ and an expenditure function of the form

$$\ln M_k(p, V_k) = \lambda_0 + \gamma' \ln p + \ln p' \Gamma \ln p + \delta_0 \ln V_k$$
$$+ \delta' \ln p \ln V_k + \alpha_0 (\ln V_k)^2 \tag{A4.3}$$

where V_k^0 and V_k^1 are the utilities attained by household k in the base and current periods.

Social cost-of-living index

Let $W(\mathbf{u})$ be a social welfare function where $\mathbf{u} = (V_1, V_2, \ldots, V_K)$ is the vector of individual welfare functions. Pollak's (1981) definition of the social cost-of-living index is

$$P(\mathbf{p}^1, \mathbf{p}^0, W) = \frac{M(\mathbf{p}^1, W)}{M(\mathbf{p}^0, W)} \tag{A4.4}$$

where $M(\ )$ is the social expenditure function. The social cost-of-living index is the ratio of the minimum level of aggregate expenditure required to attain social welfare level W at prices $\mathbf{p}^1$ to the level of aggregate expenditure required to attain the same level of social welfare at base period prices $\mathbf{p}^0$.

The group cost-of-living indexes are calculated using equation (A4.4) with social welfare defined over the subgroup of interest rather than over the entire population. The group cost-of-living index for a subset of G households is defined as

$$P_G(\mathbf{p}^1, \mathbf{p}^0, W_G) = \frac{M_G(\mathbf{p}^1, W_G)}{M_G(\mathbf{p}^0, W_G)}$$

where M_G is the expenditure function defined over the subgroup of households and W_G is the level of group welfare.

5   The standard of living

Are living standards in jeopardy? Will future generations attain levels of well-being that are comparable to those of their parents and grand-parents? There is little debate over the fact that the United States enjoys one of the highest standards of living in the world. The absence of growth in real median family income over the past thirty years, however, has prompted concern for future prospects.

The results presented in this chapter suggest that this concern is unwarranted. The data do not support the claim that the standard of living has been stagnant or falling. Consumption-based estimates of social welfare have increased substantially since 1970 and, in fact, show a rate of growth that approaches the postwar average. Although there were occasional declines from one year to the next, the long-run trend was upward, and this qualitative finding is robust across alternative measures of the standard of living.

5.1. HOUSEHOLD NEEDS AND EQUIVALENCE SCALES

Since my measure of social welfare is based on the average level of consumption per equivalent adult, accurate estimates of the con-sumption requirements of households are essential. Although there is debate as to what such estimates represent, virtually every measure of social welfare uses one. If living standards are reported on a per household basis, needs are assumed to be the same regardless of

88

household composition. If welfare is measured in per capita terms, needs are assumed to increase linearly with the number of persons sharing resources.

I begin by examining a subset of the many empirical estimates of household equivalence scales. What is most evident from this literature is the absence of a consensus as to what constitutes "reasonable" estimates of the consumption requirements of heterogeneous households. Rather than advocate the use of one scale over another, I assess the sensitivity of conclusions to alternative choices.

For the moment, I ignore the utility provided by children (or other characteristics of the household) and measure the needs of households conditional on their observed compositions.[1] In this setting, larger households require more resources to maintain the same level of well-being, and for a given level of consumption, larger families have lower welfare. The empirical issue is the magnitude by which the standard of living decreases with each additional member.

The most widely used scales are those that are easy to implement. The per capita adjustment, for example, assumes that each additional family member (regardless of age or gender) increases the needs of the household by the same amount. The Organization for Economic Cooperation and Development (OECD) uses equivalence scales to measure poverty in different countries. Its scales assign a value of 1.0 for the first adult and 0.7 for each additional adult, whereas children add 0.5 adult equivalents to the total.[2] A couple with two children is assumed, therefore, to need 2.7 times the expenditure of a single adult to attain the same level of welfare. As with the per capita estimates, economies of scale are ignored beyond the second adult. Using data from the 1972–1973 CEX, Lazear and Michael (1988) estimate that the consumption of a child is roughly 40 percent of an adult's. Based on this observation, they assign one adult equivalent for every adult in the household and 0.4 equivalents for each child. The prototypical family of four, therefore, comprises 2.8 adult equivalents.

Although these estimates have the virtue of simplicity, they are not completely satisfactory because of their implausible assumptions concerning economies of scale in consumption; each additional member increases the consumption requirements by the same

1. For more on this issue, see the discussion in the technical appendix to this chapter.
2. These scales are reported by Ruggles (1990), Table 4.4, p. 74.

amount. Moreover, important differences between households (such as age, gender, region of residence, etc.) are largely ignored. These concerns have prompted the development of alternative estimates that are based on nutritional standards, the subjective judgments of households, and the variation in spending patterns across households.

Nutritional equivalence scales

A number of equivalence scales are based on the nutritional intake required to avoid malnutrition. The costs of purchasing essential nutrients are tabulated to determine the resources needed to maintain a healthy diet for different types of households. The Amsterdam index described by Deaton and Muellbauer (1980) is a nutritional equivalence scale that takes an adult female to be 0.9 adult equivalents (relative to an adult male), children under age fourteen are 0.52 equivalents, teenage boys (age fourteen to seventeen) add 0.98 equivalents, and girls of the same age are 0.9. Since additional family members of the same age and gender are assumed to increase the food requirements in the same way, economies of scale in consumption are not accounted for.

The equivalence scales implicit in the poverty thresholds used by the Bureau of the Census are also founded on households' nutritional requirements. They were developed by Mollie Orshansky and were based on the Department of Agriculture's estimates of minimally adequate diets for a variety of households. Unlike the Amsterdam scales, they incorporate economies of scale in consumption and vary over attributes other than family size, such as the age of the head of the household, the number of related children under eighteen years old, the gender of the head of the household, and farm versus nonfarm residence. Weighted averages of the original equivalence scales used by the Census Bureau are presented in Table 5.1.[3]

Although widely used, nutritional equivalence scales have several obvious problems. They are usually founded on experts' opinions as to what constitutes a minimally adequate diet, and there is far from

3. The poverty lines differentiated by farm/nonfarm residence and gender were eliminated in 1981. See Orshansky (1965) for a description of these equivalence scales. The equivalence scales in Table 5.1 are computed from the 1964 weighted poverty thresholds reported in Orshansky (1966), Table 1, p. 23.

Table 5.1. *Census equivalence scales*
(reference: size 4, nonfarm, male)

	Nonfarm		Farm	
	Male	Female	Male	Female
Size 1, Age <65	0.53	0.49	0.37	0.34
Size 1, Age >65	0.47	0.47	0.33	0.33
Size 2, Age <65	0.66	0.63	0.46	0.43
Size 2, Age >65	0.59	0.59	0.42	0.41
Size 3	0.78	0.75	0.55	0.53
Size 4	1.00	0.99	0.70	0.69
Size 5	1.18	1.17	0.83	0.83
Size 6	1.32	1.32	0.93	0.96
Size 7+	1.63	1.60	1.14	1.09

Source: Orshansky (1966), Table 1, p. 23.

a consensus as to what this is. More significant, these scales are based on households' food intakes and ignore other critical consumption requirements. Although a family of four may need three times as much food as a single adult, it may not require three times the housing expenditure. Ignoring nonfood items biases the assessment of households' relative needs in an unknown direction. Note, also, that the measurement of the standard of living requires an answer to the question of how much additional consumption is required for a family of four to achieve the same welfare as a single adult. A nutritional scale is not designed to address this question but, instead, measures the cost of maintaining a specific physiological function.

Subjective equivalence scales

Subjective equivalence scales are estimated on the basis of households' assessments of the income needed to attain different standards of living. The responses to survey questions are used to compare the self-assessed consumption requirements across different types of households.[4]

---

4. This approach was pioneered by economists at Leyden University who were interested in subjective poverty thresholds. See Goedhart et al. (1977), van Praag et al. (1980), and van Praag et al. (1982).

Table 5.2. *Subjective equivalence scales
(reference: family of four, head <65)*

	Male	Female
Size 1, Age <65	0.65	0.45
Size 1, Age >65	0.42	0.29
Size 2, Age <65	0.81	
Size 2, Age >65	0.52	
Size 3	0.91	
Size 4	1.00	
Size 5	1.07	
Size 6	1.13	

Source: Danziger et al. (1984), p. 503.

Unfortunately, there are few survey data of this type in the United States. The Gallup Poll has, in the past, asked "What is the smallest amount of money a family of four needs to get along in your community?" This provides an estimate of different households' perceptions of what it takes for a family of four to "get along" but is of little use in estimating equivalence scales.[5]

The 1979 Income Survey Development Program posed a question that is more useful for equivalence scale estimation:

Living where you do now and meeting the expenses you consider necessary, what would be the very smallest income you (and your family) would need to make ends meet?[6]

Danziger et al. (1984) have used the responses to this question to estimate the needs of households with different compositions (see Table 5.2).[7]

Several features of these estimates are striking. They show enormous economies of scale in consumption; a family of six requires only 1.7 times the expenditure of a single adult to "make ends meet." The scales for elderly individuals and couples are roughly one-third lower

5. This quote is taken from Danziger et al. (1984). Kilpatrick (1973) finds that the answer to this question varies systematically with the income of the respondent and computes what he refers to as the income elasticity of the poverty line.
6. See Danziger et al. (1984), p. 501.
7. Families of size two are assumed to be husbands and wives living together, and larger families are husbands and wives and their children.

than their younger counterparts, and the self-assessed needs of women are one-third lower than for men.[8]

Although subjective equivalence scales provide an interesting alternative perspective, it's unclear how the results should be utilized. There is no way to assess the accuracy of individuals' responses to these hypothetical questions; de Vos and Garner (1991) find that households' responses to the "minimum income" question in the United States were almost twice the size of the official poverty threshold. Because individuals state (rather than demonstrate) their consumption requirements, the consistency and accuracy of their responses are important concerns, as is the robustness of the estimates to modest changes in the wording of the questions.[9] In addition, the scales are measured at a subsistence standard of living and cannot be used for comparisons at different welfare levels.

Full budget equivalence scales

Some of the shortcomings of nutritional and subjective equivalence scales can be avoided by using households' spending patterns to evaluate their consumption requirements. Full budget equivalence scales are defined to be the total expenditure necessary, relative to a reference household, to attain a stipulated level of well-being. If a family of four needs three times the expenditure (on all commodities) of a single adult to be as well off, its equivalence scale is 3.0. A household equivalence scale defined in this way is analogous to a cost-of-living index and will vary over not only household size but also any characteristics which influence expenditure patterns.

One of the simplest approaches to equivalence scale estimation – attributed to Engel (1895) – begins with the assumption that households that devote the same fraction of total expenditure to food are equally well off. Empirical studies invariably find that the food share falls with total spending but increases with family size. The relationship between the food share and total expenditure is illustrated in Figure 5.1 for two types of households. A family of four with total

---

8. Qualitatively similar results have been obtained by de Vos and Garner (1991) using the 1982 CEX where a similar question was posed to consumer units. van Praag (1994) reports large economies of scale in consumption for subjective equivalence scales calculated for three European countries.
9. See, for example, the discussion in Citro and Michael (1995).

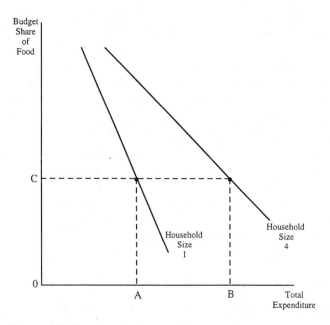

Figure 5.1. Engel equivalence scales

expenditure OB has a food share represented by OC. This share is attained at expenditure level OA for the reference household, and the Engel equivalence scale for the family of four is the ratio of OB to OA.

Although these scales are easy to implement, there are problems with them. Their simplicity depends on the assumption that the food share is inversely related to the welfare level. Although this might be true for identical households, it is unlikely to hold for households with different compositions. Nicholson (1976) gives a plausible counterexample in which a couple has a child and is compensated so as to leave its welfare unchanged. The adults' spending will be roughly the same, whereas the child will consume food almost exclusively. The food share rises even though the family is equally well off after the birth of the child, and the equivalence scale is overestimated.[10]

Implicit in Engel's method is the assumption that households' consumption requirements are the same for all goods. This, too, is

---

10. Additional arguments against the use of Engel equivalence scales are presented by Browning (1992) and Deaton and Muellbauer (1986).

unlikely since a family with children needs items such as milk and diapers but fewer adult goods such as theater tickets and restaurant meals. Note, also, that the equivalence scale depends on the share at which it is evaluated. In the example illustrated in Figure 5.1, the higher the share, the lower the scale; this suggests that the choice of the reference welfare level can have a significant influence on households' estimated consumption requirements.[11]

Engel equivalence scales have been used in the United States by the Bureau of Labor Statistics to describe the total spending of different types of households. In a research initiative called the Family Budgets Program, prototypical high-, intermediate-, and low-level budgets were developed for two types of households. These budgets were then adjusted using Engel equivalence scales to estimate the expenditures of households with different characteristics. Using a single adult as the reference, the scale for a family of two was 1.64, size three was 2.25, size four was 2.75, size five was 3.28, and size six was 3.60.[12]

Barten (1964) proposed an alternative approach in which households' needs were assumed to vary across commodities. Utility is assumed to be a function of the quantities consumed deflated by commodity-specific equivalence scales. If the food equivalence scale for a family of four is 3.0 and the housing scale is 1.5, it attains the same welfare as a reference household if it consumes three times the food and 1.5 times the housing. Barten's equivalence scale is the total expenditure, relative to the reference household, necessary to attain a stipulated level of well-being.

This model implies a direct correspondence between household compositional changes and price changes. The birth of a child not only increases the needs of the household (termed the composition effect) but also changes the "effective" prices of certain commodities (such as milk and diapers). Gorman's (1976) now famous description of this phenomenon is, "When you have a wife and a baby, a penny bun costs threepence." The changes in relative prices induce substitution across

---

11. Similar approaches have been proposed by Rothbarth (1943) using adult goods such as alcohol and tobacco and by Watts (1967) using food and necessities. These modifications do not resolve the problems with this general approach to estimating household equivalence scales. For a more complete discussion of these issues, see Browning (1992).
12. This is taken from Table 1 of Johnson (1994).

all goods, and the equivalence scale depends on both the composition and the substitution effects.

By way of illustration, assume that households consume only food and housing and that the equivalence scales for a family of four are 3.0 and 1.5, respectively. If a single adult consumes $1,000 worth of food and $500 worth of housing, then, with no substitution, the family of four would need $3,000 worth of food and $750 worth of housing to attain the same welfare. The household equivalence scale for the family is 3,750/1,500 or 2.5 adult equivalents.[13] However, in the Barten model, the increase in the effective price of food for large families induces substitution away from food toward housing. To achieve the same level of welfare as the single adult, the family of four would consume, say, $2,800 worth of food and $800 worth of housing and would have a scale of 3,600/1,500 or 2.4 adult equivalents.

Since these scales depend on households' expenditure patterns, they vary not only over household size but also over any set of demographic characteristics which influence spending. Recall the discussion of the equivalence scales for the two identical individuals who live in Boston and Los Angeles in Chapter 2. The Bostonian who takes public transportation to work has less need for gasoline (a smaller gasoline equivalence scale) than does the individual from Los Angeles. He attains the same welfare with less gasoline consumption and less total expenditure and, as a result, has a lower equivalence scale.

Barten equivalence scales have been estimated for the United States by Jorgenson and Slesnick (1987).[14] The demographic characteristics that were found to influence demand patterns (and, therefore, equivalence scales) were as follows:

> *Household Size*: 1, 2, 3, 4, 5, 6, or 7 or more.
> *Age of Household Head*: 16–24, 25–34, 35–44, 45–54, 55–64, and
> 65 and over.

13. This equivalence scale, which does not accommodate substitution, was originally proposed by Prais and Houthakker (1955). For further discussion of issues related to Prais-Houthakker equivalence scales, see Muellbauer (1980).
14. The 1987 econometric model has been reestimated to include possible gender differences in expenditure patterns. To avoid the problems caused by having the equivalence scale depend on the level of welfare at which it is evaluated, we impose the condition that the scale satisfy equivalence scale exactness. For further elaboration of these conditions, see Blackorby and Donaldson (1988b) and Lewbel (1989). Additional estimates of Barten equivalence scales using U.S. data are presented by van der Gaag and Smolensky (1982) and Johnson (1994). Muellbauer (1977) estimates Barten scales for the United Kingdom.

Table 5.3. *Barten equivalence scales (reference household: size 4, age 25–34, Northeast, nonfarm, white, male)*

Size 1	Size 2	Size 3	Size 4	Size 5	Size 6	Size 7+
0.32	0.57	0.76	1.00	1.11	1.52	1.92
Age 16–24	Age 25–34	Age 35–44	Age 45–54	Age 55–64	Age 65+	
0.65	1.00	1.39	1.53	1.39	0.93	
Northeast	Midwest	South	West	Nonfarm	Farm	
1.00	1.03	1.13	0.74	1.00	1.63	
White	Nonwhite	Male	Female			
1.00	1.12	1.00	0.62			

Source: Author's calculations using the model described by Jorgenson and Slesnick (1987).

Region of Residence: Northeast, Midwest, South, and West.
Race of Household Head: White, nonwhite.
Type of Residence: Nonfarm, farm.
Gender of Household Head: Male, female.

A subset of the 1344 possible equivalence scales is presented in Table 5.3.

The implied economies of scale in consumption are smaller than those found for the nutritional and subjective scales. The age of the head of the household has a substantial influence on the equivalence scale through the implied age of the dependent children. Regional effects are important (which may reflect differences in price levels), as are farm/nonfarm differences. Female-headed households have lower equivalence scales than those headed by males due, in part, to differences in their composition. Male-headed households with four members typically include two adults and two children, whereas female-headed households of the same size are composed of one adult and three children.[15]

Note that, unlike the Census Bureau's scales (Census scales for short), Table 5.3 shows variation over attributes such as region of

15. Lower equivalence scales for women in the United States have also been obtained using different methods and data by Danziger et al. (1984) as well as by van der Gaag and Smolensky (1982).

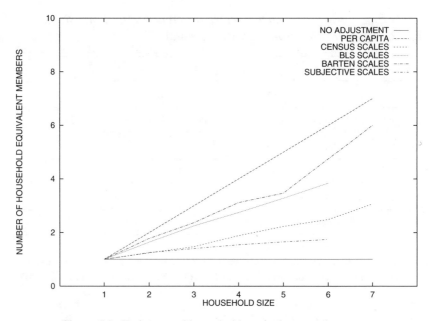

Figure 5.2. Estimates of household equivalence scales

residence and race of the head of the household. Even over shared dimensions, though, the two sets of estimates are quite different. The Census scales incorporate greater economies of scale in consumption as family size increases. The Barten scales for farm households are substantially higher than for nonfarm households, whereas the reverse is true for the official scales. The Barten scales are lower for female-headed households, whereas the Census scales show little difference between male- and female-headed households.

Figure 5.2 illustrates differences between six sets of equivalence scales as they vary with household size.[16] The per capita model incorporates no economies of scale in consumption, and failure to adjust for needs implicitly assumes the opposite. The other equivalence scales are intermediate between these two extremes, with the subjective and Census scales indicating larger economies of scale than the BLS and Barten scales. The Census scales, for example, imply that

16. The Census scale, subjective scales, and Barten scales are taken from Tables 5.1–5.3. The reference characteristics for the Barten scales are those indicated in Table 5.3. For the Census scales, the reference characteristics are male-headed nonfarm households, under 65 years of age. The BLS scales are those reported by Johnson (1994).

a family of four needs only 1.9 times the expenditure of a single individual to attain the same welfare. The comparable estimate based on the Barten scales is 3.1.

Numerous econometric estimates have appeared over the years using different techniques and data sets. My goal is not to provide an exhaustive survey of empirical estimates but rather to present a number of alternatives and to assess the extent to which estimates of the standard of living vary with the choice of equivalence scales. I perform this sensitivity analysis for four different equivalence scales: the per capita adjustment, the full budget Barten scales in Table 5.3, the Census scales, and the estimates that make no adjustment for differences in needs.

5.2. THE SOCIAL STANDARD OF LIVING

What has happened to the standard of living in the United States? The index introduced in Chapter 2 is the average level of consumption per equivalent adult:

$$W = \frac{M}{P(\mathbf{p}, \mathbf{p}_0, V)\sum_{k=1}^{K} m_0(\mathbf{p}_0, \mathbf{A}_k)} \tag{5.1}$$

where $M = \sum_{k=1}^{N} M_k$ is aggregate expenditure and $P(\mathbf{p}, \mathbf{p}_0, V)$ is a social cost-of-living index evaluated at social welfare level V. The second term in the denominator, $\Sigma m_0(\mathbf{p}_0, \mathbf{A}_k)$, is the number of adult equivalent members, which represents the aggregate consumption requirements of the population.

Figure 5.3 presents estimates of the standard of living over the period 1947 through 1995. The index is calculated using aggregate expenditures from the PCE that have been adjusted to include the services received from the stock of consumer durables. These expenditures are deflated by the social cost-of-living index described in Chapter 4 as well as by an estimate of the total number of household equivalent members based on the Barten scales presented in Table 5.3. To facilitate comparisons of growth rates over subperiods, the index is reported on a logarithmic scale.

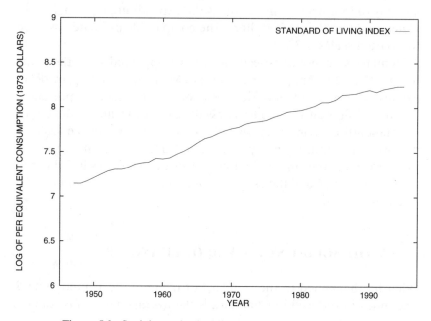

Figure 5.3. Social standard-of-living index, 1947–1995

What is most evident from Figure 5.3 is that the standard of living has grown steadily since the end of World War II. The average growth rate over the forty-eight years is 2.3 percent per year. Over the first half of the period, social welfare rose 2.6 percent per year compared to 1.9 percent since 1971. The slowdown is largely attributable to several deep recessions in the mid-1970s, the early 1980s, and the early 1990s. The variation in growth rates is more pronounced across decades, with the standard of living increasing 2.1 percent in the 1950s, 3.4 percent in the 1960s, 2.1 percent in the 1970s, 2.3 percent in the 1980s, and 0.8 percent in the first half of the 1990s.

The persistent growth arises both from an increase in aggregate consumption and from an accompanying decrease in the average consumption requirements of households.[17] In constant 1973 dollars, mean expenditures per household increased from $6,718 in 1947 to $14,490 in 1995, an average growth rate of 1.6 percent per year. Over

17. It is important to recall that the population of families and unrelated individuals is defined as households to maintain comparability with the CEX.

the same period, the average need per household, measured by the number of adult equivalent members, decreased at a rate of 0.7 percent per year, which reflects, in part, the decrease in average household size from approximately 3.2 persons in 1947 to 2.4 in 1995.

This picture of living standards contrasts sharply with the trend in real median family income. Between 1947 and 1995, its average growth rate was only 1.4 percent per year, with virtually all of the growth occurring before 1971. What accounts for this difference? The summary statistic used to represent the average standard of living is the income of the median family, which need not be representative of the entire population. If, for example, the incomes of every family below the median decreases by the same absolute amount and every other family is unaffected, the median is unchanged even though most people would agree that the average standard of living has fallen.

Using the family as the basic observational unit also ignores the fact that its average size has decreased over time, especially after 1971. This implies that the consumption requirements of families have decreased and that median family income understates the growth in the standard of living. Moreover, restricting the focus to families ignores what the Bureau of the Census defines as "unrelated individuals." These single-member households have become an increasingly important segment of the population and now account for approximately one-third of all households in the United States.

The typical measure of median family income (e.g., the series shown in Figure 1.1) is converted to constant dollars using the CPI. I have already shown that CPI-based estimates of inflation are biased upward and that the magnitudes of the errors are quite large, particularly in the late 1970s and early 1980s. This, too, leads to an understatement of the growth rate. A final, and potentially important, source of bias is the use of before-tax income, rather than expenditure, to measure the standard of living.

What is the contribution of each of these factors in the bias of median family income? In Table 5.4 I present the growth rates of five indexes to facilitate a decomposition of the differences between per equivalent consumption and real median family income. The table

Table 5.4. *Average annual growth rates, 1947–1995 (%)*

	Total	1947–1970	1971–1995
Per equivalent consumption (SCOLI deflator)	2.28	2.64	1.93
Per capita consumption (SCOLI deflator)	2.24	2.35	2.14
Per capita consumption (CPI deflator)	1.96	2.21	1.71
Per capita income (CPI deflator)	1.86	2.51	1.22
Real median family income (CPI deflator)	1.40	2.60	0.20

Source: Author's calculations from various data sources. See footnote 18.

shows clearly that the two estimates diverge over the second half of the sample.[18] The importance of changes in family size (and the inclusion of unrelated individuals) in explaining this difference can be seen by comparing the growth rates of real median family income and real per capita income. Whereas real median family income hardly changed after 1971, per capita income increased at an average rate of 1.22 percent per year; this is 59 percent of the total difference between real median family income and per equivalent consumption. Per capita consumption (deflated by the CPI) increased at an average rate of 1.71 percent per year, which accounts for another 28 percent of the difference. Substituting a price index based on the PCE deflators rather than the CPI increases the average growth rate to 2.14 percent per year, and using Barten equivalence scales rather than the number of persons reduces the average growth rate.

Although this provides a mechanical explanation for the difference between a conventional measure of social welfare and the consumption-based index, the more important question is why we've experienced such growth. Changes in per equivalent consumption reflect

18. Median family income and per capita income were obtained from various issues of the *Current Population Reports, Series P-60.* The aggregate expenditure series are the durables-adjusted PCE. The series are put in per capita terms by dividing by the Bureau of the Census (1991, 1994, 1996) population estimates. The equivalence scales used are those presented in Table 5.3. The price indexes used are self-explanatory.

changes in permanent income that are related to the level and distribution of human and physical capital. Increases in human capital can arise from the growth in productivity and real wages that results from an increase in the educational attainment of workers. Another possible explanation for the growth in per equivalent consumption is the increase in multiple-earner families over this period. Is there a decrease in leisure that offsets the increase in consumption? This question and others that address the issue of *why* living standards have risen is an important issue for future study.

I close this section with an assessment of the sensitivity of these conclusions to the assumptions that have been made. The standard-of-living index presented in Figure 5.3 is unaffected by changes in the distribution of welfare. This choice of a distributionally neutral measure was made to maintain comparability with other indexes that are frequently used to estimate social welfare. In Figure 5.4, I compare this estimate with a distributionally sensitive measure that has the property that, for a given level of aggregate expenditure, more unequal distributions lower social welfare. The vertical distance

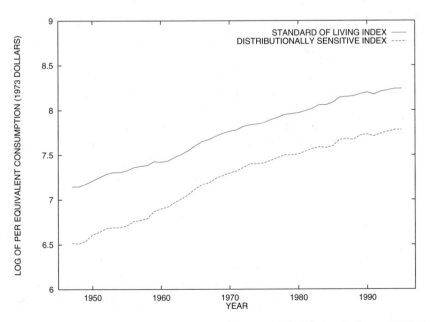

Figure 5.4. Comparisons of social standard-of-living indexes, 1947–1995

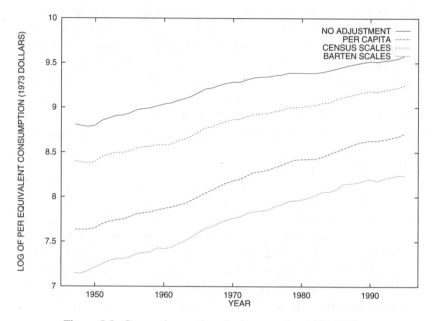

Figure 5.5. Comparisons of equivalence scales, 1947–1995

between the two indexes reflects the (proportional) loss in welfare due to inequality.[19]

Between 1947 and 1995, the distributionally sensitive index grew at an average rate of 2.6 percent per year. As with per equivalent consumption, growth in the first half of this period was higher than in the second half. The average was 2.9 percent per year in the 1950s, 4.0 percent in the 1960s, 2.1 percent in both the 1970s and the 1980s, and 1.0 percent in the first half of the 1990s. This is the same pattern as was obtained using per equivalent consumption as a measure of social welfare. Incorporating distributional considerations in the measurement of social welfare does not change the qualitative finding of a sustained increase in the standard of living in the postwar United States.

The sensitivity of the standard-of-living estimates to the choice of equivalence scales is illustrated in Figure 5.5. Each series is calculated using (5.1), the PCE estimates of aggregate expenditure and the

---

19. The specific representation of the distributionally sensitive social welfare measure is described in Appendix 1.

Table 5.5. *Average annual growth rates, 1947–1995 (%)*

	Total	1947–1970	1971–1995
Per equivalent consumption			
(Census scales)	1.77	1.95	1.58
Per equivalent consumption			
(Barten scales)	2.28	2.64	1.93
Per capita consumption	2.24	2.35	2.14
Per household consumption	1.60	1.98	1.22

Source: Author's calculations.

social cost-of-living index. Four sets of equivalence scales are examined: the Census scales, the full budget Barten scales shown in Table 5.3, the per capita adjustment, and estimates in which differences in households' consumption requirements are ignored. The average growth rates of the four indexes are shown in Table 5.5.

The highest average growth rate over the entire sample period (2.28 percent per year) is obtained using the Barten scales, whereas per capita consumption grew at a slightly lower rate of 2.24 percent. Generally, the indexes that use equivalence scales with greater economies of scale in consumption exhibit less growth because the effect of the decrease in average family size is diminished. The standard-of-living index calculated using the Census scales increased 1.77 percent per year, and the estimate that makes no adjustment for household size (the most economies of scale) grew 1.60 percent per year.

Although the average growth rates vary significantly, the qualitative conclusions are generally unaffected by the choice of equivalence scales. The 1960s were the decade with the highest growth, whereas substantially less growth occurred in the 1970s and 1990s. The indexes that make any kind of adjustment for differences in households' consumption requirements show growth in the standard of living in the 1980s that is roughly equal to the postwar average.

No matter which indexes are used, the overall conclusion is that there has been sustained growth in the standard of living. The average growth rate in the first half of the postwar period was higher than over the second half, although even in the latter period, the rate of increase was substantial. The only index, in fact, that gives a qualitatively different picture of the trend of the standard of living is CPI-deflated, median family income.

5.3. THE GROUP STANDARD OF LIVING

Have all groups shared equally in the rise in standard of living, or have some segments of the population been left behind? Whereas a macroeconomic assessment of the standard of living provides an overview, more disaggregated information is an essential ingredient to the evaluation of government programs that are targeted to specific groups. Social Security and Medicare are provided to maintain the welfare of the elderly. Are these programs appropriate and effective? Affirmative action is exercised to raise the welfare of individuals who have been subjected to discrimination. An assessment of the change in well-being over time provides circumstantial evidence of the success of these efforts. In this section I measure the standard of living for several groups that share various demographic characteristics.

The welfare of each group is measured using the average level of consumption per equivalent adult. Implementation requires information on the distribution of expenditures and the number of household equivalent members in each group, as well as a group cost-of-living index. The only data that have this information are the CEX.[20]

Since levels and growth rates are sensitive to the choice of equivalence scales (see Figure 5.5), one would expect conclusions concerning the relative levels of group welfare to also depend on how households' consumption requirements are incorporated in the welfare measure. I evaluate the group standard of living using the Barten scales, the nutritional scales used by the Bureau of the Census, and the per capita adjustment.

Age groups

Entitlement programs such as Social Security and Medicare provide a safety net for the elderly, who, presumably, cannot maintain their

---

20. The expenditures and distribution of households are interpolated between 1961 and 1972 as well as from 1973 through 1980. I also extrapolate the distribution between 1947 and 1959. The details of the method of estimating the distributions of expenditure in the years in which there are no surveys are presented in Appendix 2.

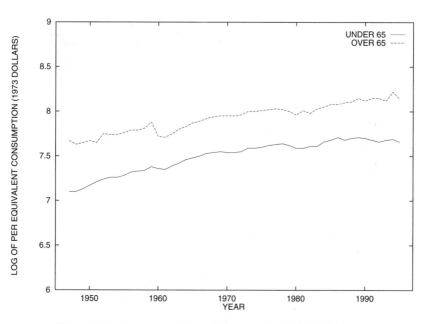

Figure 5.6. Age comparisons: Barten scales, 1947–1995

standard of living with earned income alone. Comparisons of incomes generally support the argument that the elderly are a vulnerable segment of the population. Income, however, is likely to be a particularly inaccurate measure of well-being for individuals in the later stages of the life cycle (see Slesnick 1991c). They have less earned income but, typically, more assets that can be used to maintain their consumption after retirement.

Standard-of-living indexes for groups distinguished by the age of the head of the household are presented in Figures 5.6, 5.7, and 5.8. The estimates based on the Barten scales show that those over age 65 are *substantially* better off than younger households.[21] Not only are they better off, but, since 1961, the differences have been widening. In 1961, households over 65 had a standard of living that was 36 percent higher than the welfare of the non-elderly. By 1973 the difference was 41 percent, 37 percent in 1980, 42 percent in 1990, and

21. The group indexes are calculated using expenditures in the CEX, the number of equivalent members in the group tabulated from the CEX, and the group cost of living indexes described in Chapter 4.

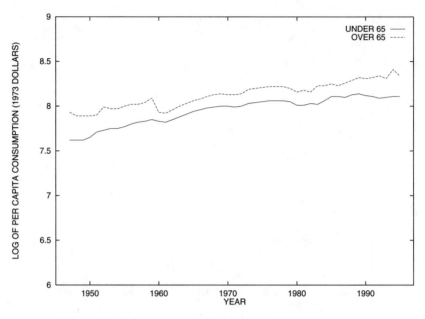

Figure 5.7. Age comparisons: Per capita, 1947–1995

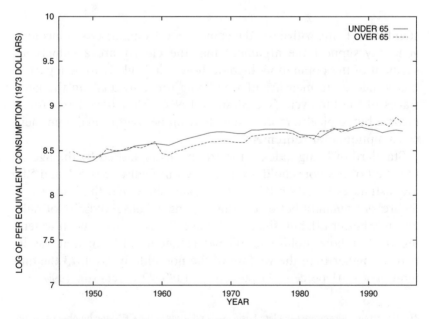

Figure 5.8. Age comparisons: Census scales, 1947–1995

Table 5.6. *Average number of persons per household – CEX*

Year	Northeast	Midwest	South	West	White	Nonwhite	Male	Female	<65	>65
1961	3.1	3.3	3.3	3.2	3.2	3.4	3.5	1.9	3.5	1.9
1973	3.0	3.0	3.0	2.9	2.9	3.3	3.3	1.9	3.3	1.7
1980	2.7	2.7	2.8	2.7	2.7	3.1	3.0	1.9	3.0	1.8
1985	2.5	2.6	2.7	2.5	2.5	2.9	2.8	1.8	2.8	1.8
1990	2.6	2.5	2.5	2.6	2.5	2.8	2.8	1.9	2.8	1.7
1995	2.6	2.6	2.5	2.6	2.5	2.8	2.8	1.9	2.8	1.7

Source: Author's calculations for consumer units in the CEX. Characteristics refer to the characteristics of the household head.

48 percent in 1995. Based on these results, the elderly do not appear to be one of the poorest segments of the population.

Differences in household composition can help explain why the elderly are not as bad off as their incomes would indicate. Elderly households do, in fact, have lower levels of both income and consumption, but their consumption requirements are also lower because they have fewer members. Table 5.6 shows that in 1961 the average size of an elderly household was 1.9 members compared to 3.5 for those under 65. Over the years, differences in the average sizes narrowed although elderly households remained significantly smaller than the non-elderly in 1995.

I recalculate the standard of living for the elderly using the per capita adjustment for needs as well as the Census equivalence scales. Figure 5.7 shows that the basic conclusions are unchanged using per capita consumption as the welfare measure. Elderly households are better off than younger households, although the differences are proportionately smaller. In 1961, average per capita consumption for the elderly was 10 percent higher than for the non-elderly. As with the Barten scales, this difference widened (to 16 percent) in 1973, 15 percent in 1980, 19 percent in 1990, and 23 percent in 1995. The estimates calculated using the Census scales show smaller differences between the two groups, with the elderly being slightly worse off in 1961 and somewhat better off in 1995.

Regardless of the method used to account for differences in needs, the elderly are at least as well off as the non-elderly and, by some measures, substantially better off. This is true even without incorpo-

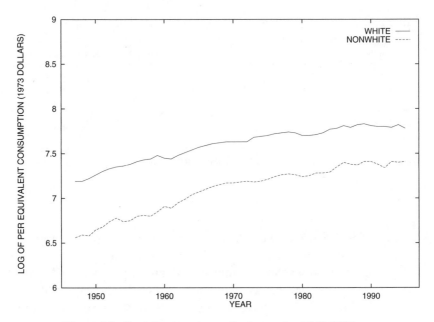

Figure 5.9. Racial comparisons: Barten scales, 1947–1995

rating the effects of in-kind transfers such as Medicare or Medicaid. A critical policy issue is the role Social Security and other transfers play in maintaining the welfare of the elderly.[22] Whatever the means, these results suggest that the elderly have been and are currently able to maintain their standard of living at levels at least as high as those of the non-elderly.

Groups differentiated by race

The standard of living for groups differentiated by the race of the head of the household is presented in Figures 5.9, 5.10, and 5.11. Non-white households have substantially lower welfare levels than whites, but there has been convergence since 1947. Using the Barten scales, there was a 63 percent difference in welfare in 1947, 55 percent in 1961, 50 percent in 1973, 46 percent in 1980, and 37 percent in 1995.

22. Using the 1972–73 CEX, Hamermesh (1984) finds Social Security to be an essential element in maintaining the consumption of retirees. This issue deserves additional scrutiny using more-recent data.

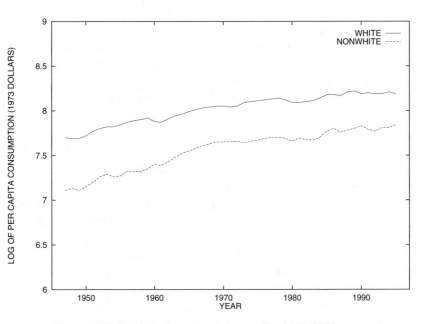

Figure 5.10. Racial comparisons: Per capita, 1947–1995

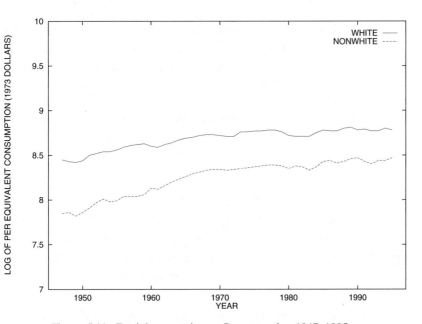

Figure 5.11. Racial comparisons: Census scales, 1947–1995

Since 1947, the average growth in the standard of living for nonwhites was 1.77 percent per year compared to 1.23 percent for whites.[23]

The per capita estimates and those tabulated using the Census equivalence scales yield qualitatively identical results. Whites have higher living standards than nonwhites, but the differences have been decreasing. Per capita consumption of nonwhites was 59 percent below that of whites in 1947 compared to 35 percent in 1995. The estimates calculated using the Census scales indicate that the gap closed from 60 percent to 31 percent. Over the critical period between 1961 and 1995, when there was (arguably) greater economic integration, per capita consumption of nonwhites grew an average of 1.32 percent per year compared to 0.94 percent per year for whites.

Although each index shows a persistent gap between whites and nonwhites, they also show progress in narrowing the differences. Understanding why this has happened is an important ingredient in the development of policies designed to reduce the gap even further. A full explanation of the convergence in the standards of living is undoubtedly quite complex. The changes in educational attainment of the two groups, however, are suggestive. One would expect per equivalent consumption to reflect levels of permanent income, which, in turn, depend on the levels of human wealth. A narrowing of the gap in the average level of human capital for whites and nonwhites would be manifested by convergence in their permanent incomes. Table 5.7 shows precisely such an effect; there was a sharp increase in the educational attainment of nonwhite heads of household between 1961 and 1995. In 1961, 23 percent of the nonwhite heads were high school graduates or more. By 1995 this fraction more than tripled to 71 percent. The educational attainment of whites remained higher, but the difference decreased significantly.

Groups differentiated by gender

Female-headed households represent another group that is considered to be particularly vulnerable. Figures 5.12, 5.13, and 5.14 show that the conclusion concerning the relative welfare levels of men and women is largely dependent on the equivalence scales used to

---

23. Note that the lower growth rates for both groups reflect the slower rate of increase of average expenditures in the CEX relative to the PCE.

Table 5.7. *Education of the head of household*

	Proportion of white heads of household					
Year	No school, not reported	Some elementary	Some high school	High school graduate	Some college	College grad or more
1961	0.02	0.32	0.18	0.26	0.10	0.11
1973	0.04	0.20	0.15	0.31	0.13	0.17
1980	0.01	0.15	0.15	0.31	0.19	0.19
1985	0.00	0.12	0.13	0.30	0.21	0.24
1990	0.01	0.10	0.11	0.30	0.23	0.24
1995	0.00	0.08	0.11	0.32	0.23	0.26
	Proportion of nonwhite heads of household					
Year	No school, not reported	Some elementary	Some high school	High school graduate	Some college	College grad or more
1961	0.07	0.49	0.20	0.16	0.04	0.03
1973	0.08	0.32	0.23	0.24	0.09	0.05
1980	0.03	0.24	0.21	0.23	0.18	0.12
1985	0.01	0.17	0.21	0.25	0.21	0.15
1990	0.00	0.14	0.21	0.29	0.19	0.17
1995	0.00	0.10	0.18	0.30	0.23	0.18

Source: Author's calculations using consumer units in the CEX.

measure their consumption requirements. The standard of living estimated using the Barten scales shows that female-headed households attain higher living standards than males throughout the sample period. In 1947, for example, the welfare of female-headed households was 56 percent higher than that of males; by 1995 the difference was 39 percent. Over the 48 years, the average growth in the standard of living for female-headed households was 0.81 percent per year compared to 1.16 percent for males.

Different conclusions are obtained if per capita consumption is used as the welfare measure. The standard of living was slightly higher for female-headed households until 1973, when the positions reversed. Figure 5.14 shows that when the Census equivalence scales are used, male-headed households had substantially higher standards of living than female-headed households in every year.

The importance of the equivalence scales in measuring differences by gender is better understood when the compositions of the two

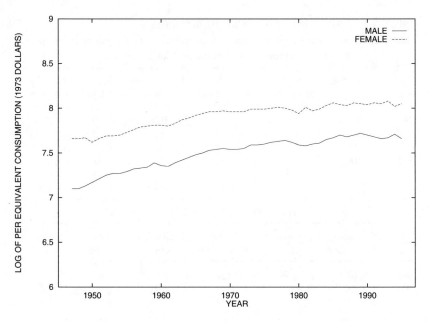

Figure 5.12. Gender comparisons: Barten scales, 1947–1995

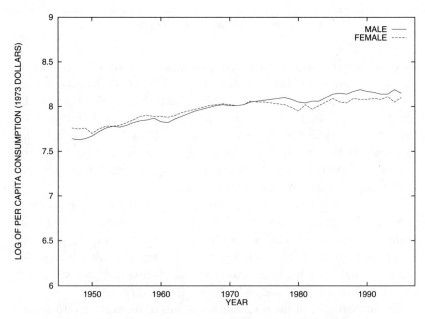

Figure 5.13. Gender comparisons: Per capita, 1947–1995

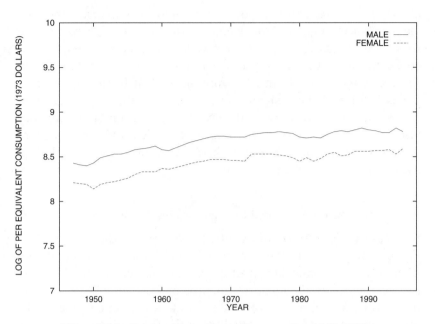

Figure 5.14. Gender comparisons: Census scales, 1947–1995

groups are analyzed more closely. Table 5.6 shows that female-headed households are, on average, smaller than their male counterparts. In contrast with the popular perception, large female-headed households are the exception rather than the rule. Tabulations over consumer units in the 1973 CEX show that, for example, approximately 60 percent of all female-headed households were single women, and half of these were over the age of 65. Almost 80 percent of the households headed by women had two or fewer members, whereas only 6 percent had five or more persons. By comparison, roughly 10 percent of all male-headed households were single men, and only 28 percent of these were over age sixty-five. More than 20 percent of the male-headed households had five or more members.[24]

These compositional differences provide insight as to why the conclusions concerning the relative welfare levels of male- and female-headed households are sensitive to the choice of equivalence scales. The Barten scales show that the female-headed households and the

24. These features are qualitatively the same at the end of the sample period, although the representation of large households among male heads falls sharply.

elderly have lower consumption requirements than men and the non-elderly. Since single, elderly women constitute a large fraction of these households, they have higher welfare levels for a given level of consumption. Given the variation in household sizes, differences in the economies of scale in consumption implicit in the equivalence scales will also have a significant influence on the relative welfare levels. Male-headed households have higher consumption, but they also have more members. The degree to which additional persons drain resources is therefore important in measuring their standard of living relative to women.

Groups differentiated by region of residence

Figures 5.15–5.17 show the average welfare for the four Census regions. Regardless of the equivalence scales used, the general conclusions are the same. For most of the sample period, the West and the Northeast had the highest standards of living, and the South had the lowest. All three sets of results show convergence. Since 1947, for example, the index calculated using the Barten scales grew at an

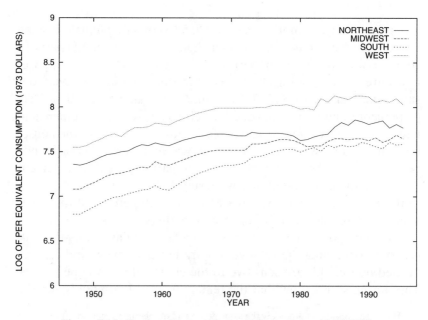

Figure 5.15. Regional comparisons: Barten scales, 1947–1995

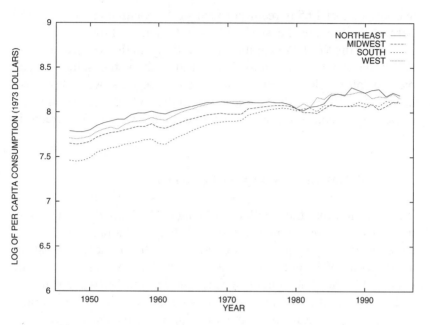

Figure 5.16. Regional comparisons: Per capita, 1947–1995

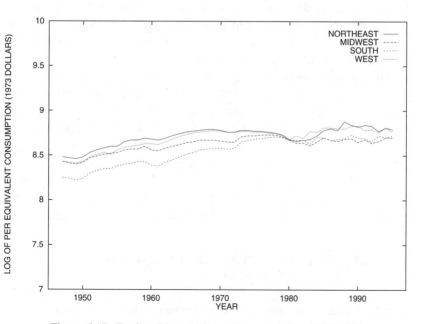

Figure 5.17. Regional comparisons: Census scales, 1947–1995

average rate of 1.65 percent per year in the South compared to 0.85 percent in the Northeast, 1.19 percent in the Midwest, and 1.00 percent in the West. Per capita consumption and the welfare measure based on the Census equivalence scales show the same general picture, although the differences across regions were less pronounced. In 1995 the difference between the highest and lowest levels of per capita consumption was 8 percent compared to 33 percent in 1947.

5.4. SUMMARY AND CONCLUSIONS

The assertion that the standard of living in the United States is stagnant or decreasing is inconsistent with the results presented in this chapter. Per equivalent consumption has been increasing at an average rate of 2.3 percent per year. The highest average growth rate occurred in the 1960s, but even as recently as the 1980s, the standard of living grew at a rate approximately equal to the postwar average. This qualitative conclusion is surprisingly insensitive to the many assumptions needed to measure social welfare. Even per capita income, suitably deflated by an index other than the CPI, exhibits sustained growth since 1947. Only median family income is consistent with the claim that living standards are in jeopardy, and this index is ill suited for measuring social welfare.

An examination of welfare at lower levels of aggregation reveals several equally surprising results. The elderly population, long regarded as the most vulnerable group, attained higher levels of well-being than the non-elderly. Although nonwhite households had lower welfare than whites, there has been convergence over time. Female-headed households had lower income and expenditure levels than males but were also smaller. As a result, their standing relative to male-headed households depends on how we incorporate the consumption requirements of households in the welfare measure.

TECHNICAL APPENDIX: HOUSEHOLD EQUIVALENCE SCALES

I briefly describe the models used to estimate household equivalence scales. More-detailed surveys of this literature are provided by

Deaton and Muellbauer (1980), Browning (1992), and Lewbel (1997). I begin with the following notation:

$\mathbf{p} = (p_1, p_2, \ldots, p_N)$ – a vector of prices of all commodities.

x_{nk} – the quantity of the nth commodity consumed by the kth household $(n = 1, 2, \ldots, N; k = 1, 2, \ldots, K)$.

$M_k = \displaystyle\sum_{n=1}^{N} p_n x_{nk}$ – total expenditure, or the dollar value of consumption.

$w_{nk} = \dfrac{p_n x_{nk}}{M_k}$ – budget share of the nth good.

$\mathbf{A}_k$ – the vector of household attributes.

$m_0(\mathbf{A}_k)$ – the general household equivalence scale.

$m_n(\mathbf{A}_k)$ – the commodity-specific equivalence scale for good n and household k.

Engel equivalence scales are the simplest to estimate and are founded on the assumption that households with the same per equivalent (total) expenditure have the same per equivalent demands:

$$\frac{x_{nk}}{m_0(\mathbf{A}_k)} = F\left(\mathbf{p}, \frac{M_k}{m_0(\mathbf{A}_k)}\right)$$

This implies that household budget shares are the same only if they have the same level of per equivalent expenditure.

Let w* be the share at which the equivalence scales are evaluated. Denote M_k^* and M_r^* as the levels of total expenditure at which this share is attained for the kth and reference households. Per equivalent expenditures must therefore be the same:

$$\frac{M_k^*}{m_0(\mathbf{A}_k)} = \frac{M_r^*}{m_r(\mathbf{A}_k)}$$

Normalizing the equivalence scale of the reference household to be 1, the Engel scale for household k is

$$m_0(\mathbf{A}_k) = \frac{M_k^*}{M_r^*}$$

Note that the index depends on the share at which it is evaluated. Engel's approach also implicitly assumes that the needs of households are the same for all goods and are represented by the general equivalence scale.

Prais and Houthakker (1955) generalized this approach by assuming that needs vary across commodities, yielding demands of the form

$$\frac{x_{nk}}{m_n(\mathbf{A_k})} = F\left(\mathbf{p}, \frac{M_k}{m_0(\mathbf{A_k})}\right)$$

Although this model was an advance over Engel's simple formulation, it is consistent with utility maximization only if preferences preclude substitution between goods. In addition, Muellbauer (1980) showed that, in general, the equivalence scales are not identified using cross-sectional data alone.

Barten (1964) extended this approach by defining household utility as a function of the levels of per equivalent consumption of each good:

$$U = U\left(\frac{x_{1k}}{m_1(\mathbf{A_k})}, \frac{x_{2k}}{m_2(\mathbf{A_k})}, \ldots, \frac{x_{Nk}}{m_N(\mathbf{A_k})}\right)$$

This implies an indirect utility function of the form

$$V(\mathbf{p}, M_k, \mathbf{A_k}) = V\left(\frac{p_1 m_1(\mathbf{A_k})}{M_k}, \frac{p_2 m_2(\mathbf{A_k})}{M_k}, \ldots, \frac{p_N m_N(\mathbf{A_k})}{M_k}\right)$$

$$(A5.1)$$

For this representation of preferences, changes in demographic composition have the same impacts on welfare and demand patterns as price changes. The addition of a child has an income or compositional effect but also increases the relative prices of "child goods" and induces substitution away from these commodities.

The expenditure function corresponding to the indirect utility function (A5.1) is

$$M_k = M(p_1 m_1(\mathbf{A_k}), p_2 m_2(\mathbf{A_k}), \ldots, p_N m_N(\mathbf{A_k}), V)$$

and the Barten equivalence scale is given by

$$m_0(\mathbf{p}, V, \mathbf{A_k}) = \frac{M(p_1 m_1(\mathbf{A_k}), \ldots, p_2 m_2(\mathbf{A_k}), \ldots, p_N m_N(\mathbf{A_k}), V)}{M(p_1, p_2, \ldots, p_N, V)}$$

Finally, note that the equivalence scales reported in this chapter are derived from demand functions. Pollak and Wales (1979) have argued that it is not possible to estimate equivalence scales in this manner because welfare comparisons require the "unconditional" assessment of welfare with a given set of characteristics. The demand patterns only measure well-being conditional on the observed demographic characteristics.

Formally, demand patterns enable the identification of the utility function conditional on the observed characteristics, say $V(\mathbf{p}, M_k, \mathbf{A}_k)$. To perform welfare economics and estimate equivalence scales, one requires the unconditional preferences, which can be represented by

$$W_k = G(V(\mathbf{p}, M_k, \mathbf{A}_k), \mathbf{A}_k)$$

The welfare level W_k will differ from $V(\ )$ to the extent that attributes influence well-being in ways other than through their consumption patterns. Indeed, the function $G(\ )$ cannot be identified by examining expenditure patterns alone.[25]

---

25. For more on this issue, see Pollak (1991), Blundell and Lewbel (1991), and Lewbel (1997). Blundell and Lewbel show that identification can be achieved by restricting the form of the equivalence to be independent of the base utility level.

6 Does a rising tide raise all ships?

There has been sustained growth in the standard of living, but what has happened to the distribution? Should growth be enhanced at the expense of a more egalitarian distribution? Is such a trade-off inevitable, or is it possible to have an increase in social welfare without a rise in inequality? Although growth in the standard of living is of central concern, its distribution is also used as an indicator of economic success. Indeed, a casual examination of the menu of government programs reveals that distributional issues, along with growth, play an influential role in the design of public policy.

As with measures of the standard of living, estimates of inequality have focused on the distribution of family income. The Bureau of the Census reports that inequality decreased over the two decades following World War II but reversed its trend in the late 1960s.[1] In 1998 it reached its highest level since 1947, and that is disheartening in light of the dramatic growth of government expenditures on social insurance and means-tested transfer programs.

What accounts for the infamous U-turn in inequality? A common and compelling explanation is based on the movements in the distribution of labor earnings, the largest component of income for most families. There is near unanimity of opinion that earnings inequality has increased.[2] Some researchers believe that over the period in

1. These estimates are based on the Census Bureau's published estimates of the Gini coefficient of family income. See, for example, Figure 1.2.
2. There is, however, far less agreement as to why this has occurred. Explanations include changes in the return on human capital or skill, demographic changes induced by the

122

which total income inequality fell, increased dispersion of earnings was more than offset by the rise in government transfers to the poor. More recently, the widening of the earnings distribution has been the dominant effect which led to the reversal in the downward trend in (total) income inequality. The policy prescription is that either something must be done to stem the increase in the dispersion of wages or the government must redouble its efforts to aid our less fortunate citizens.

Although an examination of earnings inequality reveals interesting and important features of labor markets, neither it nor the family income distribution gives an accurate picture of the distribution of household welfare. In contrast with the trend of family income inequality, I will show that per equivalent consumption inequality decreased through the early 1970s but has changed little since then.

What might account for such different conclusions? Consumption smoothing consistent with the permanent income hypothesis implies that the distribution of total expenditure will be less dispersed than the distribution of income. The demographic changes documented in Chapter 3 could also have an important influence on the trend in inequality when household compositional effects are included in the measure of welfare. The impact of such demographic changes is missed if heterogeneous households are treated symmetrically, as they are in the Census Bureau's estimates of inequality. Similarly, the distributional effects of price changes are ignored if attention is restricted to the distribution of income.

6.1. MEASURING INEQUALITY

Conceptual issues

What is the best way of summarizing differences between two distributions? What criterion, in particular, should be used to determine the relative levels of inequality? A Lorenz curve, which relates the cumulative proportion of the variable of interest to the fraction of the population (ordered from the poorest to the richest) that owns

---

baby boom, the increased labor-force participation of women, and structural changes in the composition of employment such as the increase in part-time work and the proliferation of "bad" jobs. See Levy and Murnane (1992) for a survey of this literature.

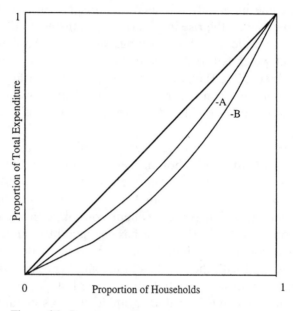

Figure 6.1. Lorenz curves

it, is frequently used to compare distributions. The farther it is from the diagonal, which represents perfect equality, the greater the inequality. Figure 6.1, for example, shows the Lorenz curves for two distributions, with A representing unequivocally less inequality relative to B.[3]

Ranking distributions is straightforward if the Lorenz curves do not intersect, as in Figure 6.1. If they do cross, however, there is no unambiguous ordering and we must rely on summary statistics to quantify the degree of inequality. For this purpose it would seem natural to use standard statistical measures of dispersion such as the sample variance or the standard deviation. These specific indexes are ill suited for inequality measurement, however, because they are not invariant to the level of well-being. If the welfare of every household doubles, most people would conclude that relative inequality is unaffected. The sample variance, though, would quadruple and the standard deviation would double.

3. Specifically, distribution A is said to "Lorenz dominate" B and can be obtained from B using a sequence of progressive transfers from the rich to the poor. A generalization of the condition of Lorenz dominance was provided by Shorrocks (1983).

What, then, constitutes an "ideal" inequality index? Some researchers have proposed a framework that limits the set of feasible indexes by requiring them to be consistent with a variety of axioms. Invariance to the scaling of each household's welfare, for example, is a property that is commonly imposed.[4] Inequality indexes are also required to satisfy a "principle of transfers" in which the measured level of inequality must fall with a mean-preserving transfer from the rich to the poor. Indexes that use only the lowest and the highest percentiles of the distribution (e.g., the ratio of aggregate expenditure attributable to the highest and lowest deciles) do not satisfy this axiom.[5]

Although an axiomatic framework eliminates a number of commonly used inequality indexes, many others remain, and the choice of one over another must ultimately be made. This choice requires subjective judgments related to the sensitivity of the index to transfers between households. The Gini coefficient, for example, is the ratio of the area between the Lorenz curve and the diagonal to the total area below the diagonal, and it is most sensitive to changes in the middle of the distribution. The coefficient of variation is the ratio of the standard deviation to the mean, and changes in the distribution have the same effect no matter where they occur. Theil's (1967) entropy index exhibits the greatest sensitivity to changes at the lower end of the distribution.[6]

The link between inequality indexes and their ethical basis is made explicit by defining inequality to be the loss in social welfare attributable to disparities in well-being. This approach was pioneered by Atkinson (1970), who demonstrated that, for a fixed mean, Lorenz dominance of one distribution over another implies a higher level of social welfare for a utilitarian social welfare function.[7] Failing such a relationship, a functional form for the household welfare function must be specified. Atkinson defined "equally distributed equivalent

4. Relative indexes are, by far, the most commonly used measures of inequality. Absolute inequality indexes, which require invariance to equal absolute additions of income, have also been proposed. See Kolm (1976a,b) and Blackorby and Donaldson (1980a).
5. A more general transfer principle has been proposed by Shorrocks and Foster (1987) which facilitates an ordering of distributions whose Lorenz curves intersect.
6. For further discussion of the properties of a wide variety of inequality indexes, see Blackorby and Donaldson (1978) and Cowell (1977).
7. See also Kolm (1969) and Sen (1973). Dasgupta, Sen, and Starett (1973) generalized Atkinson's (1970) result to include any social welfare function that is Schur-concave. Shorrocks (1983) extends the results to distributions with different means.

income" as the amount of income that, if allocated to everyone, yields the same level of social welfare as the observed distribution. The inequality index is 1 minus the ratio of equally distributed equivalent income to mean income.

Atkinson's index is illustrated in Figure 6.2 for an economy that comprises two identical households. The distribution of total expenditure is represented by point A, and the level of social welfare is W°. The curvature of the social welfare contour reflects the property that, all other things being equal, more-egalitarian distributions of expenditure increase social welfare. Point C represents the maximum level of social welfare that is attained when aggregate expenditure is divided equally among households. The equally distributed equivalent expenditure needed to attain W° is given by point B, and inequality is the ratio of BC to OC.

Note that if welfare is the same for each household, social welfare is maximized, there is no inequality, and the index is equal to zero. If one household has all of the resources and the others nothing, social welfare attains its lowest possible level and the inequality index is

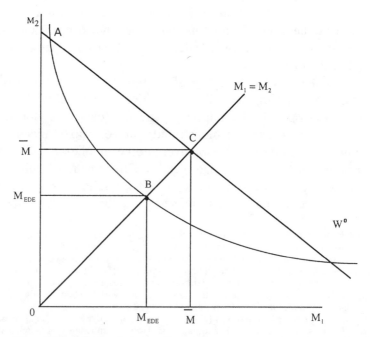

Figure 6.2. Atkinson's inequality index

equal to 1. Blackorby and Donaldson (1978) have shown that this general approach to inequality measurement has, as special cases, virtually all of the commonly used indexes such as the Gini coefficient, Theil's entropy coefficient, and the coefficient of variation.[8]

Although this method of inequality measurement is not as commonly used as statistical measures of dispersion, it has several advantages. The normative basis of the index, which is part of any measure, is made explicit. This facilitates an examination of the sensitivity of conclusions to assumptions related to the magnitude by which inequality changes with transfers from the rich to the poor. Since the index is based on an underlying social welfare function, the implied policy prescriptions are built in. The gains in social welfare, for example, that result from poverty relief are readily determined. As important, there is coherence between the inequality indexes, the measures of social welfare, and the cost of living described in previous chapters.

My consumption-based index used to measure inequality in the United States is consistent with the framework developed by Atkinson. Social welfare is maximized at the perfectly egalitarian distribution in which per equivalent consumption is the same for each household. Inequality is measured as the proportional difference between social welfare attained at the actual distribution of per equivalent consumption and the maximum level of social welfare. The specific form of the index is described in Appendix 1.

Data issues

The calculation of inequality in the distribution of per equivalent consumption requires disaggregated data on expenditures, household equivalence scales, and household-specific price indexes. Unlike the measurement of the social standard of living, in which either the PCE or the CEX can be used, only the latter provide enough detail to measure inequality.

Over the thirty-five years for which we have cross-sectional data, there have been several changes to the CEX which could influence

---

8. Many aspects of inequality measurement are multidimensional, such as the joint relationship between total expenditure and household needs. Multivariate extensions to inequality measurement are presented by Atkinson and Bourguignon (1982, 1987) and Maasoumi (1986).

the measured levels of inequality in nontrivial ways.[9] There is variation in the sample sizes which affects the relative precision of the
indexes. The 1961 survey had approximately 13,000 consumer units,
the 1972 and 1973 surveys had roughly 9,500 households, and there
were between 4,000 and 6,000 households from 1980 through 1995.

The survey response rates ranged from 80 percent to 90 percent
but did not change much over time.[10] It is widely believed that households that refuse to participate in the surveys are over-represented
by the very rich and the very poor. If this is true, estimates based on
the CEX underestimate inequality because of under-representation
of consumer units in the upper and lower tails of the distribution.
Since the response rates did not vary significantly over time, the trend
in inequality was probably unaffected.

If a respondent's expenditures were extremely high, the reported
value was sometimes replaced by an arbitrarily chosen upper bound.
This practice, referred to as topcoding, was used to preserve the con-
fidentiality of survey participants and resulted in an inequality estimate that was biased downward. There was no topcoding in the 1961,
1972, and 1973 CEX, but it was implemented in subsequent years.
For the expenditure data, topcoding was a problem primarily for
the monthly rental equivalent of owner-occupied housing, in which
approximately 10 percent of the samples in the 1980s and 1990s were
censored at $1,000. To mitigate this effect, I used the conditional
mean rental equivalent, adjusted for inflation, for the subsample that
would have been censored in 1973.[11]

In the earlier surveys, college students were classified as members
of their parents' households but were treated as independent households starting in 1980. This change could affect the distribution of
household expenditure because it increases the number of households with low levels of consumption. On a per capita or needs-
corrected basis, however, the impact on inequality was probably quite
small. The definition of the head of household also changed over time,

---

9. A more detailed description of these changes is presented by Mayer and Jencks (1992).
10. Mayer and Jencks (1992), however, contend that the response rate reported for the
    1961 survey is misleading and is actually much lower.
11. A small proportion of additional households (well under 1 percent in most years) had
    other items that were topcoded. Expenditures on these items were replaced by the
    upper bound, with little impact on the estimated level of inequality. The tabulations
    presented here differ slightly from my previous estimates (Slesnick 1994) because of
    the inclusion of these few households.

although I made an attempt to maintain consistency throughout the sample period.

Perhaps the most important change in the CEX was the shift to reporting expenditures on a quarterly basis after 1973. The high level of attrition in the sample over the calendar year precludes the possibility of obtaining an annual estimate of total expenditure, and, moreover, the resulting set of households is not representative of the U.S. population. The smaller sample size also increases the sampling variance and reduces the precision of the inequality estimates.

Some researchers have tried to deal with this problem by using all observations within a year regardless of the number of times they were interviewed.[12] If a household was in the survey for only one quarter, its expenditures were multiplied by 4 to convert them to an annual basis. The expenditures of households that were in the sample for only two quarters were multiplied by 2 and so on. Although this procedure increases the sample size, there are several potentially serious problems. Only the quarterly surveys are representative of the population, and there is no reason to expect this approach to yield an estimate of spending that is itself representative. Note also that a consumer unit observed at the beginning of the year is treated the same as a household surveyed at the end even though, because of general inflation, it likely faces different prices. There is, in addition, a strong seasonal pattern to spending, with expenditures in the fourth quarter being higher than others because of Christmas. Combining these temporally distinct samples to measure inequality could result in spurious inferences concerning relative levels of welfare and inequality.

To avoid these problems, I restrict the sample to the set of households interviewed in the second quarter of each year. Since households undoubtedly smooth their consumption over the course of a year, the quarterly estimates likely overstate the variance in the expenditures and overestimate inequality. This is important to keep in mind in examining the long-run trend in inequality. However, the transitory components of spending on many items such as food, housing, and the services from consumer durables are relatively small for most households, and that partially mitigates this upward bias.

---

12. See, for example, Cutler and Katz (1991) and Johnson and Shipp (1997).

The bottom line is that levels of inequality are likely understated in the CEX because of the undersampling of very poor and very rich households. Since this effect didn't change much over time, the estimated trend in inequality is probably unaffected. The downward bias in the level is at least partially offset by the overestimate of inequality that results from using quarterly expenditure data. This latter effect also has the effect of understating the downward trend in the index. Relative to these two primary effects, the other changes in the design of the surveys likely had little effect on the inequality estimates.

6.2. INEQUALITY IN THE UNITED STATES

I evaluate inequality using the logarithm of per equivalent consumption as the measure of household welfare:

$$W_k = \ln\left(\frac{M_k}{P_k(\mathbf{p}, \mathbf{p}_0, V_k)m_0(\mathbf{p}_0, \mathbf{A}_k)}\right) \tag{6.1}$$

The distribution of well-being is a function of the joint distribution of total expenditure M_k, the price effects P_k, and households' needs as measured by the equivalence scales. The influence of each separate component on overall inequality could be large, and the conditions under which the distribution of household welfare (6.1) coincides with the distribution of family income are quite strong. Only if households are identical, have exactly the same spending patterns, and have total expenditure equal to income will the two distributions be the same. Since these conditions do not hold, it is not surprising that there are major differences between inequality estimates based on per equivalent consumption and those based on family income.

Figure 6.3 presents inequality estimates over the period 1947 through 1995 for two indexes.[13] Among the class of inequality mea-

---

13. The inequality estimates in this chapter are based on tabulations from the CEX using the definition of expenditures described in Chapter 3. The method of evaluating the inequality index is described in Appendix 1, and the interpolation of the estimates in the years in which there was no CEX is based on a technique described in Appendix 2. Inequality estimates in Figures 6.3 and 6.4 use the Barten scales to adjust for household compositional differences and the household-specific price indexes described in Chapter 4. These indexes are calculated using the implicit price deflators of the PCE.

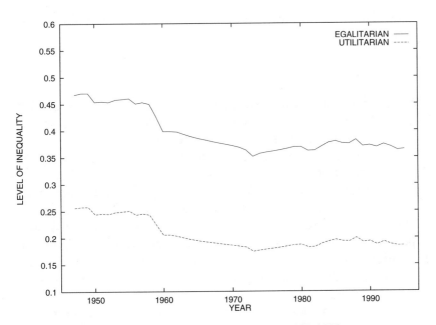

Figure 6.3. Inequality in the United States, 1947–1995

sures that I consider, the "egalitarian" index exhibits the greatest sensitivity to transfers between rich and poor households and the "utilitarian" index shows the least. The choice of index influences the level of inequality but has no effect on the trend. Both indexes show that inequality decreased between 1947 and 1972 but has changed little since then. Far from experiencing a dramatic U-turn in recent years, inequality in 1995 was roughly the same as in 1972 and substantially lower than the level attained in 1947.

There is no question that this finding is at odds with what are perceived to be the stylized facts. It is, therefore, important to assess why per equivalent consumption shows such a different picture of inequality. Possible explanations include the divergence between the income and expenditure distributions as well as differences induced by household-specific price and compositional effects. Identifying the sources of inequality can be an important ingredient in the development of sound public policy. If changes in inequality are the result of shifts in relative prices, the government should respond differently from what is appropriate if they arise from poor households having large families.

Price effects

We know that changes in prices *could* have a potentially large effect on the distribution of well-being if, for example, the relative prices of necessities increase. Inflation is often referred to as the "cruelest tax" because of its presumed reduction in the purchasing power of the poor relative to the rich. In fact, the results presented in Chapter 4 indicated that there was little variation in the inflation rates across unequally situated households. Despite substantial changes in the relative prices of some goods over the sample period, differences in spending on these items are not large enough to create significant variation in the cost of living. As a result, I would not expect prices to have large distributional effects.

To estimate the impact of price changes, I measure inequality for a welfare function that is identical to (6.1) except for the omission of the household-specific price index P_k:

$$W_k = \ln\left(\frac{M_k}{m_0(\mathbf{p}_0, \mathbf{A}_k)}\right) \tag{6.2}$$

Differences between inequality calculated using per equivalent expenditure (6.2) and using per equivalent consumption (6.1) are exclusively the result of the differential effects of price movements on well-being.

Figure 6.4 shows that, as expected, prices have had little distributional effect and no influence on the postwar trend in inequality. This is true even in periods of large changes in relative prices, such as between 1973 and 1974 as well as between 1979 and 1980. Although the effects were small, relative price changes increased inequality early in the sample period as well as between 1974 and 1985. Far from being the cruelest tax, price changes have had almost no (net) distributional impact and certainly cannot explain the divergence between the distributions of per equivalent consumption and family income.[14]

---

14. Using a different approach, Newbery (1995) also found small distributional effects of price changes in Hungary and the United Kingdom.

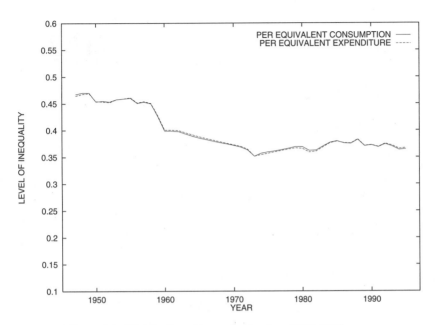

Figure 6.4. Distributional impacts of prices, 1947–1995

Household composition effects

What role does household composition play in explaining the level and trend of inequality? Are conclusions robust across alternative choices of equivalence scales? The dramatic changes in the demographic composition of the population described in Chapter 3 suggest that, in contrast with price effects, accounting for household heterogeneity in the measurement of welfare could have a substantial influence on both the level and the trend of inequality. This effect can be identified by comparing the distribution of per equivalent expenditure (6.2) to the distribution of the logarithm of total expenditure.

Figure 6.5 shows that accounting for differences in household composition (using the Barten scales) has an important effect on the distribution of welfare and its movement over time. Inequality calculated using no adjustment for needs is lower than that calculated using the Barten scales in every year. Perhaps more important, the welfare measure that incorporates differences in needs across households shows a substantially different trend in inequality. Inequality in the distribution of log expenditure (i.e., no adjustment for composi-

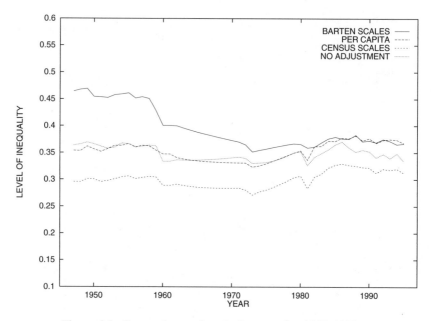

Figure 6.5. Comparisons of equivalence scales, 1947–1995

tional differences) changed little over the sample period, ranging from 0.36 in 1947 to 0.33 in 1961, 0.33 in 1973, 0.35 in 1980, 0.35 in 1990, and 0.33 in 1995. The distribution of per equivalent expenditure, in contrast, decreased from 0.46 in 1947 to 0.40 in 1961, 0.35 in 1973, 0.37 in 1980, 0.37 in 1990, and 0.37 in 1995.

Given the importance of differences in household composition to the estimates of inequality, it is essential to assess the sensitivity of conclusions to alternative representations of the household equivalence scales. Buhmann, Rainwater, Schmaus, and Smeeding (1988) showed that inequality and poverty estimates can change with different representations of households' needs. A more systematic analysis of this issue was provided by Coulter, Cowell, and Jenkins (1992), who found a U-shaped relationship between the level of inequality and the economies of scale in consumption that are implicit in the equivalence scales.[15]

15. The intuition is that, since richer households are typically larger, incorporating differences in needs with substantial economies of scale initially narrows the differences. With fewer economies of scale, however, household welfare levels are reordered to such an extent that well-being becomes more dispersed than the original distribution of household expenditure.

In light of these findings, I recalculate the level of inequality for equivalence scales that exhibit different economies of scale in consumption. Estimates that make no adjustment for needs are based on the assumption that the welfare of a family of four is the same as the welfare of a single adult who has the same expenditure. The per capita adjustment is at the opposite extreme and assumes no economies of scale in consumption. The Census scales and the Barten scales are intermediate between these two estimates, with the former exhibiting substantially greater scale economies.[16]

Figure 6.5 shows that the levels and trends of inequality are sensitive to the choice of equivalence scales. Whereas the index calculated using the Barten scales decreases over the sample period, the other estimates do not change appreciably. Per capita expenditure inequality shows a pattern that is similar to the estimates based on log expenditure (no adjustment for needs) ranging from 0.35 in 1947 to 0.35 in 1961, 0.32 in 1973, 0.35 in 1980, 0.38 in 1990, and 0.37 in 1995. The estimates based on the Census equivalence scales show similar stability over the five decades, ranging from 0.30 in 1947 to 0.31 in 1995.

No matter how I account for differences in needs, the overall conclusion is that the consumption-based inequality measures do not show the dramatic U-turn that is found when family income is used to measure welfare. The inequality measure based on per equivalent consumption shows a decline in inequality through the mid-1970s and little change thereafter. The other welfare measures show essentially no net change in inequality over the five decades since World War II. Although this result appears robust, it is possible that it reflects the choice of the functional form of the welfare function or inequality index.

As a final check of the sensitivity of the distributions to different estimates of the consumption requirements, I examine the deciles of household expenditure and per capita expenditure in Tables 6.1 and 6.2. Table 6.1 shows the proportion of aggregate expenditure owned

---

16. Buhmann et al. (1988) represent the equivalence scale as $m_0 = S^\theta$ where S is family size and θ is a scale elasticity that is between zero and 1. A value of zero assumes no adjustment for needs, whereas the per capita model is obtained when θ is 1. Note, however, that the Census scales and the Barten scales vary over dimensions other than household size. Banks and Johnson (1994) find that simply distinguishing adults from children in equivalence scales changes conclusions concerning the relationship between inequality and equivalence scales identified by Coulter, Cowell, and Jenkins (1992).

Table 6.1. *Household expenditure distribution*

	Share of aggregate expenditure by decile									
Year	1	2	3	4	5	6	7	8	9	10
1961	0.026	0.045	0.059	0.072	0.084	0.097	0.112	0.129	0.153	0.221
1973	0.027	0.046	0.060	0.072	0.084	0.097	0.111	0.129	0.153	0.222
1980	0.024	0.044	0.058	0.070	0.083	0.097	0.111	0.129	0.157	0.226
1985	0.024	0.043	0.056	0.069	0.081	0.093	0.108	0.127	0.158	0.242
1990	0.026	0.044	0.057	0.068	0.079	0.092	0.107	0.126	0.156	0.244
1995	0.028	0.047	0.059	0.070	0.081	0.094	0.108	0.127	0.153	0.235

	Cumulative share of aggregate expenditure									
Year	Bottom 10%	Bottom 20%	Bottom 30%	Bottom 40%	Bottom 50%	Bottom 60%	Bottom 70%	Bottom 80%	Bottom 90%	100%
1961	0.026	0.071	0.131	0.203	0.287	0.385	0.497	0.626	0.779	1.000
1973	0.027	0.073	0.133	0.204	0.288	0.385	0.496	0.625	0.778	1.000
1980	0.024	0.068	0.126	0.196	0.279	0.376	0.488	0.617	0.774	1.000
1985	0.024	0.067	0.122	0.191	0.271	0.365	0.473	0.600	0.758	1.000
1990	0.026	0.071	0.128	0.195	0.274	0.366	0.473	0.599	0.755	1.000
1995	0.028	0.074	0.133	0.203	0.284	0.378	0.485	0.612	0.765	1.000

	Average household size by decile									
Year	1	2	3	4	5	6	7	8	9	10
1961	1.8	2.3	2.7	3.0	3.3	3.6	3.6	3.8	4.1	4.2
1973	1.5	2.0	2.2	2.5	2.9	3.3	3.4	3.7	3.9	4.2
1980	1.4	1.9	2.3	2.4	2.8	3.2	3.0	3.3	3.5	3.7
1985	1.5	2.0	2.1	2.3	2.6	2.7	2.9	3.2	3.2	3.3
1990	1.6	1.9	2.1	2.3	2.5	2.6	2.9	3.0	3.2	3.3
1995	1.5	1.9	2.1	2.5	2.6	2.6	2.9	3.1	3.0	3.4

Source: Author's calculations from the *Consumer Expenditure Surveys*. Rows in the first panel may not sum to 1 because of rounding.

Table 6.2. *Per capita expenditure distribution*

Year	Share of aggregate expenditure by decile									
	1	2	3	4	5	6	7	8	9	10
1961	0.026	0.045	0.058	0.069	0.081	0.093	0.108	0.126	0.154	0.239
1973	0.030	0.048	0.059	0.070	0.081	0.093	0.106	0.123	0.152	0.238
1980	0.026	0.043	0.056	0.068	0.079	0.092	0.107	0.127	0.156	0.244
1985	0.024	0.042	0.055	0.066	0.078	0.091	0.106	0.126	0.157	0.254
1990	0.026	0.041	0.052	0.064	0.077	0.090	0.104	0.124	0.156	0.266
1995	0.027	0.042	0.053	0.065	0.076	0.090	0.106	0.128	0.159	0.255

Year	Cumulative share of aggregate expenditure									
	Bottom 10%	Bottom 20%	Bottom 30%	Bottom 40%	Bottom 50%	Bottom 60%	Bottom 70%	Bottom 80%	Bottom 90%	100%
1961	0.026	0.071	0.129	0.198	0.280	0.373	0.480	0.607	0.761	1.000
1973	0.030	0.077	0.137	0.207	0.288	0.381	0.487	0.610	0.762	1.000
1980	0.026	0.070	0.125	0.194	0.273	0.365	0.472	0.599	0.755	1.000
1985	0.024	0.066	0.121	0.187	0.265	0.356	0.462	0.588	0.745	1.000
1990	0.026	0.067	0.119	0.183	0.259	0.350	0.454	0.578	0.734	1.000
1995	0.027	0.068	0.121	0.186	0.262	0.352	0.459	0.586	0.745	1.000

Year	Average household size by decile									
	1	2	3	4	5	6	7	8	9	10
1961	5.7	4.4	4.1	3.8	3.5	3.3	3.0	2.8	2.4	2.0
1973	5.0	4.2	3.8	3.5	3.3	3.1	2.8	2.6	2.2	1.8
1980	4.5	3.8	3.5	3.3	3.1	2.9	2.6	2.4	2.0	1.7
1985	4.1	3.4	3.1	3.1	2.9	2.6	2.4	2.1	2.1	1.6
1990	4.1	3.7	3.6	3.0	2.7	2.5	2.4	2.2	1.9	1.6
1995	4.4	3.8	3.3	3.1	2.8	2.6	2.4	2.1	1.9	1.5

Source: Author's calculations from the *Consumer Expenditure Surveys.*

by each decile of households as well as the cumulative shares. The stability of the distribution over the thirty-five years is noteworthy. There was an increase in the share going to the highest decile; these households owned 22.1 percent of aggregate expenditure in 1961 and 23.5 percent in 1995. The proportion going to the lowest decile also increased from 2.6 percent in 1961 to 2.8 percent in 1995. In contrast with popular perception, the modest gains of the wealthiest came at the expense of those in the middle of the distribution (deciles 4 through 7) rather than those in the lower tail.

The importance of accounting for differences in needs is illustrated by the systematic variation in average household sizes across deciles. A common misperception is that households with the lowest income or consumption have the largest families. The CEX data show exactly the opposite pattern; household size is positively related to the level of expenditure. Any correction for needs, therefore, induces a reordering of welfare levels in which households with low per equivalent expenditure are different from those that have low levels of (unadjusted) total expenditure.

Table 6.2 shows the modest deterioration of the distribution of per capita expenditure that was illustrated in Figure 6.5.[17] While dispersion increased, the proportion of aggregate expenditure attributable to each decile of individuals did not change greatly between 1961 and 1995. The highest decile showed the most significant movement, increasing from 23.9 percent of aggregate expenditure in 1961 to 25.5 percent in 1995. Changes in the other deciles were smaller, and more than one-half of the increase in the share of the wealthiest individuals came at the expense of those in deciles 4 through 6. Note that average household size decreases with the level per capita expenditure, and that confirms the reordering of welfare levels when differences in needs are accounted for.

The tabulations reported in Tables 6.1 and 6.2 reinforce the finding of relative stability in the distribution of welfare over the postwar period. The estimated levels and trends of inequality are dictated, to some extent, by the choice of the equivalence scales. The central conclusion, however, that the distribution of per equivalent consumption differs significantly from the distribution of family income is robust. Instead of a dramatic U-turn in inequality, the consumption-based

17. An equal sharing rule is assumed so that each individual in a household is assumed to have the same expenditure.

inequality indexes exhibit either no net change in inequality since 1947 or a decrease, depending on the method used to adjust for needs.

6.3. THE INCOME AND EXPENDITURE DISTRIBUTIONS

Why are the income and expenditure distributions so different? Are taxes and transfers the explanation, or is there an equilibrating effect of the services received from durables and owner-occupied housing? To what extent does consumption smoothing explain the divergence? Comparisons of the income and expenditure distributions are difficult because there is evidence that the income data in the CEX (the only source of income and expenditure information) have uneven quality.

The definition of income changed little over the years and includes the following items:

1. Wages and salaries for all household members over 14 years of age.
2. Self-employment income, which is net business and farm income (gross receipts less operating income).
3. Retirement income, including the payments from Social Security, private, and government retirement programs.
4. Interest, dividends, rental, and other property income.
5. Unemployment benefits, workers' compensation, and veterans' benefits.
6. Public assistance, Supplemental Security Income, and food stamps.
7. Regular contributions for support such as alimony or child support payments.
8. Other money income such as cash scholarships, fellowships, stipends, meals and rent received as pay, and income from foster care.

As a point of reference, this is similar to the definition of income used in the *Current Population Surveys* (CPS). The primary difference is the inclusion of the net value of food stamps and the meals and rent received as pay.

Although the definition of income has remained essentially unaltered over time, a number of other changes in the CEX could affect temporal comparisons of the income distribution. As with expenditures, there was no income topcoding in the 1961, 1972, and 1973 surveys, but there was from 1980 onward. Less than 1 percent of the samples were topcoded in most years, and I assumed that these households had an income level equal to the upper bound (i.e., the topcode). This has the effect of understating the average level and dispersion of income, although the magnitude of the effect is probably small.

Consumer units in the CEX are classified as either "complete" or "incomplete" income reporters, and the method of classification changed over the years. In 1972 and 1973, a household was an incomplete reporter if the primary earner was employed but reported no earned income. The income report was also considered incomplete if there were no employed members of the household and they reported receiving retirement income, but did not report the levels. In the 1980s and 1990s, a consumer unit was classified as a complete income reporter if it reported the amounts received from major income sources such as wages and salaries, self-employment income, or Social Security income. The earlier and later definitions are obviously different, and both could have classified a consumer unit as a complete income reporter even if it was incomplete by most objective standards.

Since most income inequality studies use the CPS, it provides a useful benchmark for assessing the general quality of the income data in the CEX. Per capita income in the CEX was quite close to that tabulated from the CPS in 1961, 1972, and 1973.[18] From 1980 through 1995, however, per capita income in the CEX was approximately 20 percent *below* the CPS estimate. The lower estimates were likely the result of imputations for nonresponses which were applied to the CPS (and account for roughly 20 percent of total income) but not to the CEX. Note, however, that although the average income levels were different, Cutler and Katz (1991) found that the distributions of per capita income were quite similar.[19]

18. These and all subsequent income tabulations from the CEX are based on samples that are limited to complete income reporters.
19. Whereas expenditures in the CEX are reported on a quarterly basis after 1973, questions related to income are based on a twelve-month accounting period. For example, to determine the wages and salaries received by a member of the household, the following questions were asked. "During the past 12 months, did (consumer unit member) receive any money in wages and salaries?" "What was the amount of income received before any deductions?"

In Table 6.3 I present CEX tabulations of mean household income, mean expenditure, and their correlations in selected years. If income and expenditure were perfectly correlated, income would be a reasonable proxy for consumption in the measurement of inequality. In fact, the correlations were positive but well below 1, with the highest being 0.80 in 1961 and the lowest 0.65 in 1985. Most damaging for studies that use income as a proxy for a consumption-based welfare measure is the fact that the correlation decreased over time. This could be due to a decrease in the quality of the income data in the CEX or, more seriously, the result of systematic behavioral changes, such as variation in saving patterns, that alter the covariance between income and expenditure.

The rank correlation coefficient summarizes the correlation between households' ranks in the respective distributions. If every household has the same income and expenditure rank, the correlation coefficient is 1. A complete reversal in ranks yields a value of −1, and the coefficient is zero if the two distributions are statistically independent. As with the raw correlations, the rank correlation coefficients were low and decreased over time, from a maximum of 0.83 in 1961 to a minimum of 0.68 in 1985.

These tabulations suggest that income provides an inaccurate approximation of total expenditure and household welfare. Although formal statistical inference would strongly reject the hypothesis of independence of income and expenditure, the low correlations suggest that the two distributions are quite different. These tabulations show divergence, but they do not indicate whether expenditure is more or less equally distributed relative to income. In light of the

Table 6.3. *Moments of income and total expenditure* *(current dollars)*

Year	Mean income	Mean total expenditure	Income-expenditure correlation	Income-expenditure rank correlation
1961	6,163	5,766	0.80	0.83
1973	12,725	9,288	0.68	0.81
1980	17,897	14,497	0.66	0.72
1985	24,466	19,620	0.65	0.68
1990	30,876	23,954	0.70	0.73
1995	35,787	27,306	0.67	0.70

Source: Author's calculations using complete income reporters in the CEX.

permanent income hypothesis, one would expect the expenditure distribution to be less dispersed than the income distribution.

This prediction is borne out by comparisons of the household
income and expenditure distributions. The deciles of before-tax
income, the cumulative proportions, and the corresponding average
household sizes are presented in Table 6.4. Relative to the distribution of household expenditure shown in Table 6.1, the income
distribution was more dispersed. In fact, the Lorenz curve of the
expenditure distribution was everywhere inside that of the income
distribution in every year. The differences were most pronounced in
the upper tail of the distribution. The top 20 percent of the income
distribution accounted for 41.3 percent of total income in 1961, 43.5
percent in 1973, 43.7 percent in 1980, 46.8 percent in 1990, and 46.5
percent in 1995. The corresponding proportions for the expenditure
distributions were 37.4 percent in 1961, 37.5 percent in 1973, 38.3
percent in 1980, 40.0 percent in 1990, and 38.8 percent in 1995.

As important, there was more movement in the distribution of
income over the thirty-five years, and, consistent with the findings of
other studies, it has been getting more unequal. Table 6.5 shows that
the ratio of the income share of the top 30 percent to the share of
bottom 30 percent increased from 5.4 in 1961 to 8.4 in 1995. The ratios
for household expenditure were 3.8 in 1961 and 3.9 in 1995.

What accounts for these differences? A household's expenditure is
the level of before-tax income less its tax liabilities less savings plus
the services from owner-occupied housing and consumer durables.
A full explanation of the divergence between the income and expenditure distributions requires an analysis of the distribution
of taxes, savings, and the services from housing and durables. The
relative importance of each component can be assessed by comparing inequality in the distributions of after-tax and disposable income,
where the latter concept is defined as the after-tax income plus the
services received from owner-occupied housing and consumer
durables.[20]

---

20. After-tax income is before-tax income less the sum of federal, state, and local taxes.
    The taxes reported by each household in the CEX are the net taxes paid over the
    previous twelve months. I've made no attempt to assess the accuracy of the reported
    tax payments. Bosworth, Burtless, and Sabelhaus (1991) claimed that the tax reports
    in the 1972 and 1973 CEX appear to be accurate, whereas those in the 1980s are
    unreliable.

Table 6.4. *Household income distribution*

	Share of aggregate income by decile									
Year	1	2	3	4	5	6	7	8	9	10
1961	0.016	0.034	0.051	0.067	0.081	0.095	0.111	0.130	0.157	0.256
1973	0.012	0.030	0.045	0.061	0.077	0.094	0.112	0.133	0.163	0.272
1980	0.011	0.027	0.042	0.058	0.075	0.096	0.116	0.139	0.173	0.264
1985	0.009	0.024	0.036	0.051	0.067	0.087	0.110	0.138	0.181	0.296
1990	0.012	0.026	0.038	0.052	0.069	0.087	0.109	0.138	0.177	0.291
1995	0.010	0.025	0.038	0.052	0.069	0.090	0.112	0.140	0.182	0.283

	Cumulative share of aggregate income									
Year	Bottom 10%	Bottom 20%	Bottom 30%	Bottom 40%	Bottom 50%	Bottom 60%	Bottom 70%	Bottom 80%	Bottom 90%	100%
1961	0.016	0.051	0.101	0.168	0.250	0.345	0.456	0.587	0.744	1.000
1973	0.012	0.042	0.087	0.148	0.225	0.320	0.432	0.565	0.728	1.000
1980	0.011	0.037	0.079	0.137	0.213	0.308	0.424	0.563	0.736	1.000
1985	0.009	0.033	0.070	0.120	0.188	0.275	0.385	0.522	0.704	1.000
1990	0.012	0.038	0.076	0.128	0.198	0.285	0.394	0.532	0.709	1.000
1995	0.010	0.034	0.072	0.124	0.193	0.282	0.394	0.535	0.717	1.000

	Average household size by decile									
Year	1	2	3	4	5	6	7	8	9	10
1961	1.8	2.5	2.9	3.2	3.3	3.6	3.7	3.7	3.8	3.8
1973	1.5	2.1	2.4	2.7	2.9	3.2	3.4	3.6	3.7	3.8
1980	1.5	2.0	2.1	2.6	2.8	2.9	3.2	3.4	3.4	3.5
1985	2.0	1.9	2.3	2.4	2.4	2.7	2.8	2.9	3.3	3.2
1990	1.6	2.0	2.1	2.3	2.5	2.5	2.8	3.0	3.2	3.2
1995	1.9	1.8	2.2	2.3	2.3	2.8	2.8	3.0	3.1	3.1

Source: Author's calculations from the *Consumer Expenditure Surveys* over the sample of complete income reporters. Rows in the first panel may not sum to 1 because of rounding.

Table 6.5. *Ratio of the top 30% to the bottom 30%*

Year	Household income	Household expenditure	Per capita expenditure
1961	5.4	3.8	4.0
1973	6.5	3.8	3.7
1980	7.3	4.1	4.2
1985	8.8	4.3	4.4
1990	8.0	4.1	4.6
1995	8.4	3.9	4.5

Source: Author's calculations using the CEX over the sample of complete income reporters.

Inequality for the alternative definitions of income are presented in Figure 6.6. Consistent with the tabulations reported in Table 6.4, before-tax income inequality increased sharply over the sample period, from 0.45 in 1961 to 0.59 by 1986, and subsequently decreased to 0.55 in 1995.[21] In 1961, the payment of federal, state, and local taxes reduced inequality from 0.45 to 0.42, and that implies progressivity of the tax system.[22] Between 1961 and 1995, differences between the before- and the after-tax income distributions shrank and by 1995 the two indexes were very close. The upward trend in inequality is preserved using after-tax income; differences in tax liabilities over this period cannot explain the divergence between the income and expenditure distributions.

Adding the services from durables and owner-occupied housing to after-tax income had an equilibrating effect on the income distribution. In 1961, disposable income inequality was 0.39 compared to 0.42 for the after-tax income distribution. Inequality in the distribution of total expenditure was 0.33, so approximately half of the difference between before-tax income inequality and total expenditure inequality can be explained by taxes and the service flows from durables and housing. The remainder is due to the distribution of saving and

21. For these and subsequent calculations, the inequality index is assumed to exhibit the greatest sensitivity to transfers between the rich and the poor and is consistent with the "egalitarian" index shown in Figure 6.3. Inequality levels are linearly interpolated in the years in which there were no surveys.
22. This definition of tax progression is due to Musgrave and Thin (1948).

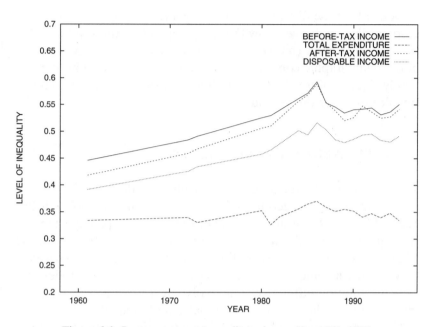

Figure 6.6. Income versus expenditure inequality, 1961–1995

dissaving.[23] The service flows from durables and housing remained inequality-reducing in 1995 but accounted for a smaller fraction of the difference between the before-tax income and total expenditure distributions. Before-tax income inequality was 0.55, after-tax income inequality was 0.54, disposable income inequality was 0.49, and total expenditure inequality was 0.33.

The distribution of saving is, therefore, the most important component of the wedge between the before-tax income and expenditure distributions. It is consumption smoothing and the manner in which it changed between 1961 and 1995 that are most influential in explaining the differences in the levels and trends of the income and expenditure inequality indexes. Although a detailed examination of the

23. Given the nature of the data, this interpretation must be qualified. As noted previously, the difference between disposable income and total expenditure is also the "dumping ground" of measurement errors associated with each component of disposable income and consumption. The extent to which there are differential errors of measurement at different points of the distribution will distort the estimate of the impact of consumption smoothing on differences between the income and expenditure distributions.

movements in the distribution of saving and dissaving is beyond the scope of this study, we know that they depend on the level and distribution of wealth (human and nonhuman) as well as the changes in the demographic composition of the population (such as age and family size). Both of these determinants of saving patterns changed significantly over this period.

6.4. BETWEEN-GROUP INEQUALITY

To what extent can inequality be explained by differences between male- and female-headed households or between households distinguished by race? Are differences between age groups important, or is inequality primarily the result of disparities within these groups? I have shown that the distribution of saving is an important wedge between the income and expenditure distributions. This implies that age-consumption differences that evolve over the life cycle could be important in explaining the overall pattern of inequality.

There are a number of ways to decompose inequality into within- and between-group components. The theoretical literature has focused on descriptions of indexes for which total inequality can be represented as the weighted sum of inequality indexes defined over the within- and between-group distributions.[24] This type of decomposition typically requires the inequality index to be additive, a restriction that has strong normative implications. As an alternative approach, I define between-group inequality as the inequality that remains after the differences in welfare within groups are eliminated.[25] Whatever inequality exists is solely the result of differences in welfare between subgroups of the population.

Between-group inequality calculated in this way depends on the relative welfare levels as well as the number of households in each group. If, for example, the proportion of households in each group is

---

24. A partial list of contributions includes Blackorby, Donaldson, and Auersperg (1981), Bourguignon (1979), Cowell (1980), and Shorrocks (1980, 1984).
25. Specifically, each individual within the group is assumed to have the welfare attained when group expenditure is reallocated to equalize well-being within the group. Inequality is then measured using the indexes defined in sections 6.3 and 6.4. An alternative approach has been proposed by Blackorby, Donaldson, and Auersperg (1981) in which each individual receives the "equally distributed equivalent income" of the group to which he or she belongs.

constant, then, all other things being equal, the greater the disparity in group welfare, the greater the inequality. Any change in inequality, moreover, can be attributed solely to changes in the relative levels of group welfare.

The influence of the composition of the population on between-group inequality is more subtle. Assume that there is a demographic group that historically attains higher welfare levels than another group. If representation of the low welfare group falls, there are fewer households with low welfare, the social welfare loss due to dispersion decreases, and between-group inequality falls. In the limit, if the low-welfare group disappears (as actually occurs for farm households in the United States), inequality between groups is eliminated.

Inequality between age groups

If the life-cycle hypothesis is true, a certain degree of inequality is unavoidable because of the systematic variation of consumption (and income) with age. Paglin (1975) pointed out that even if life-time incomes are identical across the population, "snapshots" of the (current) income distribution will show inequality because a cross section comprises individuals at different stages of the life cycle. It becomes important, therefore, to assess the inequality that is due solely to differences between age groups.[26]

The potential importance of life-cycle effects is illustrated in Figure 6.7. The age profile of total expenditure in the 1995 CEX is shown for six groups distinguished by the age of the head of the household: 16–24, 25–34, 35–44, 45–54, 55–64, and 65 and over. There is substantial variation in the average expenditure across the different groups; total expenditure increases until age 45–54 and subsequently falls. At first glance, this profile is surprising since the life-cycle hypothesis predicts a smoother path of consumption as households age. Note, however, that the age groups vary systematically in terms of their average household size. Figure 6.8 shows a strong life-cycle pattern of household size across the six age groups. The average household

---

26. There is also reason to believe that there is a link between age and the within-group distribution. Deaton and Paxson (1994) have pointed out that the permanent income hypothesis implies that dispersion in consumption should increase within cohorts as they age. Evidence from three different countries supports this prediction. See also the discussion by Blundell and Preston (1998).

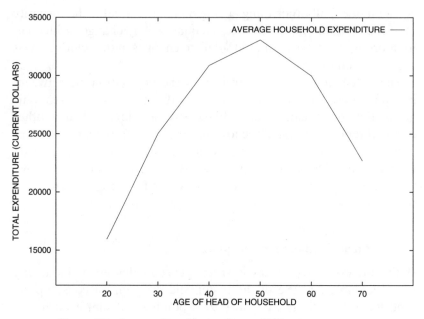

Figure 6.7. Age profile of expenditure: 1995

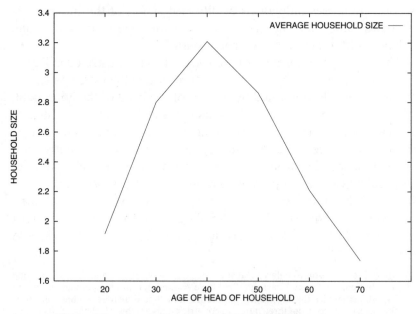

Figure 6.8. Age profile of household size: 1995

size peaks for those with a household head between 35 and 44 years of age, so on a per capita basis, the age profile of consumption will appear smoother than what is shown in Figure 6.7.

The relative welfare levels for households at different stages of the life cycle (within a particular year) depend on how needs are measured. It is not surprising, therefore, that conclusions concerning both the levels and the trends of inequality between age groups are also dependent on the choice of equivalence scales (Figure 6.9). The inequality index calculated using the Barten equivalence scales initially decreased from 0.10 in 1947 to 0.08 in 1961 and then increased to 0.12 in 1980. By the end of the sample period, between-group inequality was 0.10. The index based on per capita consumption shows a different trend after 1961, decreasing from 0.07 in 1961 to 0.05 in the early 1980s. Instead of decreasing further, between-group inequality almost doubled over the remainder of the sample period. Inequality calculated using the Census scales showed little change between 1961 and the early 1980s and then, like the per capita index, increased through 1995.

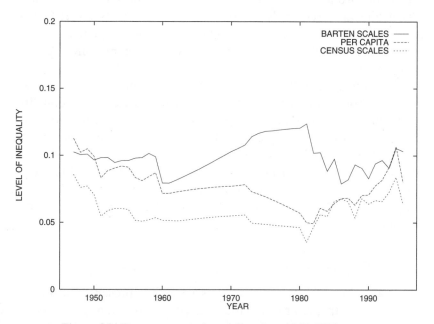

Figure 6.9. Between-group inequality: Age, 1947–1995

Table 6.6. *Between-group inequality as a fraction of total inequality (%)*

	Age			Region			Race			Gender		
Year	Barten scales	Per capita	Census scales	Barten scales	Per capita	Census scales	Barten scales	Per capita	Census scales	Barten scales	Per capita	Census scales
1947	22	32	29	28	15	14	14	17	20	10	3	9
1961	20	21	18	31	18	19	17	16	19	9	1	9
1973	32	23	18	24	9	9	18	16	17	12	0	13
1980	33	16	15	17	2	1	20	19	18	11	4	15
1990	22	19	20	25	10	12	16	14	13	14	4	15
1995	28	22	20	20	4	5	16	15	14	16	2	12

Source: Author's calculations based on between-group inequality indexes.

Table 6.6 shows the percentage of total inequality that can be explained by differences between various demographic groups. Although most inequality can be attributed to disparities within rather than between age groups, age-consumption differences explain a nontrivial fraction of total inequality. Regardless of the equivalence scales used, between-group differences accounted for approximately one-fifth to one-third of the total depending on the year. If these disparities are exclusively the result of life-cycle differences (which need not be the case), this fraction of total inequality is, in a sense, "inevitable" and simply reflects the age composition of the population.

The life-cycle pattern of consumption and its impact on inequality in any particular year also influence the overall trend in inequality. In Figure 6.10 I present estimates of inequality within the different age groups over the sample period. When between-group age effects are removed, the Barten equivalence scales show a much sharper decrease in inequality since 1947 until the early 1970s. Within-group inequality calculated using the other equivalence scales does not show qualitatively different trends relative to the estimates of total inequality.

Inequality between regions, races, and genders

Inequality between the four Census regions is presented in Figure 6.11, and the trends are similar across choices of equivalence scales. Inequality between regions decreased between 1947 and 1980 but

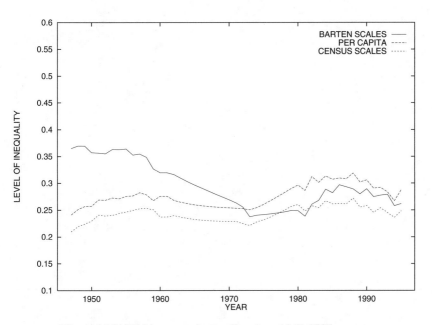

Figure 6.10. Within-group inequality: Age, 1947–1995

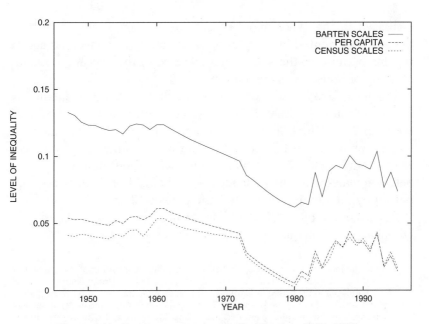

Figure 6.11. Between-group inequality: Region, 1947–1995

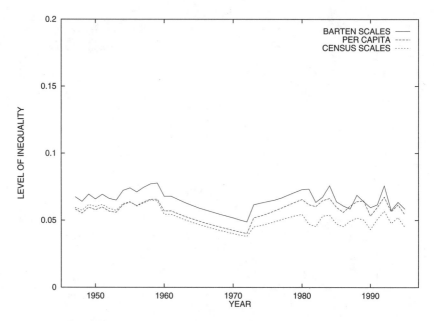

Figure 6.12. Between-group inequality: Race, 1947–1995

increased in the 1980s and 1990s. These estimates reflect the fact that, as documented in Chapter 5, living standards converged across regions because of the substantial increase in the average standard of living of households living in the South.[27]

The most striking sets of results are those related to inequality between groups differentiated by the race and gender of the head of the household. The popular perception is that much of the inequality that exists in the United States can be explained by differences in the living standards of white and nonwhite households as well as between male- and female-headed households. This claim is not supported by the tabulations shown in Figures 6.12 and 6.13.

Regardless of the equivalence scales used, Figure 6.12 shows little net change in inequality between groups differentiated by race.

27. One of the most dramatic changes in the demographic composition of the population is the disappearance of households living on farms. In 1947, approximately 16 percent of all families and unrelated individuals lived on farms compared to between 1 and 2 percent at the end of the sample period. This population shift had the effect of decreasing between-group inequality not because of improvements in the living standards of farm families but because of their marked decrease in representation in the population.

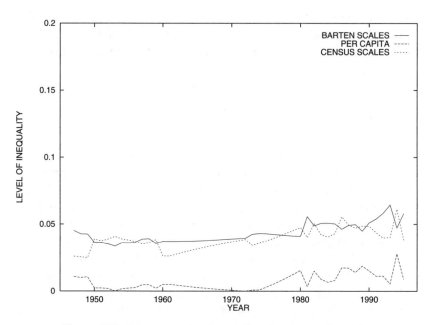

Figure 6.13. Between-group inequality: Gender, 1947–1995

Although there was convergence in the average welfare levels of whites and nonwhites (documented in Chapter 5), the narrowing of the gap was offset by an increase in the proportion of nonwhite households whose standards of living remained well below those of whites. Perhaps more surprising is the fact that inequality between groups distinguished by race explains less than 20 percent of the total. Using the Barten scales to measure household welfare, Table 6.6 shows that between-group inequality accounted for only 14 percent of the total in 1947 and 16 percent in 1995. The inequality estimates based on the Census scales and the per capita adjustment yield qualitatively similar results.

As with inequality between groups distinguished by race, inequality between male- and female-headed households did not change much over the past five decades. The levels of inequality remained roughly the same using the Barten and Census equivalence scales, but the reasons for the disparities are different. Recall that the average welfare of female-headed households exceeded that of their male counterparts using the Barten scales, whereas the reverse was true for the Census scales. Per capita consumption of male- and female-headed households was roughly the same, and that explains the fact that between-group inequality was close to zero throughout the sample period.[28]

6.5. SUMMARY AND CONCLUSION

I have presented results in this chapter that show that the widely reported U-turn in inequality in the United States is an artifact of the inappropriate use of family income as a measure of welfare. When well-being is defined to be a function of per equivalent consumption, inequality either decreased over the sample period or remained essentially unchanged depending on the choice of equivalence scales. This conclusion arises because the distribution of consumption differs sharply from the distribution of income, which, in turn, is due to the distribution of savings and dissavings across the population. Household composition is also important in explaining the observed levels and trends of inequality, but the impacts of relative price changes are small.

The fact that one obtains an inaccurate picture of inequality by restricting consideration to the distribution of income has important policy implications. The conventional wisdom is that rising earnings inequality has been offset by income transfers until 1973.[29] The increasing level of income inequality since 1973 has led some analysts to the conclusion that the government must redouble its efforts to bring about greater equality in the distribution of well-being. My results suggest there is no U-turn to explain and no increase in inequality to overcome. One could make the case, however, that in 1995 the level of inequality in household welfare remained high and that substantial gains could be realized through the equalization of the distribution of welfare. Is the government able to change the distribution of well-being in a substantive way? I haven't addressed this question directly. Household composition, however, has been shown to be an important determinant of inequality. Changes in the demo-

28. Cowell and Jenkins (1995) have also found that between-group inequality is relatively unimportant in explaining overall dispersion using a different method of decomposition, a different measure of welfare, and a different data set.
29. See Levy (1987), p. 165.

graphic composition of the population therefore influence levels and trends of inequality, and these changes are beyond the control of policy makers. It remains for further research to examine the extent to which government tax and transfer programs can truly influence the distribution of household welfare.

7 Consumption and poverty

The declaration of war on poverty by President Johnson marked the beginning of a comprehensive government initiative to reduce the incidence of poverty in the United States. New social programs were created and old programs were expanded in an effort to provide a safety net for those at the lower end of the income distribution. To monitor the success of this effort, a statistical program was implemented by the Bureau of the Census to provide annual estimates of poverty. The results have not been encouraging; although the proportion of the population living below the poverty line fell sharply between 1959 and 1973, little progress has been made since then. Inevitably, causal linkages between past public policies and the high poverty rate have been sought in an effort to solve the riddle of the persistence of poverty.[1]

Many aspects of poverty and poverty measurement have been debated. Is the poverty line too high or too low? Is it appropriate to differentiate between male- and female-headed households in setting the poverty line? Which price index should be used to adjust the thresholds over time? Should in-kind transfers be included in measuring household resources and welfare? Although these issues and others have been discussed extensively, it seems to have escaped notice that the Census continues to measure poverty using income as an indicator of well-being. As with inequality, this practice undoubtedly distorts the poverty estimates.

1. See, for example, Murray (1984) and Sawhill (1988).

156

Tabulations from the CEX indicate that consumption-based poverty rates are substantially lower than those tabulated using income. This finding is surprising in light of what is commonly assumed of low-income households. It is widely believed, for example, that consumption and income cannot differ significantly for the poor. They have no financial assets and cannot dissave, cannot possibly qualify to own a home, and certainly cannot afford to purchase consumer durables. The evidence from the CEX suggests that all these presumptions are false. A substantial fraction of the "income poor" are homeowners. The service flows from their stock of consumer durables account for between 11 percent and 14 percent of total spending, and, consistent with predictions of the permanent income hypothesis, there is strong evidence of consumption smoothing. Each factor contributes to the bias that results from using income to measure poverty.

7.1. MEASURING POVERTY

Poverty measurement requires two separate steps: identifying who is poor and then aggregating the information on their well-being to determine the extent of poverty. The concept of absolute poverty identifies the poor using a fixed threshold that is typically associated with a subsistence level of well-being. Anyone below the cut-off is classified as poor regardless of his position relative to others. As a result, it is possible for everyone (or no one) in the population to be identified as poor.

An alternative view is that deprivation cannot be assessed without comparing individuals' living standards to societal norms. The degree of impoverishment is related to households' relative levels of well-being.[2] Operationally, the "relative poverty line" is defined as a fraction of the mean or median welfare level so that, for realistic distributions, poverty can never be eliminated.[3]

These two methods of identifying the poor have different implications for both the level and the trend of poverty. With distributionally neutral growth in the standard of living, for example, absolute

2. Arguments in favor of the relative approach to poverty measurement are presented by Townsend (1985) and Sen (1983).
3. Fuchs (1967) suggested that the "relative poverty line" be 50 percent of median income.

poverty decreases while the number of "relatively poor" individuals is unchanged. If there is widespread famine and compression of the distribution, absolute poverty rises but relative poverty falls even though a large fraction of the population is starving. This has led some analysts to conclude that relative poverty is best interpreted as an indicator of inequality rather than a measure of impoverishment.

A less commonly used approach to setting the poverty line is based on individuals' perceptions of the resources needed to maintain a subsistence standard of living. In previous chapters I described surveys, administered primarily in Europe, Canada, and the United States, in which participants are asked to provide an estimate of the minimum income necessary to "make ends meet." If households' incomes fall below the stated minima, they are classified as poor.[4] Since perceptions of what it takes to make ends meet depend on lifestyles and on how one is doing compared to others, there is a relative component to this method of identifying the poor. Indeed, it is frequently observed that subjective poverty thresholds increase with the incomes of the respondents and exceed the official thresholds by significant amounts. Application of this approach to identification requires the judgment that it is reasonable to measure poverty on the basis of individuals' subjective assessments rather than observed economic circumstances.

Once the poverty population has been identified, how should the information on their well-being be aggregated to measure the extent of poverty? Sen (1976) stated that poverty indexes should satisfy three basic conditions. First and foremost, they should be functions only of the welfare of the poor so that changes in the well-being of the nonpoor leave the indexes unaffected. Second, the poverty measures should be negatively related to the welfare of the poor so that, all other things being equal, an improvement in their standard of living results in a decrease in the measured level of poverty. The final condition requires the indexes to increase with transfers from the poor to anyone who is richer.[5]

---

4. Examples of subjective poverty thresholds are provided by Danziger et al. (1984), de Vos and Garner (1991), Goedhart et al. (1977), Hagenaars (1986), and Kilpatrick (1973).
5. These conditions are referred to as the focus axiom, the monotonicity axiom, and the weak transfer axiom. Foster (1984) provides a survey of the voluminous literature on the axiomatic approach to the measurement of poverty that was largely stimulated by Sen's work.

Sen's axiomatic framework provides a benchmark that can be utilized to evaluate widely used measures of poverty. Let W_k be the welfare of the kth individual and define W_z as the poverty threshold. If L individuals have welfare levels below W_z and if N is the size of the total population, the head-count ratio is the fraction of the population that is poor:

$$P_0 = \frac{L}{N} \tag{7.1}$$

This simple index is probably the most commonly used measure of poverty. Although it depends only on the welfare of the poor, it is independent of the "intensity" of poverty because it is unaffected by the distance of the poor from the poverty line. Moreover, regressive transfers among the poor either leave the index unchanged or cause it to decrease.[6]

The average poverty gap measures the (normalized) average distance of the poor from the poverty line:

$$P_1 = (1/N) \sum_{k=1}^{L} \frac{W_z - W_k}{W_z} \tag{7.2}$$

In most applications, welfare is represented by the individual's income so that the numerator in (7.2) is the additional income needed to eliminate poverty. It satisfies the focus and monotonicity axioms, but regressive transfers among the poor have no effect on the poverty measure.

Foster, Greer, and Thorbecke (1984) (FGT) developed a general approach to poverty measurement that has the head-count ratio and the average poverty gap as special cases. Their index is a function of the average distance of the poor from the poverty line:

$$P_\alpha = (1/N) \sum_{k=1}^{L} \left(\frac{W_z - W_k}{W_z} \right)^\alpha \tag{7.3}$$

If α is zero, the FGT index is the head-count ratio, whereas a value of 1 produces the average poverty gap. If α is greater than 1, the index satisfies all of Sen's axioms, with higher values assigning greater weight to the well-being of the poorest individuals.

---

6. This occurs when the recipient escapes poverty as a result of the transfer.

The framework developed by Sen is widely used, but several alternatives have been proposed. Analogous to inequality measurement, one approach measures poverty as the loss in social welfare due to the existence of a group of individuals below the poverty line. Blackorby and Donaldson (1980b), for example, developed an index that is a function of the proportional difference between the poverty line and the monetary equivalent of the welfare of the poor. Jorgenson and Slesnick (1989), Pyatt (1987), and Vaughn (1987) measure poverty as the gain in social welfare that results from an optimal sequence of transfers that raise the welfare of the poor above the poverty line.

All these approaches depend on the poverty threshold as well as the aggregation procedure. Another strand of research has identified the conditions under which it is possible to discern a change in the level of poverty irrespective of the choice of the poverty line or index. A definitive assessment is possible if the poverty index is additive, the population is homogeneous, and the cumulative proportion of persons (ranked from the lowest welfare level to the highest) is higher for one distribution than another up to the highest possible value of the poverty line.[7]

7.2. POVERTY IN THE UNITED STATES

The official poverty rate (i.e., the head-count ratio) reported by the Bureau of the Census is based on a definition of absolute poverty developed in the mid-1960s by Mollie Orshansky of the Social Security Administration. It began with an estimate of the level of food consumption, termed the Economy Food Plan, that is required to avoid the risk of malnutrition. Under the assumption that food constituted one-third of all expenditures for poor households, the poverty line was defined to be three times the Economy Food Plan. This accounted for other consumption items in the subsistence

---

7. If this "first order dominance" condition does not hold, one must compare the generalized Lorenz curves up to the maximum threshold. If one distribution "second order dominates" another, poverty will be lower for all poverty indexes other than the head-count ratio. See Atkinson (1987) as well as Foster and Shorrocks (1988). Ravallion (1994) presents an excellent summary of the use of stochastic dominance conditions to measure poverty.

budget such as housing, utilities, medical care, transportation, and so on.[8]

Households having different compositions were recognized as having different needs. The subsistence consumption of an elderly individual is not the same as that of a family of four with two teenagers. To account for such heterogeneity, the cost of subsistence diets was tabulated for households distinguished by their size, age, gender, and farm/nonfarm residence. As before, the poverty thresholds were obtained by scaling these estimates upward to account for other consumption items. This was equivalent to adjusting the poverty lines across different types of households using nutritional equivalence scales.

As prices rise, the costs of purchasing the subsistence market baskets increase. Unless the nominal poverty lines are adjusted upward, they represent the expenditures for lower and lower levels of well-being. To ensure that the thresholds represented a constant standard of living, the Census Bureau adjusted the poverty lines over time using the CPI. Prior to 1969 the thresholds were adjusted on the basis of changes in the cost of food rather than the CPI itself.

When the Bureau of the Census began estimating the poverty rate in the mid-1960s, the only available annual data were the income estimates provided by the *Current Population Surveys*. Out of practical necessity, households' incomes were used as proxies for consumption. In terms of the welfare function W_k, the official poverty measure can be summarized as follows. All members of a household are identified as poor if $W_k < W_z$ where[9]

$$W_k = \frac{Y_k}{\Pi m_f(\mathbf{A}_k)} \tag{7.4}$$

and Y_k is the household's before-tax income, $\mathbf{A}_k$ is the vector of attributes, $m_f(\mathbf{A}_k)$ is the nutritional equivalence scale, and Π is the CPI.

Although reasonable people can differ in their opinion as to what constitutes a subsistence level of consumption, the conceptual basis

8. See Orshansky (1965) for a complete description the original poverty thresholds. For households with fewer than three members, the multiplier was higher.
9. The poverty population is actually identified by comparing nominal income to the monetary value of the poverty threshold W_z, which is $\Pi m_f(\mathbf{A}_k)W_z$ for the kth household. Thus, W_z can be interpreted as the consumption needed for the reference household to attain the subsistence level of welfare.

of the poverty index developed by the Social Security Administration was quite reasonable. The subsequent implementation by the Census Bureau, however, was plagued by several problems. Household welfare was evaluated using before-tax income even though poverty was defined using the concept of consumption. The substitution of income for consumption was rationalized by the assumption that the two must be the same for the poverty population. The needs of households, in addition, were represented by the nutritional equivalence scales presented in Table 5.1 rather than equivalence scales defined over all commodities in the budget. Note also that only absolute price effects were incorporated in the welfare function even though the impact of relative price changes on the poor could be important. As demonstrated in previous chapters, the estimates of inflation based on the CPI were biased upward in the 1970s and 1980s, implying that the poverty lines were overinflated over this period.

The availability of annual expenditure data in the CEX obviates the need to use income as a proxy for consumption in the measurement of poverty. Taking per equivalent consumption to be the measure of well-being, I can define a consumption-based poverty index that does not have the shortcomings of the approach used by the Census Bureau. This welfare function, introduced in Chapter 2, is represented as follows:

$$W_k = \frac{M_k}{P_k(\mathbf{p}, \mathbf{p}^0, V_k) m_0(\mathbf{p}^0, V_k, \mathbf{A}_k)} \tag{7.5}$$

In contrast with (7.4), this function depends on total expenditure M_k, includes relative price effects through the household-specific price indexes P_k, and incorporates needs through full budget equivalence scales.

The consumption-based definition of poverty is completed by choosing a poverty threshold that is conceptually consistent with the original intent of the Social Security Administration. Let M_z be the total expenditure required to purchase the Economy Food Plan and other subsistence items for a reference household (with characteristics $\mathbf{A}_r$) facing prices $\mathbf{p}$. The threshold level of welfare is given by

$$W_z = \frac{M_z}{P_r(\mathbf{p}, \mathbf{p}^0, V_r^z) m_0(\mathbf{p}^0, V_r^z, \mathbf{A}_r)} \tag{7.6}$$

where V_r^z is the welfare of the reference household facing prices $\mathbf{p}$ with total expenditure M_z. All members of the household are classified as poor if $W_k < W_z$ for the welfare function defined by (7.5) and the poverty threshold (7.6).

To facilitate comparisons with the official statistics, the poverty line is chosen to be consistent with the threshold used by the Census Bureau. For this purpose, I begin by noting that the 1964 Low Cost Food Plan developed by the U. S. Department of Agriculture (1964) for a nonfarm family of four was $24.60 per week.[10] Taking the Economy Food Plan to be 75 percent of this level, the minimally nutritious annual level of food expenditure was $959.40. Statistical estimates of household demand functions reveals that this household required an expenditure level of $2,998 in 1964 to purchase the subsistence market basket.[11] Utilizing this as the estimate of the subsistence level of total expenditure, the 1964 implicit price deflators from the PCE, and the Barten equivalence scale for the nonfarm family of four, the poverty threshold W_z is computed using (7.6).

Using per equivalent consumption and the corresponding poverty line, I tabulate the proportion of persons living in poverty using the expenditure data reported in the CEX. In intervening years I estimate poverty using the interpolation procedure described in Appendix 2. I present consumption-based poverty rates for the United States in Figure 7.1 and compare them to the Census Bureau's estimates. As described earlier, the latter index is calculated using before-tax income (reported in the CPS), the CPI, and nutritional equivalence scales. Between 1959 and 1973 the official estimate of poverty fell sharply from 0.224 to a postwar low of 0.111. After 1973 there was little change in the poverty rate until the recession years of the early 1980s, when it jumped to 0.152 in 1983. Poverty subsequently decreased through 1989 and then reversed trend until 1993, when the fraction of the population living in poverty reached 0.151. This was higher than the 1966 poverty rate. This suggests that, over this period of almost three decades, there was no apparent progress

---

10. The family is assumed to have two school-age children. See Table 7, p. 21, of the October 1964 issue of the Department of Agriculture's *Family Economics Review*.
11. This is slightly higher than the threshold used in Slesnick (1993) because of the revision in the PCE prices. Note that for this household type, the budget share of food is 0.32. Despite all of the protestations to the contrary (e.g., Ruggles 1990), Orshansky's procedure of multiplying the food share by 3 to obtain the subsistence level of total expenditure seems to provide a good approximation.

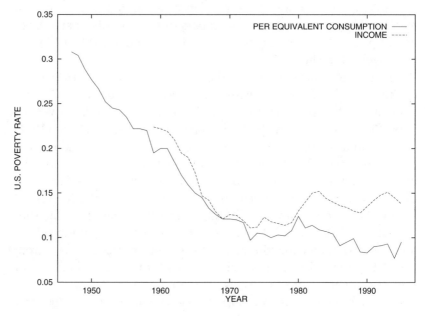

Figure 7.1. Aggregate poverty, 1947–1995

in rectifying the plight of the poor despite concerted efforts by federal, state, and local governments.

The consumption-based poverty estimates shown in Figure 7.1 tell a different story. There has been a substantial decrease in poverty since World War II, with most of the reduction occurring between 1947 and 1978. Over this period the fraction of the population living below the poverty line fell from its highest level of 0.308 to 0.102. Poverty increased between 1979 and 1980 but subsequently fell by approximately one-fourth over the remainder of the sample period. Although the Census Bureau reports no net change in the incidence of poverty since the late 1960s, the poverty rate computed using consumption data decreased from 0.145 in 1966 to 0.095 in 1995.

Is the conclusion of declining poverty robust across choices of the poverty index? Measures which incorporate the intensity of poverty lead to similar conclusions. In fact, the Foster-Greer-Thorbecke (FGT) indexes (7.3) tabulated for different values of the parameter α show even larger proportionate reductions in poverty. The average poverty gap (α equal to 1) shown in Figure 7.2 decreased from 0.124

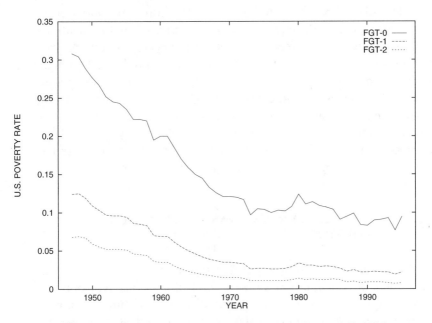

Figure 7.2. Foster-Greer-Thorbecke poverty indexes, 1947–1995

in 1947 to 0.022 in 1995, an average decrease of 3.6 percent per year. By comparison, the poverty rate (α equal to zero) fell 2.5 percent per year over the same period. The FGT index for α equal to 2 fell at an even faster rate of 4.5 percent per year.

Why was there a decrease in poverty? Does a rising tide raise all ships? It is worth noting that there is an obvious correlation between the growth rate of the standard of living and the reduction in the poverty rate. The fastest rate of increase in per equivalent consumption occurred in the 1960s, and over this decade, the poverty rate fell from 0.200 to 0.121. The slowest growth occurred in the 1970s, and the poverty rate remained virtually unchanged from a level of 0.121 in 1970 to 0.124 in 1980. The experience of the 1950s and 1980s also supports the conclusion that the fraction of persons living in poverty fell most precipitously when the general standard of living grew most rapidly. Although these results are suggestive, correlation does not imply causation. A definitive answer to the question of why we observe this trend can be found only with further research.

The divergence in trends between the consumption-based index and the Census Bureau's estimate has important ramifications for assessments of the effectiveness of antipoverty programs. Arguments both for and against social welfare policy are predicated on high and persistent poverty rates. The poverty rate computed using per equivalent consumption indicates that poverty has actually decreased over the postwar era. As important, the Census Bureau's figures exaggerate the extent of poverty in all but four years. By 1995 the official poverty rate is 0.138 compared to 0.095 computed using welfare functions based on per equivalent consumption.

7.3. INCOME- VERSUS CONSUMPTION-BASED POVERTY

The official estimates of poverty differ from those based on per equivalent consumption along several dimensions. Not only is consumption used to measure household welfare, but different price indexes and equivalence scales are used to adjust the poverty line. What role does consumption alone play in the differences shown in Figure 7.1? I answer this question by calculating the poverty rate using the welfare function (7.4) after substituting total expenditure for income. Differences between this index and the official poverty rate are largely due to the substitution of consumption for income in the measurement of the standard of living.[12] To measure the effect of the CPI bias on the poverty rate, another consumption-based poverty estimate is tabulated using household expenditures, the same equivalence scales, and the PCE price index.

Figure 7.3 shows that the poverty rates tabulated using households' expenditures (and the CPI) are lower than the official estimates throughout the postwar period, and in most years the differences are very large. In 1961, for example, the poverty rate tabulated using total expenditure was 0.096 compared to the Census Bureau's estimate of 0.219. This gap persists over the intervening years, and by 1995 the

---

12. There are other minor differences. I use $2,998 as the poverty line for a family of four in 1964 and adjust the threshold using the same equivalence scales (shown in Table 5.1) and price index (the CPI) throughout the sample period. As mentioned previously, the official estimates embody a number of changes in the equivalence scales and the price adjustments.

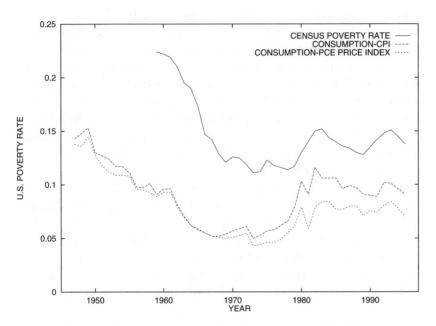

Figure 7.3. Income versus consumption poverty, 1947–1995

official poverty rate was 0.138 compared to 0.091. Note that although the poverty rates tabulated using expenditures are lower than comparable income-based estimates, the trends of the two indexes are similar.

The differences between the two consumption-based indexes in Figure 7.3 illustrate the biases that arise from inflating the poverty lines over time using the CPI. The differences were small until the mid-1970s, when the two indexes began to diverge. In 1973 the poverty rate computed using the CPI was 0.050 compared to 0.043 using the PCE index, but by 1982 the gap had widened to 0.116 and 0.079. More important, in virtually every year the consumption-based poverty rate computed using a more accurate price index was approximately half the income-based estimate reported by the Census Bureau. By 1995 the official poverty rate was 0.138 compared to 0.070 obtained using expenditures and the PCE price index.

The extent of poverty in the United States has been overstated, and Figure 7.3 shows that an important source of the biases in the Census Bureau's estimates can be attributed to the use of income as

a welfare measure. Why might this be the case? If consumption decisions are based on permanent income and if current income is the
sum of the permanent and the transitory components, households
with low incomes will have high ratios of consumption to income.
Since household welfare depends on the level of consumption, a fixed
absolute poverty threshold becomes a smaller and smaller fraction of
the overall level of well-being as the average standard of living rises.
The income poor will, therefore, have increasing consumption-to-
income ratios and current income will deteriorate over time as a
proxy for total expenditure.

I illustrate this phenomenon in Figure 7.4. Let $\overline{Y}^P_{1961}$ denote the
average level of (real) permanent income in 1961, and let Y_{pov} be the
level of real income representing the poverty line. At this level of
current income, the consumption of the poor household is $\overline{C}^{1961}_{pov}$ and
the consumption-to-income ratio exceeds 1. Suppose that the stan-
dard of living increases in 1973 so that average permanent income
is $\overline{Y}^P_{1973}$. If the poverty threshold is fixed in real terms, the (average)

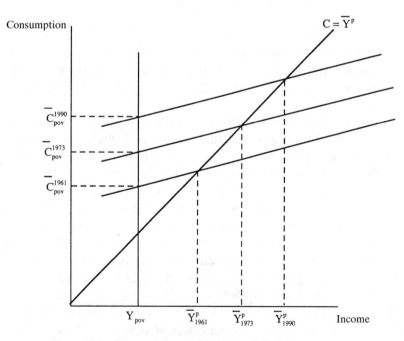

Figure 7.4. Consumption and income of the poor

permanent income of individuals classified as poor based on their current income increases and their new consumption level is $\overline{C}_{pov}^{1973}$. Thus, in 1973, the ratio of consumption to income for "poor" individuals increases, and income deteriorates as an indicator of household welfare. If the standard of living continues to increase in 1990, the consumption-to-income ratio at the poverty line will also increase.

The hypothesis that households with low incomes are able to smooth consumption is best assessed using longitudinal data on expenditures and incomes. Since such data are unavailable in the United States, the evidence must be examined using the CEX. Recall, though, that the income data in the CEX have uneven quality. With this in mind, I measure poverty using income from the CEX, the CPI to adjust the thresholds, and the nutritional equivalence scales shown in Table 5.1 developed by Orshansky.[13] This population will be referred to as the "income poor." The "consumption poor" are those classified as poor using exactly the same criterion except for the substitution of total expenditure for income in the welfare function.

To what extent is the prediction of an increasing consumption-to-income ratio for the income poor consistent with the CEX data? In Figure 7.5 I present the ratio of consumption to (disposable) income for households classified as poor based on their income. The tabulations are generally consistent with the pattern implied by the permanent income hypothesis, with the ratio increasing from 1.17 in 1961 to 1.69 in 1984. Although this provides circumstantial evidence of consumption smoothing, the trend of the consumption-to-income ratio in Figure 7.5 is probably understated because the poverty line was not held fixed in real terms. In the 1980s, the ratio would have been even higher had the poverty line not been overinflated by the CPI.

An implication of these results is that a substantial number of individuals are misclassified as poor when income is used to measure poverty. In fact, of all the individuals who are income poor, a minority are also identified as poor based on their consumption levels. Of the income poor, 59 percent were also consumption poor in 1961, 44 percent in 1973, 42 percent in 1980, 39 percent in 1985, 39 percent in

---

13. The welfare function used is (7.4), and the poverty line is the welfare level of the reference family of four with $2,998 in 1964. Tabulations are over complete income reporters only.

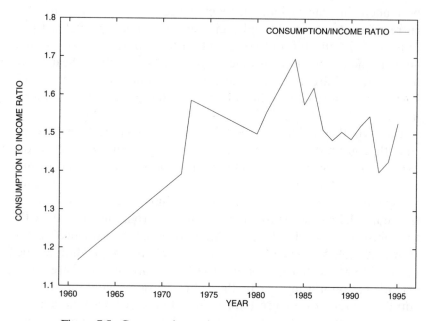

Figure 7.5. Consumption-to-income ratio: Income poor, 1961–1995

1990, and 33 percent in 1995. This supports the notion that some households are income poor because income is transitorily low, either because they are at the beginning or the end of the life cycle or because of random fluctuations in income. Of the households that are income poor but not consumption poor (i.e., those who are misclassified as poor), 49 percent in 1961 had a head of household who was either over 65 or under 25. These households constituted 50 percent of those misclassified in 1973, 55 percent in 1980, 35 percent in 1985, 45 percent in 1990, and 36 percent in 1995.[14]

A full explanation of the differences between the income- and the consumption-based poverty rates requires an examination of the components of the wedge between total expenditure and income. The means of each component are tabulated for the income poor and are presented in Table 7.1. Consistent with Figure 7.5, average total

14. In keeping with expectations, the "permanent income" or consumption poor also tend to have low income. In 1961, 83 percent of the consumption poor were also income poor; the overlap was 64 percent in 1973, 59 percent in 1980, 66 percent in 1985, 63 percent in 1990, and 61 percent in 1995.

Table 7.1. *Summary statistics of the income poor*

	Financial characteristics of the poor (current dollars)					
Year	Mean before-tax income	Mean tax liability	Mean service flows	Mean saving	Mean total expenditure	Proportion homeowners
1961	1,533	16	645	−361	2,523	0.41
1973	1,794	65	1,003	−1,602	4,335	0.40
1980	3,411	57	2,052	−2,699	8,106	0.39
1985	4,220	106	3,660	−4,478	12,252	0.44
1990	5,470	−45	3,247	−4,258	13,019	0.35
1995	5,936	119	4,740	−5,570	16,127	0.36

			Budget shares			
Year	Energy	Food	Consumer goods	Consumer durables	Housing	Consumer services
1961	0.075	0.281	0.125	0.113	0.229	0.177
1973	0.089	0.274	0.074	0.108	0.255	0.200
1980	0.129	0.280	0.049	0.106	0.252	0.184
1985	0.126	0.222	0.051	0.135	0.262	0.204
1990	0.100	0.250	0.049	0.120	0.260	0.220
1995	0.090	0.226	0.046	0.139	0.294	0.204

			Distribution of dissaving households by age				
Year	Total	16–24	25–34	35–44	45–54	55–64	65+
1961	0.585	0.026	0.081	0.091	0.079	0.095	0.214
1973	0.663	0.105	0.098	0.066	0.083	0.110	0.201
1980	0.726	0.149	0.127	0.069	0.063	0.095	0.222
1985	0.765	0.156	0.131	0.118	0.117	0.112	0.131
1990	0.746	0.169	0.126	0.122	0.078	0.076	0.175
1995	0.784	0.123	0.152	0.132	0.110	0.091	0.176

Education of the head of household

			Proportion by educational category			
Year	0 yrs, no report	1–8 yrs	9–11 yrs	HS grad	Some college	College grad or more
1961	0.076	0.635	0.149	0.088	0.032	0.021
1973	0.122	0.431	0.187	0.167	0.053	0.041
1980	0.027	0.311	0.200	0.203	0.204	0.056
1985	0.016	0.242	0.196	0.233	0.221	0.090
1990	0.019	0.232	0.190	0.260	0.227	0.073
1995	0.007	0.171	0.221	0.262	0.247	0.092

Source: Author's calculations over complete income reporters in the CEX.

expenditure exceeded mean income in each year. The averages of the components of the differences between income and consumption indicate that tax liabilities were essentially zero, whereas the average consumption of owner-occupied housing and consumer durables was unexpectedly high, ranging, in current dollars, from $645 in 1961 to $4,740 in 1995.[15]

These levels may be surprising since we do not expect the poor to own their home or to have an inventory of consumer durables. Note, though, that between 35 percent and 44 percent of the income poor were homeowners, and the services from the stock of consumer durables accounted for 10.8 percent to 13.9 percent of total expenditure depending on the year. Measuring the well-being of households using before-tax income ignores substantial service flows from housing and durables, understates household welfare, and overstates the level of poverty.

The service flows from housing and durables are not the entire story. A comparison of total expenditure with disposable income reveals substantial dissaving among the income poor, ranging from $361 in 1961 to $5,570 in 1995. Given that saving is evaluated as a residual and that there is measurement error in each of the components of the difference between income and total expenditure, it is important to assess the plausibility of these estimates of dissaving.

In the absence of reliable data on the change in net worth, I gauge the accuracy of the levels of dissaving using an indirect approach. In the third panel of Table 7.1 I present the fraction of the income poor who are dissavers and their corresponding age distribution. The overall proportion increased from 58.5 percent of the income poor in 1961 to 78.4 percent in 1995. In 1961, 1973, and 1980, approximately one-third of the dissavers were more than 65 years of age. In 1985, 1990, and 1995, the proportion fell to slightly more than one-fifth. Heavy representation of the elderly among the dissavers seems reasonable since one would expect them to have assets they can draw upon in retirement. Note, however, that young households with a head age 16–24 also accounted for a substantial fraction of the dissavers in the 1980s and 1990s. Life-cycle effects would lead one to predict over-representation of the young among the dissavers.

---

15. The tax liabilities are those reported for the previous twelve months and are net of the refunds received.

However, one would not expect these households to have assets. If the dissaving levels are accurate, young households are, in all likelihood, borrowing.

On balance, the profile of the poor shown in Table 7.1 is at odds with popular perceptions. Approximately 40 percent of the income poor were homeowners compared to roughly 60 percent of the entire population. In the 1980s and 1990s more than 50 percent of the heads of households of the income poor had at least a high school diploma and more than 30 percent had some college.[16] The consumption of durable services was substantial, and the levels and distribution of dissaving, if accurately reported, indicate either access to credit or the ownership of financial assets. Perhaps most telling is the surprisingly low share of spending devoted to food in each year. Engel's Law implies an inverse relationship between the level of well-being and the budget share of food. The food shares of the income poor (Table 7.1), however, were not greatly different from those of the entire sample. Over the same six years, the aggregate shares in the CEX were, respectively, 0.243, 0.229, 0.234, 0.195, 0.197, and 0.183.

If one accepts the hypothesis of consumption smoothing by those with low incomes, a very different profile is expected for households classified as poor based on their expenditures. These households have low levels of permanent income and should have characteristics which reflect that. In Table 7.2 I report the tabulations of the characteristics of the consumption poor.[17] They had incomes substantially below the mean but did not exhibit, on average, dissaving. Their saving rates were positive and not very different from those of the entire sample. Compared to the income poor, the services from owner-occupied housing and durables were substantially lower, both absolutely and as a fraction of total expenditure. A smaller fraction were homeowners.

The consumption poor also had substantially higher budget shares of food compared to the income poor. The share of the other necessity in the budget, energy, was also higher, whereas shares of consumer durables, housing, and consumer services were lower. The third panel of Table 7.2 shows that fewer poor households were dissavers,

16. For all households in the United States, the comparable estimates from the CEX were 70 percent and 45 percent.
17. The nature of the tabulations requires us to restrict the sample to include only the consumption poor who are also "complete" income reporters.

Table 7.2. *Summary statistics of the consumption poor*

	Financial characteristics of the poor (current dollars)					
Year	Mean before-tax income	Mean tax liability	Mean service flows	Mean saving	Mean total expenditure	Proportion homeowners
1961	1,926	21	257	217	1,945	0.17
1973	3,386	99	393	1,035	2,645	0.19
1980	6,346	259	596	2,126	4,556	0.15
1985	7,647	187	913	2,518	5,855	0.21
1990	9,516	60	1,054	3,195	7,315	0.13
1995	10,747	144	1,310	3,271	8,641	0.14

	Budget shares					
Year	Energy	Food	Consumer goods	Consumer durables	Housing	Consumer services
1961	0.081	0.365	0.144	0.089	0.162	0.159
1973	0.089	0.328	0.084	0.110	0.227	0.162
1980	0.144	0.370	0.054	0.086	0.192	0.154
1985	0.138	0.322	0.051	0.097	0.204	0.188
1990	0.120	0.326	0.056	0.103	0.210	0.184
1995	0.108	0.318	0.054	0.108	0.227	0.185

	Distribution of dissaving households by age						
Year	Total	16–24	25–34	35–44	45–54	55–64	65+
1961	0.365	0.019	0.060	0.062	0.056	0.061	0.108
1973	0.219	0.042	0.042	0.034	0.017	0.038	0.046
1980	0.294	0.102	0.057	0.032	0.029	0.035	0.040
1985	0.334	0.128	0.083	0.030	0.028	0.038	0.027
1990	0.317	0.123	0.068	0.043	0.024	0.016	0.043
1995	0.361	0.087	0.091	0.047	0.056	0.016	0.065

Education of the head of household

	Proportion by educational category					
Year	0 yrs, no report	1–8 yrs	9–11 yrs	HS grad	Some college	College grad or more
1961	0.092	0.676	0.137	0.072	0.017	0.006
1973	0.179	0.461	0.173	0.132	0.029	0.026
1980	0.034	0.314	0.198	0.209	0.204	0.042
1985	0.022	0.274	0.248	0.234	0.171	0.051
1990	0.013	0.224	0.234	0.268	0.231	0.029
1995	0.015	0.195	0.266	0.272	0.216	0.037

Source: Author's calculations over complete income reporters in the CEX.

ranging from a maximum of 36.5 percent of the poor in 1961 to a minimum of 21.9 percent in 1973. The dissavers were concentrated among the elderly and the young, with more than one-third of all dissavers falling in the 16–24 age group in the 1980s and early 1990s. Perhaps most revealing is the fact that the consumption poor were less educated than the income poor. In general, proportionately fewer heads of households had gone to college, and a larger fraction had not graduated from high school.

This coincides with prior notions of the "permanent income poor." In addition to lower educational attainment, they had fewer physical assets such as homes and consumer durables. A large proportion of their total expenditures was devoted to necessities such as food and energy, and there was substantially less dissaving. However, although the permanent income hypothesis represents a plausible explanation for the differences, there are other possible explanations.

Total expenditure could be overstated for those in the lower tail of the distribution. Although we have no alternative estimates of the distribution of total expenditure, the relationship between the aggregate levels in the CEX and the PCE, even accounting for definitional and coverage differences, casts doubt on this as a plausible explanation. Jencks and Edin (1990) suggest that there is systematic under-reporting of income by the poor and present evidence from twenty-five welfare families in Chicago. A comparison of the CPS with administrative records also indicates an understatement of transfer income. There is certainly incentive for poor (and rich) households to understate their income, and disproportionate under-reporting by the income poor would inflate the levels of dissaving presented in Table 7.1 and increase the number of persons classified as poor. Further investigation and additional data are necessary to settle this issue.

7.4. SENSITIVITY ANALYSIS

The consumption-based poverty estimates are at odds with the stylized facts. In the preceding section I showed that much of the difference in any given year can be explained by the substitution of consumption for income in the measurement of household welfare. What roles do the other factors play? Is the decrease in the incidence of poverty robust across choices of the poverty line? Is the lower poverty rate the result of an overstatement of consumption? What is the impact of relative price variation? How sensitive are the estimates to alternative choices of the equivalence scales? In this section I assess the sensitivity of my results to the assumptions that have been made to compute the poverty rate.

Poverty thresholds

The poverty rate has been tabulated using a threshold that represents the welfare of a family of four with $2,998 in 1964. If the PCE price index is used to inflate this threshold, by 1995 the poverty line would be $13,565. By current standards this is a paltry sum for a family of four. Furthermore, one wonders why it is reasonable to classify a family with expenditures of, say, $13,500 as poor but not a family with expenditures of $13,600. Although a threshold of roughly $3,000 in 1964 is consistent with the poverty line used by the Census Bureau, its selection is completely arbitrary.

Indeed, a number of alternative thresholds have been proposed over the years. Ruggles (1990) suggested that the poverty line be redrawn because households with low *incomes* have budget shares of food that are roughly 20 percent rather than 33 percent of total spending. Her conclusion was that the cost of the Economy Food Plan should be multiplied by 5 rather than by 3, as proposed by Orshansky.

Of course, the flaw in this argument is that households with low incomes do not necessarily have low welfare levels. The poverty line should represent a constant (subsistence) utility level which, in turn, depends on the level of consumption. An examination of the expenditure patterns of households with low consumption (and welfare) levels reveals that the food share is, in fact, approximately one-third rather than one-fifth of total spending. The Ruggles poverty line is substantially higher, in real terms, than the standard originally set by Orshansky.

Nevertheless, a higher real threshold is as defensible as any other. The critical issue is whether the pattern of movement in the poverty rate is robust across choices of the poverty line. I assess the sensitivity of the trend by recomputing the poverty rates using cut-offs that

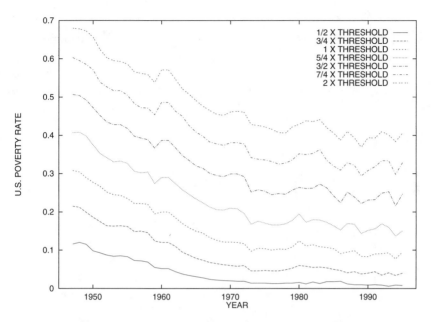

Figure 7.6. Threshold sensitivity, 1947–1995

represent the welfare levels of the reference family with different multiples of $2,998 in 1964. Figure 7.6 shows that although the levels are sensitive to the increase in the threshold, the trends are largely unaffected. Poverty decreased through the late 1970s, increased in the early 1980s, and subsequently fell over the remainder of the sample period. All other things being equal, the secular decline in the poverty rate is robust across alternative choices of the poverty line.

The consumption concept

The low poverty rate obtained using per equivalent consumption may lead to the suspicion that expenditures in the CEX are overestimated. The only other annual consumption data are the PCE, which are uniformly higher than the CEX (see Figure 3.2 and the related discussion). To get a rough idea as to what the poverty rate would be if consumption is defined as it is in the national accounts, I tabulate the head-count ratios at expenditure levels that are consistent with those

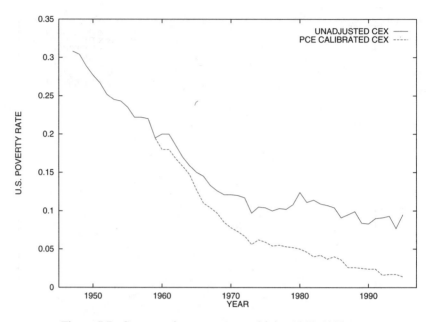

Figure 7.7. Consumption concept sensitivity, 1947–1995

reported in the PCE.[18] The adjusted poverty rate is presented in
Figure 7.7 using the original poverty line of $2,998 for the reference
family. The downward trend in the poverty rate using the PCE-
calibrated expenditures is certainly more pronounced. The poverty
rate decreased from 0.308 in 1947 to 0.056 in 1973, increased between
1973 and 1974, and then decreased over the remainder of the sample
period. By 1995, the poverty rate tabulated using the adjusted estimates of consumption was 0.014 compared with 0.095 obtained using
the unadjusted expenditures.

This alternative definition of consumption yields poverty rates that
are much lower than those presented in section 7.2 and a trend that
shows greater progress in reducing poverty. Moreover, one could reasonably argue that these estimates are themselves too low because
they do not include the full complement of in-kind transfers avail-

18. Specifically, the CEX expenditures are multiplied by the ratio of the PCE to CEX per
    capita expenditure levels. It is implicitly assumed that there is no differential under-
    statement of spending across unequally situated households.

able to the poor.[19] The overall conclusion is that the results presented in section 7.2 (and section 7.3) are probably conservative because of the dramatic growth of these benefits since 1960 and the substantial underestimate of expenditures in the CEX after 1980. The consumption-based poverty rates are undoubtedly lower than those reported, and the progress against poverty is greater.

Relative price effects

To what extent are the divergent poverty estimates attributable to the inclusion of household-specific price effects? In Chapter 6 I found that relative price changes had little impact on inequality. Despite this, one cannot preclude the possibility that changes in the structure of prices have hurt households in the lower tail of the distribution. To measure the sensitivity of the poverty rate to relative price variation, I tabulate the number of persons who belong to households with $W_k < W_z$, where the welfare function is defined by

$$W_k = \frac{M_k}{Pm_0(\mathbf{p}_0, \mathbf{A}_k)} \tag{7.7}$$

This function is distinguished from (7.5) in that expenditures are deflated by the PCE price index P rather than by household-specific price indexes. Differences between the poverty rates computed using (7.5) and (7.7) are exclusively due to the effect of relative price variation on the well-being of the poor.

The two sets of poverty rates are presented in Figure 7.8. As with the estimates of the standard of living and inequality, relative price variation has had little effect on the poverty rate. The levels and trends of the two indexes were virtually identical until the late 1980s, when they began to differ slightly. Dramatic fluctuations in the relative prices, such as between 1973 and 1974 and again between 1979 and 1980, had surprisingly little impact. To the extent that there was an effect, relative price changes have tended to lower the poverty rate in most years; the largest difference was 1.4 percentage points in 1994.

---

19. The impact of in-kind benefits on the level of poverty has been considered by Smeeding (1982) and Slesnick (1996). The Census Bureau has several "experimental" measures of poverty that include in-kind transfers.

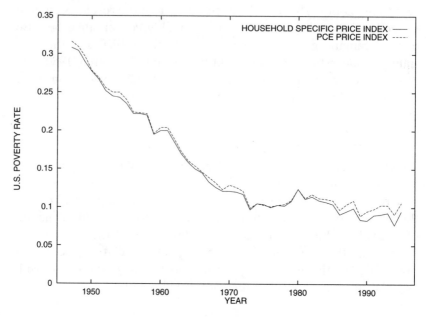

Figure 7.8. Price sensitivity, 1947–1995

Sensitivity to equivalence scales

The effect of changing the equivalence scales is illustrated in Figure 7.9.[20] Comparisons of the poverty rates based on the Barten scales and those used by the Census Bureau indicate that the effect of using the Barten scales is to increase the estimated poverty levels in every year. Prior to the 1980s, the differences were enormous, such as in 1961, when the poverty rate calculated using the Barten scales was 0.204 compared to 0.093 for the Census scales. In 1973 the corresponding rates were 0.099 and 0.043, but by 1995 the difference narrowed to 0.106 and 0.070.

An implication is that the choice of equivalence scales has a pronounced effect on the trend in the poverty rate. Whereas poverty tabulated using the Barten scales decreased sharply between 1947 and 1973, the decline was more attenuated when the Census scales were used. Both indexes show an increase in poverty in the early 1980s but exhibited more modest changes thereafter. The poverty

20. To isolate the effect of the equivalence scales, I use the welfare function presented in (7.7).

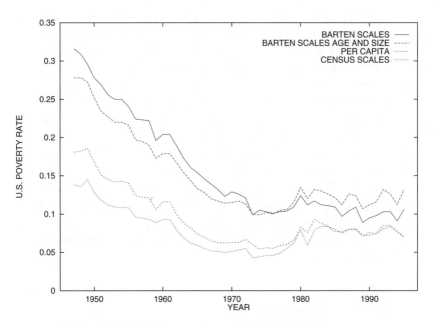

Figure 7.9. Equivalence scale sensitivity, 1947–1995

rate calculated using the Barten scales decreased from 0.124 in 1980 to 0.106 in 1995 compared to the decrease from 0.079 to 0.070 when the Census scales were used.

The differences between the two poverty rates suggest that conclusions concerning the levels and trends are dependent on how welfare levels are compared across heterogeneous households. To what extent are these two sets of estimates anomalous? The former scales depend on the region of residence, race, and gender of the head of the household, which, for political reasons, are unlikely to be used to distinguish the official poverty lines. What if these dimensions are ignored in comparing the welfare levels? As a further assessment of the sensitivity of the poverty rate to the equivalence scales, I measure poverty using the Barten scales as they vary over age and family size alone. I also tabulate the poverty rate using per capita consumption as the welfare measure.

Figure 7.9 shows that the variation in the estimated poverty rates persists with these two additional sets of equivalence scales. The tabulations based on the per capita adjustment of the thresholds show higher levels of poverty than do the Census scales and greater progress in reducing poverty. The levels and the trend of the index, however, are closer to those based on the Census scales. The Barten scales, which vary only by household size and the age of the head of the household, show higher poverty rates than does the per capita index but greater reduction in poverty over the entire period. The downward trend is more attenuated than for the Barten scales which vary over all the dimensions shown in Table 5.3.

Consistent with the simulations of Coulter et al. (1992), there is substantial variation in the poverty estimates across choices of equivalence scales. The Census scales yield the lowest estimates and show the least progress against poverty. The Barten scales, with and without variation across characteristics other than age and size, are at the other extreme, revealing the highest level and the greatest reduction in the poverty rate.

7.5. WITHIN-GROUP POVERTY

Are there groups of individuals who are at greater risk of falling into poverty? How has the poverty profile changed over time? Answers to these questions are particularly important to the design of an effective system of transfers to the most needy. I examine the poverty profiles using the Barten scales and assess the sensitivity of the results by repeating the calculations using the Census scales.

In Figure 7.10 I present the poverty rates tabulated using per equivalent consumption (equation 7.5) for three age groups: households with a head who is less than twenty-five years of age (young), households with a head over age sixty-five (elderly), and those with a head between the ages of thirty-five and forty-four (middle-aged). Middle-aged individuals were over-represented in the poverty population, and the young and elderly were under-represented. This is generally consistent with the finding in Chapter 5 that, on average, the standard of living of the elderly was higher than for the non-elderly. For the elderly, poverty was virtually eliminated, decreasing from 0.154 in 1948 to 0.006 in 1994.

The variation of the overall poverty rate to the choice of equivalence scales would suggest similar sensitivity of the poverty profile. Retabulating the within-group poverty rates using the Census scales

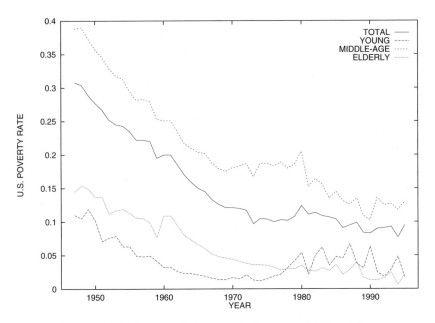

Figure 7.10. Poverty rate by age: Barten scales, 1947–1995

and welfare measure (7.7) confirms this prediction. Figure 7.11 shows that, in most years, the young were over-represented among the poor, whereas middle-aged households exhibited a poverty rate that was similar to that of the entire population. The elderly were over-represented until the early 1980s and then had poverty rates well below the national average. Poverty among the young exhibited a U-turn, falling sharply between 1947 and 1967 and subsequently increasing. The poverty rate for the elderly decreased from 0.142 in 1949 to 0.032 in 1994.

Regional poverty rates exhibited convergence similar to that found for the standard-of-living indexes. Figure 7.12 shows that the South had, by far, the highest poverty rate but also exhibited the greatest reduction since World War II. The poverty rate was 0.510 in 1947 but fell to its lowest level of 0.118 by 1994. Poverty in the Midwest had a trend that was virtually identical to the overall poverty rate. Individuals living in the Northeast and the West were under-represented in the poverty population over the entire period. Relative to those of

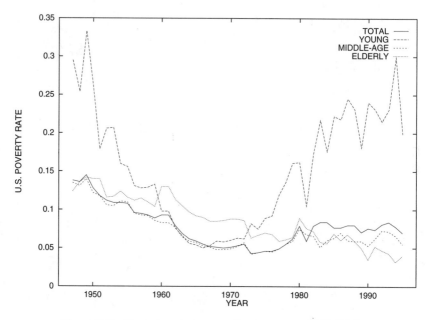

Figure 7.11. Poverty rate by age: Census scales, 1947–1995

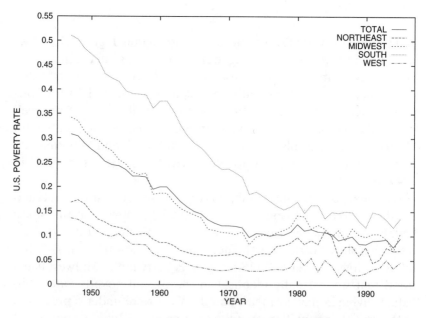

Figure 7.12. Poverty rate by region of residence: Barten scales, 1947–1995

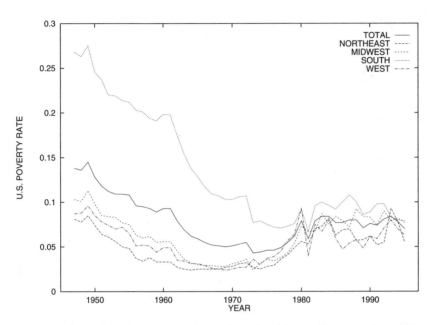

Figure 7.13. Poverty rate by region of residence: Census scales, 1947–1995

the Midwest and the South, the downward trends within these regions were more attenuated.

The general conclusions concerning regional variation in poverty are robust across the choice of equivalence scales. The poverty rates tabulated using the Census scales are presented in Figure 7.13. As with the Barten scales, the highest incidence and the sharpest reduction in the poverty rate were found in the South. The other three regions were under-represented among the poor until 1979, and, as in Figure 7.12, there was convergence over time.

It is not surprising that nonwhites were over-represented among the poor, although the persistence of the gap between the two groups is disturbing. Figure 7.14 shows that the poverty rate for nonwhites was more than twice that of whites in every year. In 1947 the fraction of nonwhites living in poverty was 0.598 compared to 0.279 for whites, and, by 1995, the rates were 0.208 and 0.073. There also appears to be greater fluctuation in the incidence of poverty from year to year for nonwhites. In the recession years of the early 1980s, the poverty rate for nonwhites increased from 0.296 in 1979 to 0.321 in 1981 compared

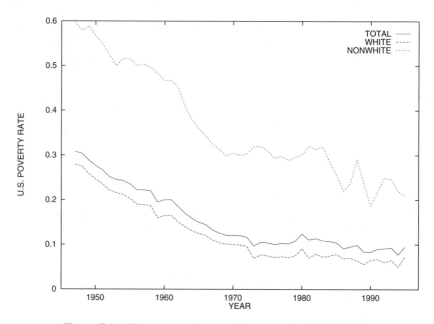

Figure 7.14. Poverty rate by race: Barten scales, 1947–1995

to a decrease from 0.075 and 0.070 for whites. The same pattern of movement is observed during the recession in the early 1990s.

Qualitatively identical conclusions are obtained when household welfare is measured using the Census equivalence scales. Figure 7.15 shows that the poverty rate tabulated using the official scales was much higher for nonwhites than whites but exhibited a sharper decrease since 1947; it fell from 0.498 in 1947 to 0.169 in 1995. Over the same period, poverty for whites fell from 0.101 and 0.051. As with the Barten scales, there were significant fluctuations in the incidence of poverty for nonwhites, particularly in the 1980s and early 1990s.

The most surprising feature of the poverty profile is the poverty rate among members of female-headed households. Using the Barten scales to measure household welfare (see Figure 7.16), individuals belonging to households headed by women were under-represented in the poverty population in all but a few years. This is because the equivalence scale for female-headed households is much lower than the scale for their male counterparts. Whereas poverty among male-headed households fell precipitously over the postwar

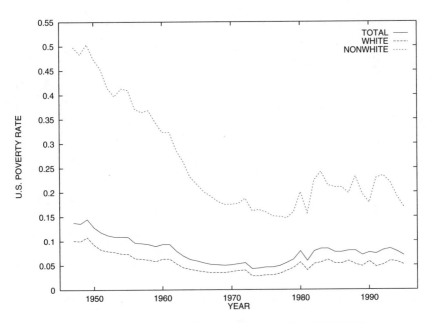

Figure 7.15. Poverty rate by race: Census scales, 1947–1995

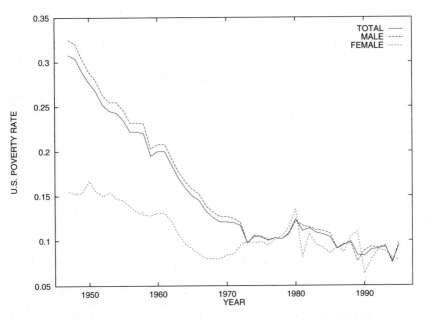

Figure 7.16. Poverty rate by gender: Barten scales, 1947–1995

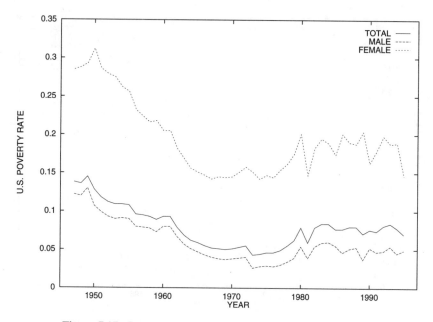

Figure 7.17. Poverty rate by gender: Census scales, 1947–1995

period, poverty changed more gradually for women. In 1947, just over 15 percent of all persons belonging to female-headed households were poor compared to slightly less than 8 percent in 1995. The comparable levels for male-headed households were 32 percent and 10 percent. The use of the Census scales yields exactly the opposite conclusion (see Figure 7.17). Female-headed households were dramatically over-represented in the poverty population and, as with nonwhites, had poverty rates that fell precipitously from 0.285 in 1947 to 0.146 in 1995. The corresponding poverty rates for members of male-headed households were 0.122 and 0.049.[21]

7.6. SUMMARY AND CONCLUSION

A consumption-based poverty measure provides a strikingly different perspective on the evolution of the level and the trend of poverty

---

21. The sensitivity of the poverty profile to the equivalence scales used to adjust the thresholds has also been demonstrated by van der Gaag and Smolensky (1982) as well as by Lazear and Michael (1980).

in the postwar United States. Using expenditure data, a set of equivalence scales defined over the entire budget, and household-specific
price indexes, I find that the poverty rate has fallen sharply since 1947.
It would be premature, however, to proclaim victory in the War on
Poverty. In 1995 nearly twenty-five million persons had consumption
levels below the minimum standard set by the Social Security Administration in the mid-1960s. Certain subgroups of the population
remained particularly vulnerable to the threat of poverty. Nevertheless, the results presented in this chapter suggest that important
progress has been made.

In contrast, the Census Bureau has reported that poverty has been
on the rise since the late 1960s, when many of the poverty alleviation
programs began to take effect. This has led analysts across the
political spectrum to classify the War on Poverty as an abysmal
failure. Conservatives attribute this to "dependency" attitudes and
labor supply disincentives induced by government transfer programs.
Liberals claim that the government effort simply fell short of what
was required to aid our less fortunate citizens. The relatively low
and declining consumption-based poverty rate suggests that these
arguments need to be reexamined.

In an era of tight fiscal budgets and a large number of competing
social problems, effective targeting of government transfers to the
most needy is of critical importance. The empirical results presented
in this chapter suggest that income gives a very distorted view of a
household's welfare level. To make further reductions in the poverty
rate we must focus attention on the persons who need assistance the
most – namely, those with the lowest levels of consumption.

8   Conclusions

There is little doubt that family income is the predominant indicator of living standards and their distribution in the United States. The Bureau of the Census reports estimates of real median family income and the Gini coefficient of family income, and it tabulates poverty rates every year using survey data on income. These statistics show a stagnant standard of living, rising inequality, and persistent poverty.

Although it is widely used, I've noted repeatedly that there is little basis in economic theory for using income as a measure of welfare. The standard theoretical paradigm of consumer behavior describes households as constrained utility maximizers, where utility is a function of the goods and services consumed. This implies that, for a "snapshot" estimate of the standard of living, the relevant summary variable is total expenditure rather than income. Moreover, there are reasons to believe that consumption provides a more accurate proxy for intertemporal well-being.

I've shown that consumption-based welfare measures provide a distinctly different perspective on the evolution of living standards and their distribution in the postwar United States. Using established principles of welfare economics and alternative data sources, the picture that emerges is much more optimistic. In this concluding chapter, I summarize the key findings and highlight their differences from the stylized facts that are based on tabulations obtained using income data.

THE COST OF LIVING

Changes in the cost of living are most commonly measured using the CPI despite increasing evidence of sustained, systematic upward biases in the estimates of inflation. The recent report of the Boskin Commission stated that substitution biases, quality changes in existing goods, and the introduction of new goods have resulted in a serious overstatement of the inflation rate. This is in addition to the permanent bias in the price level that was introduced as a result of the inappropriate treatment of owner-occupied housing prior to 1983.

Using cost-of-living indexes which treat housing correctly throughout the sample period (and partially accounting for substitution biases), I have corroborated the finding that inflation is overstated when measured using the CPI. Between 1948 and 1995, the upward bias averaged 0.2 percent per year. Over subperiods, however, the differences were amplified. From 1978 through 1982, for example, the average annual bias was 1.2 percent, and in some years the difference was between two and three percentage points.

These problems have important implications both for the analysis of living standards and for fiscal policy. Inflation estimates that are too high imply growth rates of real variables (e.g., real family income) that are understated when the CPI is used as a price deflator. Variables that are indexed to the CPI, such as Social Security benefits and the Census Bureau's poverty thresholds, are overinflated. This results in an increase in the real incomes of transfer recipients and estimated poverty rates that are biased upward.

Another important empirical issue relates to the accuracy with which national price indexes reflect the cost of living of subgroups of the population. Because of differences in spending patterns, changes in prices can have different effects on unequally situated households. This issue is quite important because many transfers are targeted to specific groups. Should we, for example, use a separate cost-of-living index for the elderly? In indexing welfare benefits, should we use a price index that accounts for possible differences in the spending patterns of the poor?

I found that differences in the cost of living were small for households distinguished by race, gender, and the average standard of living. Perhaps more important, however, is the finding that price indexes defined over the elderly showed higher inflation rates than those tabulated for the non-elderly at the end of the sample period (Table 4.2). Even though the differences weren't large, it may be appropriate to adjust Social Security benefits using a separate price index that accounts for differences in the spending habits of the elderly. Indexes for both the elderly and the non-elderly, however, diverged sharply from the CPI, and this suggests that the current method of indexation needs to be changed.

THE STANDARD OF LIVING

Whereas real (CPI-deflated) median family income increased 2.6 percent per year between 1947 and 1970, there has been little change since then; the average annual growth rate over the entire sample period (1947 through 1995) was only 1.4 percent. The consumption-based estimate of the standard of living (shown in Figure 8.1) shows a distinctly different pattern of growth. This index increased at an average rate of 2.6 percent per year between 1947 and 1970, but,

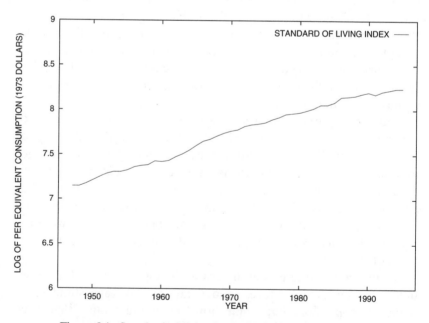

Figure 8.1. Standard of living in the United States, 1947–1995

unlike median family income, continued to increase 1.9 percent per year from 1971 through 1995. On the basis of these estimates, there is little evidence that living standards are in jeopardy, nor is there support for the prediction that future generations are at risk of attaining standards of living that are below those of their parents.

A natural question is, why does per equivalent consumption show such a different pattern of growth than median family income over the latter half of the sample period? Close to 60 percent of the difference can be attributed to the fact that the former index accounts for the decrease in average family size over this period, whereas the latter estimate does not. Approximately 30 percent of the difference results from using consumption rather than income to measure social welfare.

Given the changes in household composition since 1947, it is possible that the method of accounting for differences in the consumption requirements of households influences the growth rates of the standard of living. Since there is no consensus as to the right way to adjust for differences in needs, it is important to assess the sensitivity of qualitative conclusions to the choice of equivalence scales. Whereas the estimated growth rates differ, the general conclusion of sustained growth after 1970 is unaltered. Per capita consumption grew at an average rate of 2.1 percent per year, whereas per equivalent consumption grew 1.6 percent per year or 1.9 percent depending on the scales used. Each of these estimates contrasts sharply with those based on real median family income, which changed very little over this period.

What can be said of the welfare of different subgroups of the population? This is of significant policy relevance because subsidies and transfers are often targeted to specific demographic groups. Social Security, for example, is intended to help maintain the standard of living of the elderly, whereas AFDC provides support mainly for female-headed households with children.

As I did with the average standard of living, I tabulated the levels of per equivalent consumption for a number of demographic groups using three sets of equivalence scales. Several conclusions are unaffected by the method used to account for differences in household consumption requirements. I found, for example, that the standard of living of the elderly exceeded that of the non-elderly; the choice of equivalence scales affected only the magnitude of the difference. Not surprisingly, whites were substantially better off than nonwhites, although there was convergence in their relative welfare levels over time. Differences across geographic regions have narrowed, with the South showing dramatic progress. Conclusions concerning the living standards of female-headed households, relative to their male counterparts, depend critically on the choice of equivalence scales. This is not surprising in light of the fact that these households are, on average, smaller and have a higher ratio of children to adults.

INEQUALITY

The Census Bureau reported that family income inequality decreased through the late 1960s and then increased to its highest postwar level in 1998. Inequality in the distribution of per equivalent consumption, shown in Figure 8.2, showed a similar decrease through the mid-1970s but has changed little since then. There is no obvious U-turn in inequality.

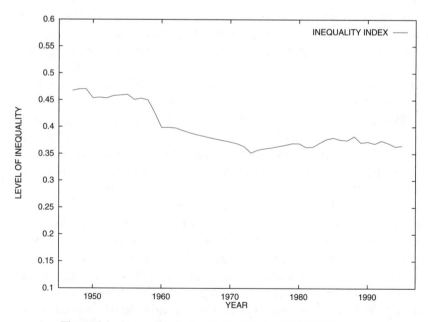

Figure 8.2. Inequality in the United States, 1947–1995

These different conclusions can be explained by several factors. Income is much more unequally distributed than expenditures, and most of this difference is due to consumption smoothing. There is, in addition, more temporal movement in the distribution of income than in the distribution of expenditures. Consistent with the findings of the Census Bureau, I found that household income became more unequally distributed, whereas, in contrast, the expenditure distribution changed much less.

Another important source of the difference between the distributions of family income and per equivalent consumption arises from the fact that the latter measure accounts for variation in household composition. There is a strong positive correlation between household size and the level of total expenditure. This suggests that adjusting household expenditures for differences in their consumption requirements should have a significant effect on the distribution. Accounting for household heterogeneity does, in fact, influence both levels and trends of inequality. The overall conclusion, though, is that inequality in per equivalent consumption has either decreased or changed very little since 1947 depending on the equivalence scales used.

How much inequality is there between different demographic groups, and how much of it can be explained by disparities within groups? We know that, due to life-cycle differences, there may be significant disparities in welfare across age groups that are largely inevitable. I found that most inequality is within age groups but that one-third to one-fifth of the total can be explained by differences between groups of households of different ages. Looking at within-age-group inequality alone, however, does not change the qualitative conclusions concerning both the levels and the trends of inequality.

The popular perception is that much of the inequality in the United States can be attributed to disparities between groups distinguished by race or gender. Regardless of the method used to account for differences in the consumption requirements of households, inequality between races or gender is significantly smaller than within-group differences. Inequality between regions exhibited large changes over time, decreasing through the early 1980s and then increasing.

A natural question is what role, if any, the government can play in reducing inequality through a system of taxes and transfers. This is an issue of fundamental importance that has not been addressed directly. We did learn, however, that between-group age effects account for a significant fraction of total inequality, which would be difficult to mitigate even if it was desirable to do so. An open question is the role of demographic changes in the population (which are generally unaffected by policy) in explaining both the levels and the trends of inequality for certain measures of household welfare.

POVERTY

As with the standard of living and inequality, the poverty statistics produced by the Census Bureau paint a discouraging picture. The official poverty rate decreased through the mid-1970s and then reversed trend. As recently as 1993, 15.1 percent of the population was classified as poor, a number that exceeded the poverty rate attained roughly three decades earlier. Naturally, a number of analysts at both ends of the political spectrum have raised questions about the effectiveness of the government programs that were designed to eliminate poverty.

Relative to the official statistics, the consumption-based poverty estimates shown in Figure 8.3 indicate lower levels of poverty and greater progress in reducing poverty. In contrast with what is indicated by the Census Bureau's estimates, there was a substantial reduction in the fraction of the population that was classified as poor over the thirty years since the beginning of the War on Poverty. This suggests that many of the arguments predicated on high and persistent poverty rates in the United States need to be reexamined.

What is it about the consumption-based poverty estimates that yield such different conclusions? As with inequality measurement, the substitution of consumption for income in the measurement of welfare is particularly important in explaining differences in both the levels and the trends of poverty. In particular, replicating the Census Bureau's methodology – but using expenditures instead of income to identify the poor – lowers the 1995 poverty rate from the official estimate of 0.138 to 0.091. Replacing the CPI with a PCE price deflator lowers the poverty rate even further to 0.070, a level that is roughly one-half the official estimate.

Upon closer examination, income-based poverty estimates perform poorly because there is a large segment of the population

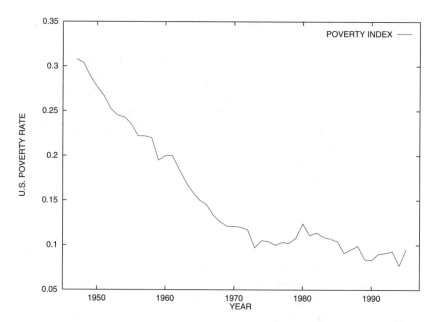

Figure 8.3. Poverty in the United States, 1947–1995

whose income does not accurately reflect its well-being. These individuals include the young, the elderly, and, more generally, those who have had transitory reductions in income. Tabulations from the CEX suggest that consumption-based poverty estimates more accurately identify the permanent income poor. Relative to those classified as poor based on their income, the consumption poor have lower levels of educational attainment, fewer consumer durables, a larger fraction of spending on food, and lower rates of homeownership.

There has been debate as to what the poverty line should be. Clearly, making any sort of adjustment upward or downward will affect the level of poverty. I've found, however, that it has little effect on its trend. It is worth reiterating, moreover, that the consumption-based poverty estimates presented in Chapter 7 are probably conservative. There is evidence that expenditures in the CEX are under-reported and, if they are adjusted to account for this, would show even lower poverty rates and greater progress in reducing poverty no matter what equivalence scales are used to adjust the poverty line.

DATA RECOMMENDATIONS

The results presented in this study are clearly descriptive rather than prescriptive. I have offered little or no explanation for the observed pattern of growth in the standard of living and the movements in the distribution. For policy purposes, however, it is precisely these issues that are of primary importance. What accounts for the high growth rate in the 1960s? Why did inequality decrease through the 1970s and then level off? Perhaps most important, is there a plausible explanation for the decrease in poverty following World War II? Is it the result of government policy initiatives, or is it the result of economic growth?

Clearly, these are the more interesting and important questions. The first step, however, in explaining the observed movements in the standard of living is to accurately describe the movements. My results suggest that the standard practice of using family income to measure welfare gives an inaccurate picture of the evolution of living standards in the United States. If social welfare statistics are to be calculated using information on consumption rather than income, efforts must be directed toward developing data that are tailored to this task.

This requires that the *Consumer Expenditure Surveys* replace the *Current Population Surveys* as the primary data source for the measurement of the standard of living and its distribution. The existing structure of the CEX, however, can be improved to increase the reliability of the estimates. First and foremost, the sample size must be increased from its current level of approximately 5,000 households. This would certainly make the surveys more expensive to administer, although there is no obvious need for the current practice of reporting the data on a quarterly basis. I would guess that moving to an annual survey would offset some of the additional expense of increasing the sample size.[1]

For the CEX to play a central role in the measurement of living standards, additional effort is required to gauge the accuracy of the data. I've presented evidence here and elsewhere of under-reporting of both income and expenditures in the CEX; a serious effort is

---

1. The best of all possible outcomes would have longitudinal information on income and expenditures. This would enable the assessment of the long-term welfare of households. The cost of such data, however, is prohibitive.

required to reconcile the differences between the survey data and personal consumption expenditures in the national accounts. If the CEX is to be used to measure social welfare, we must have confidence in its accuracy.

Price information would also be an invaluable addition to the CEX. The surveys currently report the expenditures on goods and services but not the prices paid for them. Although it is probably too much to expect households to accurately report the prices paid for each item purchased, it is certainly reasonable for the BLS to report local prices for groups of goods. This would go a long way toward accurately estimating the cost of living at lower levels of aggregation. Although some information on the stock of consumer durables is currently reported, a more detailed inventory for each household would eliminate the necessity of imputing the services of durables for many households.

Finally, additional effort must be directed toward developing a consensus as to the appropriate means of comparing households with different compositions. Almost by default, the current practice is to use nutritional equivalence scales or simply to compare welfare on the basis of per capita income or expenditures. I've shown that in some instances, the choice of equivalence scales influences critical conclusions, and additional research is required to provide a set of scales that can be used for the measurement of household welfare.

The infrastructure is in place for federal statistical agencies to move from the current practice of using income to measure the standard of living to a more accurate approach founded on the application of consumption-based methods. Although such a shift would be expensive, the costs pale in comparison to the benefits that would accrue from measuring the standard of living of households accurately. Indeed, expensive social programs are often launched (or expanded) on the basis of average income levels. Moving to consumption-based social welfare statistics will help determine whether such programs are actually necessary and, if so, more accurately identify those who need the assistance the most.

Measuring individual and social welfare

HOUSEHOLD WELFARE

I briefly summarize the empirical model used to evaluate household welfare using the following notation:

$\mathbf{p} = (p_1, p_2, \ldots, p_N)$ – a vector of prices of all commodities.

x_{nk} – the quantity of the nth commodity group consumed by the kth household ($n = 1, 2, \ldots, N; k = 1, 2, \ldots, K$).

$M_k = \sum_{n=1}^{N} p_n x_{nk}$ – total expenditure, or the dollar value of consumption of the kth household ($k = 1, 2, \ldots, K$).

$\mathbf{A_k}$ – the vector of household attributes of the kth household ($k = 1, 2, \ldots, K$).

Using the formulation introduced by Jorgenson, Lau, and Stoker (1982), household preferences are represented by an indirect utility function of the form[1]

$$\ln V(\mathbf{p}, M_k, \mathbf{A_k}) = F(\mathbf{A_k}) + \ln \mathbf{p}'\alpha_p + \frac{1}{2}\ln \mathbf{p}'B_{pp}\ln \mathbf{p}$$
$$- D(\mathbf{p})\ln M_k + \ln \mathbf{p}'B_{pA}\mathbf{A_k} \qquad (AA1.1)$$

---

1. This is an exactly aggregable translog indirect utility function. The translog utility function was introduced by Christensen, Jorgenson, and Lau (1975) and has been used extensively in empirical demand modeling. See Deaton and Muellbauer (1980) and Blundell (1988) for surveys.

where $D(\mathbf{p}) = -1 + \iota' B_{pp} \ln \mathbf{p}$, ι is a vector of ones, and α_p, B_{pp}, and B_{pA} are unknown parameters. If demographic attributes affect demand patterns in the same way as price changes (as suggested by Barten 1964) the translog indirect utility function is of the form[2]

$$\ln V(\mathbf{p}, M_k, \mathbf{A}_k) = \ln \frac{\mathbf{pm}(\mathbf{A}_k)}{M_k}' \alpha_p$$
$$+ \frac{1}{2} \ln \frac{\mathbf{pm}(\mathbf{A}_k)}{M_k}' B_{pp} \ln \frac{\mathbf{pm}(\mathbf{A}_k)}{M_k} \qquad (AA1.2)$$

In this model, the elements of $\mathbf{m}(\mathbf{A}_k)$ can be interpreted as commodity-specific household equivalence scales. To be consistent with (AA1.1), these scales must be of the form

$$\ln \mathbf{m}(\mathbf{A}_k) = B_{pp}^{-1} B_{pA} \mathbf{A}_k$$

A household's general equivalence scale is the ratio of the expenditure required to attain a given level of well-being at fixed prices to the expenditure needed by the reference household (with attributes $\mathbf{A}_r$) to achieve the same welfare:

$$m_0(\mathbf{p}, \mathbf{A}_k) = \frac{M(\mathbf{p}, V_k, \mathbf{A}_k)}{M(\mathbf{p}, V_k, \mathbf{A}_r)}$$

For the indirect utility function (AA1.2), the parameterization of the equivalence scale is

$$\ln m_0(\mathbf{p}, \mathbf{A}_k) = \frac{1}{D(\mathbf{p})} \Big(\ln \mathbf{m}(\mathbf{A}_k)' \alpha_p + 1/2 \ln \mathbf{m}(\mathbf{A}_k)' B_{pp} \ln \mathbf{m}(\mathbf{A}_k)$$
$$+ \ln \mathbf{m}(\mathbf{A}_k)' B_{pp} \ln \mathbf{p} \Big) \qquad (AA1.3)$$

This is the full budget Barten equivalence scale referred to in the text, and it is independent of the welfare level at which it is evaluated. Blackorby and Donaldson (1988b) refer to this property as equivalence scale exactness.

With household equivalence scales of this form, the indirect utility function can be rewritten as

---

2. For further details, see Jorgenson and Slesnick (1987). This method of introducing demographic attributes into the utility function has been referred to as "demographic scaling" by Pollak and Wales (1981).

$$\ln V(\mathbf{p}, M_k, \mathbf{A}_k) = \ln \mathbf{p}'\alpha_p + \frac{1}{2}\ln \mathbf{p}'B_{pp}\ln \mathbf{p}$$

$$- D(\mathbf{p})\ln [M_k/m_0(\mathbf{p}, \mathbf{A}_k)] \qquad (AA1.4)$$

We can solve for total expenditure as a function of the level of utility to obtain the expenditure function

$$\ln M(\mathbf{p}, V, \mathbf{A}_k) = \frac{1}{D(\mathbf{p})}\left[\ln \mathbf{p}'\left(\alpha_p + \frac{1}{2}B_{pp}\ln \mathbf{p}\right) - \ln V\right]$$

$$+ \ln m_0(\mathbf{p}, \mathbf{A}_k) \qquad (AA1.5)$$

In Chapter 2, household welfare was defined as the level of real expenditure per household equivalent member:

$$U_k = \frac{M_k}{P_k(\mathbf{p}, \mathbf{p}_0, V_k)m_0(\mathbf{p}_0, \mathbf{A}_k)}$$

$$= M(\mathbf{p}_0, V_k, \mathbf{A}_r)$$

If base period prices $\mathbf{p}_0$ are normalized to be 1, the welfare of the kth household reduces to

$$U_k = \ln V_k,$$

$$= \ln \mathbf{p}'\alpha_p + \frac{1}{2}\ln \mathbf{p}'B_{pp}\ln \mathbf{p} - D(\mathbf{p})\ln[M_k/m_0(\mathbf{p}, \mathbf{A}_k)]$$

Implementation of this model of welfare measurement requires information on the prices faced by households, their total expenditure, and their demographic characteristics. The unknown parameters α_p, B_{pp}, and B_{pA} must also be estimated. For this purpose, Roy's identity is applied to the indirect utility function (AA1.4) to yield the following system of demand equations:

$$\mathbf{w}_k = \frac{1}{D(\mathbf{p})}(\alpha_p + B_{pp}\ln \mathbf{p} - \iota'B_{pp}\ln M_k + B_{pA}\mathbf{A}_k)$$

where $\mathbf{w}_k$ is the vector of budget shares of the goods and services consumed by the household.

This model aggregates exactly to yield a model of aggregate demand:[3]

---

3. For further discussion of the concept of exact aggregation, see Gorman (1953, 1981), Lau (1982), and the survey by Stoker (1993).

$$\mathbf{w} = \frac{\sum_{k=1}^{K} M_k \mathbf{w}_k}{\sum_{k=1}^{K} M_k}$$

$$= \frac{1}{D(\mathbf{p})} \left(\alpha_\mathbf{p} + B_\mathbf{pp} \ln \mathbf{p} - \iota' B_\mathbf{pp} \frac{\sum M_k \ln M_k}{\sum M_k} + B_\mathbf{pA} \frac{\sum M_k \mathbf{A}_k}{\sum M_k} \right)$$

Information on both micro and macro demand patterns is analyzed for five commodity groups:

1. Energy – expenditures on electricity, natural gas, heating oil, and gasoline.
2. Food – expenditures on all food products, including tobacco and alcohol.
3. Consumer Goods – expenditures on all other nondurable goods included in consumer expenditures.
4. Capital Services – the service flow from consumer durables and the service flow from housing.
5. Consumer Services – expenditures on consumer services, such as car repairs, medical care, entertainment, and so on.

To ensure that the demand model is consistent with the framework used to measure household welfare, it is estimated subject to the integrability conditions of summability, nonnegativity, homogeneity of degree zero in prices and total expenditure, Slutsky symmetry, and quasiconvexity of the indirect utility function.[4] Micro and macro demand models are combined using cross-section and time series data to provide estimates of the unknown parameters $\alpha_\mathbf{p}$, $B_\mathbf{pp}$, and $B_\mathbf{pA}$.

SOCIAL WELFARE

To describe the social welfare function, I introduce some additional notation:

X is a matrix with elements $\{x_{nk}\}$ describing the social state.
U_k is the welfare function of household k.
$\mathbf{u} = (U_1, U_2, \ldots, U_K)$ is a vector of welfare functions of all K households.

---

4. See Jorgenson and Slesnick (1987) and Jorgenson (1990) for further details.

If the underlying social ordering satisfies the Arrovian properties of unrestricted domain, independence of irrelevant alternatives, the weak Pareto principle, and cardinal full comparability, the canonical form of the underlying social welfare function is

$$W(\mathbf{u}, X) = \overline{U} + g(U_1 - \overline{U}, U_2 - \overline{U}, \ldots, U_K - \overline{U})$$

where

$$\overline{U} = \sum_{k=1}^{K} a_k U_k$$

and g( ) is a linearly homogeneous function.[5]

The specific form of the social welfare function is chosen to be the sum of the mean welfare plus an index of deviations from the mean:

$$W(\mathbf{u}, X) = \overline{U} - \gamma \left[\Sigma a_k |U_k - \overline{U}|^{-\rho} \right]^{-1/\rho} \qquad (AA1.6)$$

with $\Sigma a_k = 1$. The parameter γ is assigned a value that ensures that (AA1.6) satisfies the Pareto principle. The parameter ρ is an inequality aversion parameter that determines the curvature of the social welfare function. It ranges from minus 1 to minus infinity, with a value of minus 1 giving the greatest weight to equity relative to efficiency.

Principles of horizontal equity are accommodated by assuming that the weights a_k are the same for identical households. They are also chosen to ensure that a transfer of expenditure from one household to another that is worse off increases the social welfare function and decreases inequality. The exact form of the weights that satisfy this condition depends on the specification of the household welfare function.

For a welfare function of the form

$$U_k = \ln \mathbf{p}' \alpha_p + \frac{1}{2} \ln \mathbf{p}' B_{pp} \ln \mathbf{p} - D(\mathbf{p}) \ln[M_k / m_0(\mathbf{p}, \mathbf{A_k})] \quad (AA1.7)$$

the weights in the social welfare function must be of the form $a_k = m_0(\mathbf{p}, \mathbf{A_k})/\Sigma m_0(\mathbf{p}, \mathbf{A_k})$. Given prices and a fixed level of aggregate expenditure $M = \Sigma M_k$, the maximum level of social welfare is attained when each household has the same welfare:

$$W_{max} = \ln \mathbf{p}' \alpha_p + \frac{1}{2} \ln \mathbf{p}' B_{pp} \ln \mathbf{p} - D(\mathbf{p}) \ln[M/\Sigma m_0(\mathbf{p}, \mathbf{A_k})]$$

$$(AA1.8)$$

5. Further details are provided in the technical appendix to Chapter 2.

Social welfare can be converted to monetary equivalents using a social expenditure function (Pollak 1981). It is defined as the minimum level of aggregate expenditure required to attain a given level of social welfare, say W, at prices **p**:

$$M(\mathbf{p}, W) = \min\left\{ M : W(\mathbf{u}, \mathbf{X}) \geq W; M = \sum_{k=1}^{K} M_k \right\}$$

For the social welfare function represented in (AA1.6) and the household welfare function (AA1.7), the parametric representation of the social expenditure function is

$$\ln M(\mathbf{p}, W) = \frac{1}{D(\mathbf{p})} (\ln \mathbf{p}'(\alpha_p + 1/2 B_{pp} \ln \mathbf{p}) - W)$$

$$+ \ln\left(\sum_{k=1}^{K} m_0(\mathbf{p}, \mathbf{A_k}) \right) \qquad (AA1.9)$$

Money metric measures of social welfare form the foundation for the measurement of the cost of living, the standard of living, and inequality.

To illustrate, the monetary measure of social welfare used in Chapter 5 can be represented as

$$SOL = \frac{M}{P(\mathbf{p}, \mathbf{p}_0, W_{max}) \sum_{k=1}^{K} m_0(\mathbf{p}_0, \mathbf{A_k})}$$

$$= \frac{M(\mathbf{p}_0, W_{max})}{\sum_{k=1}^{K} m_0(\mathbf{p}_0, \mathbf{A_k})} \qquad (AA1.10)$$

Normalizing the reference prices to be 1 and using (AA1.9) as the functional form of the social expenditure function, this index of the standard of living simplifies to $\exp(W_{max})$.

If we are interested in measuring the welfare of a subgroup of G households (where $1 \leq G \leq K$), the maximum attainable level of group welfare is

$$W_G^{max} = \ln \mathbf{p}'\alpha_p + \frac{1}{2} \ln \mathbf{p}' B_{pp} \ln \mathbf{p} - D(\mathbf{p}) \ln\left[M_G \Big/ \sum_{g=1}^{G} m_0(\mathbf{p}, \mathbf{A_g}) \right]$$

$$(AA1.11)$$

where M_G is the aggregate expenditure of the group. The corresponding group expenditure function is obtained by solving for M_G as a function of group welfare:

$$\ln M_G(\mathbf{p}, W_G) = \frac{1}{D(\mathbf{p})}(\ln \mathbf{p}'(\alpha_{\mathbf{p}} + 1/2 B_{\mathbf{pp}} \ln \mathbf{p}) - W_G)$$

$$+ \ln\left(\sum_{g=1}^{G} m_0(\mathbf{p}, \mathbf{A_g})\right) \tag{AA1.12}$$

where W_G is the level of group welfare.

The group standard-of-living index tabulated in Chapter 5 is

$$SOL_G = \frac{M_G}{P_G(\mathbf{p}, \mathbf{p}_0, W_G^{\max}) \sum_{g=1}^{G} m_0(\mathbf{p}_0, \mathbf{A_g})}$$

$$= \frac{M_G(\mathbf{p}_0, W_G^{\max})}{\sum_{g=1}^{G} m_0(\mathbf{p}_0, \mathbf{A_g})} \tag{AA1.13}$$

Using the same normalization as before, (AA1.13) simplifies to $\exp(W_G^{\max})$.

INEQUALITY

Every inequality measure is based on implicit normative judgments related to the sensitivity of the index to shifts in the distribution. These assumptions are made explicit by defining inequality as the proportional loss in social welfare attributable to an inequitable distribution of household welfare. If W^0 is the actual level of social welfare and W^1 is the social welfare attained at the perfectly egalitarian distribution of household welfare, a measure of relative inequality is given by

$$I(\mathbf{p}, W^0, W^1) = 1 - \frac{M(\mathbf{p}, W^0)}{M(\mathbf{p}, W^1)} \tag{AA1.14}$$

This index is the proportion of money metric social welfare lost due to an inequitable distribution of household welfare. It lies between zero and 1 and is equal to zero when every household has the same level of welfare.

If per equivalent consumption is used to measure household welfare as in (AA1.7) and if the social expenditure function is represented by (AA1.9), the relative inequality index simplifies to

$$I(\mathbf{p}, W^0, W^1) = 1 - \exp\left(\frac{1}{D(\mathbf{p})}(W^1 - W^0)\right) \qquad (AA1.15)$$

If the household welfare function is the log of before-tax income ($U_k = \ln Y_k$), the weights of the social welfare function are $a_k = 1/K$ and the income inequality index reduces to

$$I^Y = 1 - \frac{\exp(W^0)}{\overline{Y}} \qquad (AA1.16)$$

where $\overline{Y} = \Sigma Y_k/K$. This is identical to the index proposed by Atkinson (1970) where the equally distributed equivalent income is represented by $\exp(W^0)$. Inequality in the distribution of total expenditure is defined similarly.

Interpolating and extrapolating the expenditure distribution

The *Consumer Expenditure Surveys* are the only sources of disaggregated expenditure data in the United States. These surveys were administered approximately every ten years until 1980, at which time they were given annually. To obtain estimates of the standard of living, inequality, and the extent of poverty in the years in which surveys were not administered, the simplest and most common approach is to linearly interpolate each summary statistic between survey years. This approach does not exploit all of the information available, and, moreover, there is no guarantee that the resulting estimates will be mutually consistent.

In this appendix, I describe an alternative method of estimating the distribution of total expenditure in the years for which there are no survey data. This covers the years 1947–1959, 1962–1971, and 1974–1979. The fundamental assumption is that total expenditure is lognormally distributed within 1,344 cells cross-classified according to the following characteristics:

Household Size: 1, 2, 3, 4, 5, 6, 7 or more.
Age of Head of the Household: 16–24, 25–34, 35–44, 45–54, 55–64, and 65 and over.
Region of Residence: Northeast, Midwest, South, and West.
Race of Head of the Household: White, Nonwhite.
Type of Residence: Farm, Nonfarm.
Gender of Head of the Household: Male, Female.

The assumption of lognormality greatly simplifies the interpolation of the distribution of total expenditure between survey years.

The critical issue is whether the estimated expenditure distribution accurately approximates the empirical distribution. Although lognormality is an inadequate representation of the income distribution, I find that it performs reasonably well as an approximation of the expenditure distribution.

Figure A2.1 shows the within-sample performance of the inequality index tabulated for household expenditures under the assumption of lognormality. Although the simulated distribution produces inequality estimates that are slightly higher than those based on the empirical distribution, the two sets of estimates are very close to each other, which suggests that lognormality is a reasonable distributional assumption. How does it perform in modeling the lower tail of distribution? In Figure A2.2 I compare the poverty rates tabulated using the CEX (using the Barten scales and the household-specific price indexes) with those calculated under the assumption of lognormality. Again, the two sets of estimates are not very different, and that provides further support for the distributional assumption.

Under the assumption of lognormality, the interpolation of the distribution in the years for which we do not have survey data involves

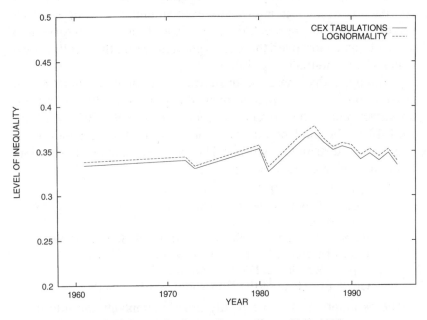

Figure A2.1. Inequality in total expenditure, 1961–1995

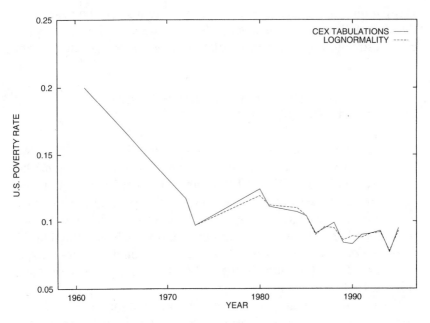

Figure A2.2. Aggregate poverty, 1961–1995

estimating the log variances of total expenditure, the cell means, and the number of households per cell. The log variances are interpolated linearly by cell for the years 1962–1971 and 1974–1979. The cell variances are assumed to be constant at the 1961 levels for the period 1947 through 1959. The estimation of the mean expenditure levels and the number of households per cell requires incorporating information from other data sources.

ESTIMATING THE NUMBER OF HOUSEHOLDS PER CELL

Over the period 1947 through 1959, the number of households per cell is estimated using the method of iterative proportional fitting described by Bishop et al. (1975). Interaction effects are captured using tabulations from the 1961 CEX. The number of households per cell in 1961 is adjusted in each year from 1947 to 1959 using the number of families and unrelated individuals (reported in the *Current*

Population Reports, Series P-60) as control totals. For the years 1962 through 1971 and 1974 through 1979, the number of households per cell is estimated by linear interpolation between cross-section years.

ESTIMATING THE MEAN HOUSEHOLD EXPENDITURE PER CELL

The mean expenditure levels are interpolated linearly by cell over the years for which we have two end points – namely, between 1962 and 1971 and from 1974 to 1979. From 1947 to 1959, the cell means are estimated indirectly. Average household expenditure is assumed to be equal to the aggregate expenditure reported in the PCE divided by the number of families and unrelated individuals presented in the *Current Population Reports*. Although this estimate differs sharply from the CEX tabulations in the 1980s, the two estimates are quite close in 1961.

The fraction of aggregate expenditure attributable to each demographic group is estimated using a bridge equation between total expenditure and income. The average propensity to consume is assumed to be a function of the level of income and the demographic characteristics of the household:

$$\frac{M_k}{Y_k} = \gamma_1 + \gamma_2 Y_k + \gamma'_A \mathbf{A}_k + \varepsilon_k \quad (k = 1, 2, \ldots, K) \qquad (AA2.1)$$

where M_k is total expenditure, Y_k is before-tax income, and $\mathbf{A}_k$ is the vector of demographic attributes. The unknown parameters $\gamma_1, \gamma_2,$ and γ_A are estimated using the 1961 CEX.[1]

This relationship between the average propensity to consume and the regressors Y_k and A_k is assumed to be stable between 1947 and 1959. From equation (AA2.1), we have[2]

$$\Sigma M_k = \gamma_1 \Sigma Y_k + \gamma_2 \Sigma Y_k^2 + \gamma'_A \Sigma Y_k \mathbf{A}_k \qquad (AA2.2)$$

and

---

1. This equation is used only to provide an empirical link between a household's expenditure and its income. No behavioral model is assumed or used to justify the specification.
2. This obviously requires that the distribution of income by demographic group be similar in the 1961 CEX and the corresponding CPS. This was found to be the case.

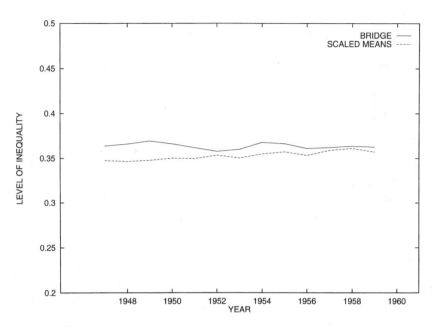

Figure A2.3. Extrapolations of expenditure inequality, 1947–1959

$$\Sigma M_k A_k = \gamma_1 \Sigma Y_k A_k + \gamma_2 \Sigma Y_k^2 A_k + \gamma_A' \ \Sigma Y_k \ A_k A_k' \qquad (AA2.3)$$

Given income distributional data from the *Current Population Reports* from 1947 through 1959, both (AA2.2) and (AA2.3) can be used to determine the share of total expenditure by demographic group, $\Sigma M_k A_k / \Sigma M_k$. For each of the twenty-three demographic groups, these shares are used as control totals to estimate the fraction of expenditure by cell using the method of iterative proportional fitting. Given the overall (mean) expenditure level, the cell means are obtained directly.

In Figures A2.3 and A2.4 I examine the sensitivity of the estimated levels of expenditure inequality and poverty (calculated using (7.5) and the Barten scales) to alternative methods of simulating the distribution of expenditure between 1947 and 1959. I compare the method described earlier (which uses the bridge equation (AA2.1)) to a simpler approach in which the cell means are scaled by a factor representing the change in the average expenditure level. Although there are some differences over the early years, the trend and the

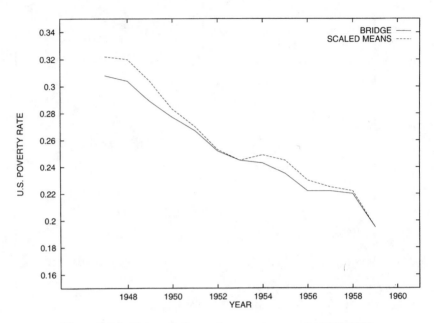

Figure A2.4. Extrapolations of aggregate poverty, 1947–1959

general levels of the poverty and inequality reported in Chapters 6 and 7 are unaffected. The method of estimating the distribution does not appear to affect the qualitative conclusions.

References

Afriat, S.N. (1967) "The Construction of Utility Functions from Expenditure Data," *International Economic Review*, Vol. 8, No. 1, February, pp. 67–77.

——— (1977) *The Price Index*, Cambridge: Cambridge University Press.

Aizcorbe, A.M., and P.C. Jackman (1993) "The Commodity Substitution Effect in CPI Data," *Monthly Labor Review*, Vol. 116, No. 12, December, pp. 25–33.

Altonji, J., F. Hayashi, and L. Kotlikoff (1992) "Is the Extended Family Altruistically Linked? Direct Tests Using Micro Data," *American Economic Review*, Vol. 82, pp. 1177–1198.

Anand, S., and M. Ravallion (1993) "Human Development in Poor Countries: On the Role of Private Incomes and Public Services," *Journal of Economic Perspectives*, Vol. 7, No. 1, Winter, pp. 133–150.

Apps, P.F., and E.J. Savage (1989) "Labour Supply, Welfare Rankings and the Measurement of Inequality," *Journal of Public Economics*, Vol. 39, No. 3, August, pp. 335–364.

Arrow, K.J. (1951) *Social Choice and Individual Values*, New York: John Wiley and Sons.

Atkinson, A.B. (1970) "On Measurement of Inequality," *Journal of Economic Theory*, Vol. 2, No. 3, September, pp. 244–263.

——— (1987) "On the Measurement of Poverty," *Econometrica*, Vol. 55, pp. 749–764.

——— (1991) "Comparing Poverty Rates Internationally: Lessons from Recent Studies in Developed Countries," *World Bank Economic Review*, Vol. 5, pp. 3–22.

——— and F. Bourguignon (1982) "The Comparison of Multi-Dimensioned Distributions of Economic Status," *Review of Economic Studies*, Vol. 49, No. 156, April, pp. 183–201.

——— and ——— (1987) "Income Distribution and Differences in Needs," in G.R. Feiwel (ed.), *Arrow and the Foundation of the Theory of Economic Policy*, London: Macmillan, pp. 350–370.

Auerbach, A.J., and L.J. Kotlikoff (1989) "Demographics, Fiscal Policy, and U.S. Saving in the 1980s and Beyond," National Bureau of Economic Research Working Paper No. 3150, October.

Balk, B.M. (1990) "On Calculating Cost-of-Living Index Numbers for Arbitrary Income Levels," *Econometrica*, Vol. 58, No. 1, January, pp. 75–92.

Banks, J., and P. Johnson (1994) "Equivalence Scale Relativities Revisited," *Economic Journal*, Vol. 104, No. 425, July, pp. 883–890.

Banks, J., R. Blundell, and A. Lewbel (1993) "Quadratic Engel Curves and Welfare Measurement," Institute for Fiscal Studies Working Paper, March.

Banks, J., R. Blundell, and I. Preston (1994) "Measuring Life-Cycle Consumption Costs of Children," R. Blundell, I. Preston, and I. Walker (eds.), *The Measurement of Household Welfare*, Cambridge: Cambridge University Press, pp. 192–214.

Barro, R. (1974) "Are Government Bonds Net Wealth?" *Journal of Political Economy*, Vol. 82, No. 6, November, pp. 1095–1117.

Barten, A.P. (1964) "Family Composition, Prices, and Expenditure Patterns," in P. Hart, G. Mills, and J.K. Whitaker (eds.), *Econometric Analysis for National Economic Planning: 16th Symposium of the Colston Society*, London: Butterworth, pp. 277–292.

Becker, G.S. (1981) *A Treatise on the Family*, Cambridge, MA: Harvard University Press.

Behrman, J.R., and A.B. Deolalikar (1987) "Will Developing Country Nutrition Improve with Income? A Case Study for Rural South India," *Journal of Political Economy*, Vol. 95, No. 3, June, pp. 492–507.

Bergson, A. (1938) "A Reformulation of Certain Aspects of Welfare Economics," *Quarterly Journal of Economics*, Vol. 52, No. 1, February, pp. 310–334.

Bishop, Y.M., S.E. Fienberg, and P.W. Holland (1975) *Discrete Multivariate Analysis: Theory and Practice*, Cambridge, MA: M.I.T. Press.

Blackorby, C., and D. Donaldson (1978) "Measures of Relative Inequality and Their Meaning in Terms of Social Welfare," *Journal of Economic Theory*, Vol. 18, No. 1, June, pp. 651–675.

————and————(1980a) "A Theoretical Treatment of Indices of Absolute Inequality," *International Economic Review*, Vol. 21, No. 1, February, pp. 107–136.

————and————(1980b) "Ethical Indices for the Measurement of Poverty," *Econometrica*, Vol. 48, No. 1, May, pp. 1053–1060.

————and————(1985) "Consumers' Surpluses and Consistent Cost-Benefit Tests," *Social Choice and Welfare*, Vol. 1, pp. 251–262.

————and————(1988a) "Money Metric Utility: A Harmless Normalization?" *Journal of Economic Theory*, Vol. 46, No. 1, October, pp. 120–129.

————and————(1988b) "Adult-Equivalence Scales and the Economic Implementation of Interpersonal Comparisons of Well-Being," University of British Columbia Working Paper No. 88-27.

————and————(1990) "A Review Article: The Case Against the Use of the Sum of Compensating Variations in Cost-Benefit Analysis," *Canadian Journal of Economics*, Vol. 23, No. 3, August, pp. 471–495.

Blackorby, C., D. Donaldson, and M. Auersberg (1981) "A New Procedure for the Measurement of Inequality Within and Among Population Subgroups," *Canadian Journal of Economics*, Vol. 14, No. 4, November, pp. 665–685.

Blundell, R. (1988) "Consumer Behaviour: Theory and Empirical Evidence – A Survey," *Economic Journal*, Vol. 98, March, pp. 16–65.

——— and A. Lewbel (1991) "The Information Content of Equivalence Scales," *Journal of Econometrics*, Vol. 50, No. 1/2, October/November, pp. 49–68.

Blundell, R., P. Pashardes, and G. Weber (1993) "What Do We Learn About Consumer Demand Patterns from Micro Data?" *American Economic Review*, Vol. 83, No. 3, June, pp. 570–597.

Blundell, R., and I. Preston (1998) "Consumption Inequality and Income Uncertainty," *Quarterly Journal of Economics*, Vol. 113, No. 2, May, pp. 603–640.

Boskin, M., and M. Hurd (1985) "Indexing Social Security: A Separate Index for the Elderly?" *Public Finance Quarterly*, Vol. 13, No. 4, October, pp. 436–449.

Boskin, M., and D. Jorgenson (1997) "Implications of Overstating Inflation for Indexing Government Programs and Understanding Economic Progress," *American Economic Review*, Vol. 87, No. 2, May, pp. 89–93.

Boskin, M., E. Dulberger, R. Gordon, Z. Griliches, and D. Jorgenson (1997) "The CPI Commission: Findings and Recommendations," *American Economic Review*, Vol. 87, No. 2, May, pp. 78–83.

Bosworth, B., G. Burtless, and J. Sabelhaus (1991) "The Decline in Saving: Evidence from Household Surveys," *Brookings Papers on Economic Activity*, No. 1, pp. 183–241.

Bourguignon, F. (1979) "Decomposable Income Inequality Measures," *Econometrica*, Vol. 47, pp. 901–920.

——— and P.A. Chiappori (1994) "The Collective Approach to Household Economic Behavior," in R. Blundell, I. Preston, and I. Walker (eds.), *The Measurement of Household Welfare*, Cambridge: Cambridge University Press, pp. 70–85.

Braithwait, S.D. (1980) "The Substitution Bias of the Laspeyres Price Index," *American Economic Review*, Vol. 70, pp. 64–77.

Branch, E.R. (1987) "Comparing Medical Care Expenditure of Two Diverse U.S. Data Sources," *Monthly Labor Review*, Vol. 110, No. 3, March, pp. 15–18.

——— (1994) "The Consumer Expenditure Survey: A Comparative Analysis," *Monthly Labor Review*, Vol. 117, No. 12, December, pp. 47–55.

Browning, M. (1992) "Children and Household Economic Behavior," *Journal of Economic Literature*, Vol. 30, No. 3, September, pp. 1434–1475.

Browning, M., F. Bourguignon, P. Chiappori, and V. Lechene (1994) "Incomes and Outcomes: A Structural Model of Intrahousehold Allocation," *Journal of Political Economy*, Vol. 102, No. 4, December, pp. 1067–1096.

Buhmann, B., L. Rainwater, G. Schmaus, and T. Smeeding (1988) "Equivalence Scales, Well-Being, Inequality and Poverty: Sensitivity Estimates Across Ten Countries Using the Luxembourg Income Study (LIS) Database," *Review of Income and Wealth*, Series 34, No. 2, June, pp. 115–142.

Bureau of the Census (various annual issues), *Current Population Reports, Consumer Income*, Series P-60, Washington, D.C., U.S. Department of Commerce.

Bureau of the Census (1967) *Trends in the Income of Families and Persons in the United States, 1947–1964*, Technical Paper No. 17, Washington, D.C., U.S. Department of Commerce.

Bureau of the Census (1975a) *Historical Statistics of the United States, Colonial Times to 1970*, Washington, D.C., U.S. Department of Commerce.

Bureau of the Census (1975b) *Statistical Abstract of the United States*, Washington, D.C., U.S. Department of Commerce.

Bureau of the Census (1980) *Statistical Abstract of the United States*, Washington, D.C., U.S. Department of Commerce.

Bureau of the Census (1990) *Statistical Abstract of the United States*, Washington, D.C., U.S. Department of Commerce.

Bureau of the Census (1991) *Statistical Abstract of the United States*, Washington, D.C., U.S. Department of Commerce.

Bureau of the Census (1992) *Statistical Abstract of the United States*, Washington, D.C., U.S. Department of Commerce.

Bureau of the Census (1994) *Statistical Abstract of the United States*, Washington, D.C., U.S. Department of Commerce.

Bureau of the Census (1996) *Statistical Abstract of the United States*, Washington, D.C., U.S. Department of Commerce.

Bureau of Economic Analysis (various annual issues), *Survey of Current Business*, Washington, D.C., U.S. Department of Commerce.

Bureau of Labor Statistics (1989) *Consumer Expenditure Interview Survey: Quarterly Data, 1984–1987*, Bulletin No. 2332, Washington, D.C., U.S. Department of Labor.

Carson, C.S. (1987) "GNP: An Overview of Source Data and Estimating Methods," *Survey of Current Business*, Vol. 67, July, pp. 103–127.

Chaudhuri, S., and M. Ravallion (1994) "How Well Do Static Welfare Indicators Identify the Chronically Poor?" *Journal of Public Economics*, Vol. 53, No. 3, March, pp. 367–394.

Chiappori, P.A. (1988) "Rational Household Labor Supply," *Econometrica*, Vol. 56, pp. 63–89.

———(1992) "Collective Labor Supply and Welfare," *Journal of Political Economy*, Vol. 100, No. 3, June, pp. 437–467.

Chipman, J.S., and J. Moore (1971) "The Compensation Principle in Welfare Economics," in A. Zarley and J. Moore (eds.), *Papers in Quantitative Economics*, Lawrence: University Press of Kansas, pp. 1–77.

———and———(1973) "Aggregate Demand, Real National Income, and the Compensation Principle," *International Economic Review*, Vol. 14, No. 1, February, pp. 153–181.

———and———(1976) "The Scope of Consumer's Surplus Arguments," in A.M. Tang et al. (eds.), *Evolution, Welfare and Time in Economics: Essays in Honor of Nicholas Georgescu-Roegen*, Lexington: Heath-Lexington Books, pp. 69–123.

——and——(1980) "Compensating Variation, Consumer's Surplus, and Welfare," *American Economic Review*, Vol. 70, No. 5, December, pp. 933–949.

Christensen, L.R., and D.W. Jorgenson (1969) "The Measurement of U.S. Real Capital Input, 1929–1967," *Review of Income and Wealth*, Series 15, December, pp. 293–320.

——and——(1973) "The Measurement of U.S. Real Capital Input, 1929–1967," *Review of Income and Wealth*, Series 19, December, pp. 329–362.

Christensen, L., D. Jorgenson, and L. Lau (1975) "Transcendental Logarithmic Utility Functions," *American Economic Review*, Vol. 65, No. 3, June, pp. 367–383.

Citro, C.F., and R.T. Michael (1995) *Measuring Poverty: A New Approach*, Washington, D.C.: National Academy Press.

Cochrane, J. (1991) "A Simple Test of Consumption Insurance," *Journal of Political Economy*, Vol. 99, pp. 957–976.

Cooter, R., and P. Rappoport (1984) "Were the Ordinalists Wrong About Welfare Economics?" *Journal of Economic Literature*, Vol. 22, No. 2, June, pp. 507–530.

Coulter, F., F. Cowell, and S. Jenkins (1992) "Equivalence Scale Relativities and the Extent of Inequality and Poverty," *Economic Journal*, Vol. 102, September, pp. 1067–1082.

Cowell, F.A. (1977) *Measuring Inequality*, New York: Halsted Press.

——(1980) "On the Structure of Additive Inequality Measures," *Review of Economic Studies*, Vol. 47, pp. 521–531.

——and S. Jenkins (1995) "How Much Inequality Can We Explain? A Methodology and an Application to the United States," *Economic Journal*, Vol. 105, No. 429, March, pp. 421–430.

Cutler, D., and L. Katz (1991) "Macroeconomic Performance and the Disadvantaged," *Brookings Papers on Economic Activity*, No. 2, pp. 1–74.

Danziger, S., J. van der Gaag, M. Taussig, and E. Smolensky (1984) "The Direct Measurement of Welfare Levels: How Much Does It Cost to Make Ends Meet?" *Review of Economics and Statistics*, Vol. 66, No. 3, August, pp. 500–505.

Dasgupta, P., and D. Ray (1990) "Adapting to Undernutrition: The Clinical Evidence and Its Implications," in J. Dreze and A. Sen (eds.), *The Political Economy of Hunger*, Oxford: Oxford University Press.

Dasgupta, P., A. Sen, and D. Starrett (1973) "Notes on the Measurement of Inequality," *Journal of Economic Theory*, Vol. 6, No. 2, April, pp. 180–187.

Deaton, A. (1977) "Equity, Efficiency, and the Structure of Indirect Taxation," *Journal of Public Economics*, Vol. 8, No. 3, December, pp. 299–312.

——(1992) *Understanding Consumption*, Oxford: Oxford University Press.

——and J. Muellbauer (1980) *Economics and Consumer Behavior*, Cambridge: Cambridge University Press.

——and——(1986) "On Measuring Child Costs: With Applications to Poor Countries," *Journal of Political Economy*, Vol. 94, No. 4, August, pp. 720–744.

Deaton, A., and C. Paxson (1994) "Intertemporal Choice and Inequality," *Journal of Political Economy*, Vol. 104, No. 1, February, pp. 437–468.

Department of Agriculture (1964) "Family Food Plan, Revised 1964," *Family Economics Review*, October, pp. 11–21.

de Vos, K., and T. Garner (1991) "An Evaluation of Subjective Poverty Definitions: Comparing Results from the U.S. and the Netherlands," *Review of Income and Wealth*, Series 37, No. 3, September, pp. 267–285.

Diewert, W.E. (1973) "Afriat and Revealed Preference Theory," *Review of Economic Studies*, Vol. 40, pp. 419–425.

———(1974) "Intertemporal Consumer Theory and the Demand for Durables," *Econometrica*, Vol. 42, No. 3, May, pp. 497–516.

———(1976) "Exact and Superlative Index Numbers," *Journal of Econometrics*, Vol. 4, No. 2, May, pp. 115–145.

———(1981) "The Economic Theory of Index Numbers: A Survey," in A. Deaton (ed.), *Essays in the Theory and Measurement of Consumer Behavior*, Cambridge: Cambridge University Press, pp. 163–208.

———(ed.) (1990) *Price Level Measurement*, Amsterdam: North Holland.

———(1995) "Axiomatic and Economic Approaches to Elementary Price Indexes," National Bureau of Economic Research, Working Paper No. 5104, Cambridge, MA.

Duggan, J., R. Gillingham, and J. Greenlees (1995) "Housing Bias in the CPI and Its Effects on the Budget Deficit and the Social Security Trust Fund," unpublished manuscript.

Dupuit, J. (1844) "De la mesure de l'utilite des travaux publics," *Annales des Ponts et Chausees, Memoires et documents relatifs a l'art des constructions et au service de l'ingenieur*, Vol. 8, pp. 332–375.

Engel, E. (1895) "Die Lebenskosten Belgischer Arbeiter-Familien Fruher und Jetzt," *International Statistical Institute Bulletin*, Vol. 9, pp. 1–74.

Fisher, F.M. (1987) "Household Equivalence Scales and Interpersonal Comparisons," *Review of Economic Studies*, Vol. 54, pp. 519–524.

Fisher, F.M., and Z. Griliches (1995) "Aggregate Price Indices, New Goods and Generics," *Quarterly Journal of Economics*, Vol. 110, No. 1, February, pp. 229–244.

Fisher, I. (1922) *The Making of Index Numbers*, Boston: Houghton-Mifflin.

Fixler, D. (1993) "The Consumer Price Index: Underlying Concepts and Caveats," *Monthly Labor Review*, Vol. 116, No. 12, December, pp. 3–12.

Foster, J. (1984) "On Economic Poverty: A Survey of Aggregate Measures," in R.L. Basmann and G.F. Rhodes, Jr. (eds.), *Advances in Econometrics*, Vol. 3, Greenwich, CT: JAI Press, pp. 215–251.

———and A.F. Shorrocks (1988) "Poverty Orderings," *Econometrica*, Vol. 56, No. 1, January, pp. 173–177.

Foster, J., J. Greer, and E. Thorbecke (1984) "A Class of Decomposable Poverty Measures," *Econometrica*, Vol. 52, pp. 761–765.

Friedman, M. (1957) *A Theory of the Consumption Function*, Princeton, NJ: Princeton University Press.

Fuchs, V. (1967) "Redefining Poverty and Redistributing Income," *Public Interest*, Vol. 8, Summer, pp. 88–95.

Fullerton, D., and D. Rogers (1993) *Who Bears the Lifetime Tax Burden*, Washington, D.C.: Brookings Institution.

van der Gaag, J., and E. Smolensky (1982) "True Household Equivalence Scales and Characteristics of the Poor in the United States," *Review of Income and Wealth*, Vol. 28, No. 1, pp. 17–28.

Gieseman, R.W. (1978) "A Comparison of the 1972–1973 Consumer Expenditure Survey Results with Personal Consumption Expenditures in the National Income and Product Accounts," Bureau of Labor Statistics, January.

———(1987) "The Consumer Expenditure Survey: Quality Control by Comparative Analysis," *Monthly Labor Review*, March, pp. 8–14.

Gillingham, R., and W. Lane (1982) "Changing the Treatment of Shelter Costs for Homeowners in the CPI," *Monthly Labor Review*, Vol. 105, June, pp. 9–14.

Goedhart, T., V. Halberstadt, A. Kapteyn, and B. van Praag (1977) "The Poverty Line: Concept and Measurement," *Journal of Human Resources*, Vol. 12, Fall, pp. 503–520.

Gorman, W.M. (1953) "Community Preference Fields," *Econometrica*, Vol. 21, pp. 63–80.

———(1955) "The Intransitivity of Certain Criteria Used in Welfare Economics," *Oxford Economic Papers*, New Series 7, pp. 25–35.

———(1976) "Tricks with Utility Functions," in M. Artis and M. Nobay (eds.), *Essays in Economic Analysis*, Cambridge: Cambridge University Press, pp. 211–243.

———(1981) "Some Engel Curves," in A. Deaton (ed.), *Essays in the Theory and Measurement of Consumer Behavior*, Cambridge: Cambridge University Press.

Gronau, R. (1988) "Consumption Technology and the Intrafamily Distribution of Resources: Adult Equivalence Scales Reexamined," *Journal of Political Economy*, Vol. 96, pp. 1183–1205.

Haddad, L., and R. Kanbur (1990) "How Serious Is the Neglect of Intra-Household Inequality?" *Economic Journal*, Vol. 100, No. 3, September, pp. 866–881.

Hagemann, M. (1982) "The Variability of Inflation Rates across Household Types," *Journal of Money, Credit and Banking*, Vol. 14, No. 1, Part 1, November, pp. 494–510.

Hagenaars, A. (1986) *The Perception of Poverty*, Amsterdam: North Holland.

Hall, R.E., and F.S. Mishkin (1982) "The Sensitivity of Consumption to Transitory Income: Estimates from Panel Data on Households," *Econometrica*, Vol. 50, March, pp. 461–481.

Hamermesh, D.S. (1984) "Consumption During Retirement: The Missing Link in the Life Cycle," *Review of Economics and Statistics*, Vol. 66, No. 1, February, pp. 1–7.

Hammond, P.J. (1976) "Equity, Arrow's Conditions, and Rawls' Difference Principle," *Econometrica*, Vol. 44, No. 4, July, pp. 793–804.

Hausman, J.A. (1981) "Exact Consumer's Surplus and Deadweight Loss," *American Economic Review*, Vol. 71, No. 4, September, pp. 662–676.

Hausman, J., and W. Newey (1995) "Nonparametric Estimation of Exact Consumer's Surplus and Deadweight Loss," *Econometrica*, Vol. 63, pp. 1445–1476.

Haveman, R., M. Gabay, and J. Andreoni (1987) "Exact Consumer's Surplus and Deadweight Loss: A Correction," *American Economic Review*, Vol. 77, No. 3, June, pp. 494–495.

Hayashi, F. (1995) "Is the Japanese Extended Family Altruistically Linked?" *Journal of Political Economy*, Vol. 103, pp. 661–674.

Hicks, J.R. (1942) "Consumer's Surplus and Index Numbers," *Review of Economic Studies*, Vol. 9, No. 2, Summer, pp. 126–137.

Houthakker, H.S., and L.D. Taylor (1970) *Consumer Demand in the United States: Analyses and Projections*, 2nd ed., Cambridge: Harvard University Press.

Hulten, C.R., and F.C. Wykoff (1981a) "The Measurement of Economic Depreciation," in C.R. Hulten (ed.), *Depreciation, Inflation and the Taxation of Income from Capital*, Washington, D.C.: Urban Institute, pp. 81–132.

———and——— (1981b) "The Estimation of Economic Depreciation Using Vintage Asset Prices," *Journal of Econometrics*, Vol. 15, No. 3, April, pp. 367–396.

Hurd, M.D. (1990) "Research on the Elderly: Economic Status, Retirement and Consumption and Saving," *Journal of Economic Literature*, Vol. 28, No. 2, June, pp. 565–637.

Hurst, E., M. Luoh, and F. Stafford (1996) "Wealth Dynamics of American Families, 1984–1994," University of Michigan, unpublished manuscript.

Hurwicz, L., and H. Uzawa (1971) "On the Integrability of Demand Functions," in J. Chipman et al. (eds.), *Preferences, Utility and Demand*, New York: Harcourt, Brace, Jovanovich, pp. 114–148.

Jencks, C., and Edin, K. (1990) "The Real Welfare Problem," unpublished manuscript, Evanston, IL: Northwestern University.

Johnson, D.S. (1994) "Equivalence Scales and the Distribution of Well-being Across and Within Households," Bureau of Labor Statistics, August.

Johnson, D.S., and S. Shipp (1997) "Trends in Consumption Inequality in the United States," *Review of Income and Wealth*, Series 43, No. 2, June, pp. 133–152.

Jorgenson, D.W. (1990) "Aggregate Consumer Behavior and the Measurement of Social Welfare," *Econometrica*, Vol. 58, No. 5, September, pp. 1007–1040.

———and B.M. Fraumeni (1989) "The Accumulation of Human and Nonhuman Capital, 1948–1984," in R.E. Lipsey and H.S. Tice (eds.), *The Measurement of Saving, Investment and Wealth: Studies in Income and Wealth*, Vol. 52, Chicago: University of Chicago Press, pp. 227–282.

Jorgenson, D.W., and Z. Griliches (1971) "Divisia Index Numbers and Productivity Measurement," *Review of Income and Wealth*, Vol. 17, No. 2, June, pp. 227–229.

Jorgenson, D.W., L.J. Lau, and T.M. Stoker (1980) "Welfare Comparison and Exact Aggregation," *American Economic Review*, Vol. 70, No. 2, May, pp. 268–272.

———, ———, and ——— (1981) "Aggregate Consumer Behavior and Individual Welfare," in D. Currie, R. Noby, and D. Peel (eds.), *Macroeconomic Analysis*, London: Croom-Helm, pp. 35–61.

———, ———, and ——— (1982) "The Transcendental Logarithmic Model of Aggregate Consumer Behavior," in R.L. Basmann and G.F. Rhodes, Jr. (eds.), *Advances in Econometrics*, Vol. 1, Greenwich, CT: JAI Press, pp. 97–238.

Jorgenson, D.W., and D.T. Slesnick (1983) "Individual and Social Cost of Living Indexes," in W.E. Diewert and C. Montmarquette (eds.), *Price Level Measurement*, Ottawa: Statistics Canada, pp. 241–323.

——— and ——— (1984) "Aggregate Consumer Behavior and the Measurement of Inequality," *Review of Economic Studies*, Vol. 51(3), No. 166, July, pp. 369–392.

——— and ——— (1987) "Aggregate Consumer Behavior and Household Equivalence Scales," *Journal of Business and Economic Statistics*, Vol. 5, No. 2, April, pp. 219–232.

——— and ——— (1989) "Redistributional Policy and the Measurement of Poverty," in D.J. Slottje (ed.), *Research on Economic Inequality*, Greenwich, CT: JAI Press, Vol. 1, pp. 1–48.

Jorgenson, D.W., D.T. Slesnick, and P.J. Wilcoxen (1992) "Carbon Taxes and Economic Welfare," *Brookings Papers in Economic Activity: Microeconomics*, pp. 393–431.

Kaldor, N. (1939) "Welfare Propositions of Economics and Interpersonal Comparisons of Utility," *Economic Journal*, Vol. 49, September, pp. 549–552.

Kilpatrick, R.W. (1973) "The Income Elasticity of the Poverty Line," *Review of Economics and Statistics*, Vol. 55, August, pp. 327–332.

King, M.A. (1983) "Welfare Analysis of Tax Reforms Using Household Data," *Journal of Public Economics*, Vol. 21, No. 2, July, pp. 183–214.

Kirman, A.P. (1992) "Whom or What Does the Representative Individual Represent?" *Journal of Economic Perspectives*, Vol. 6, pp. 117–136.

Kokoski, M.F. (1987) "Problems in the Measurement of Cost-of-Living Indexes," *Journal of Business and Economic Statistics*, Vol. 5, No. 1, January, pp. 39–46.

——— (1993) "Quality Adjustment of Price Indexes," *Monthly Labor Review*, Vol. 116, No. 12, December, pp. 34–46.

Kolm, S.C. (1969) "The Optimal Production of Social Justice," in J. Margolis and H. Guitton (eds.), *Public Economics*, London: Macmillan, pp. 145–200.

——— (1976a) "Unequal Inequalities I," *Journal of Economic Theory*, Vol. 12, No. 3, June, pp. 416–442.

——— (1976b) "Unequal Inequalities II," *Journal of Economic Theory*, Vol. 13, No. 1, August, pp. 82–111.

Konus, A.A. (1939) "The Problem of the True Index of the Cost-of-Living," *Econometrica*, Vol. 7, No. 1, January, pp. 10–29.

Kuznets, S. (1946) *National Product Since 1869*, New York: National Bureau of Economic Research.

Lau, L.J. (1982) "A Note on the Fundamental Theorem of Exact Aggregation," *Economic Letters*, Vol. 9, pp. 119–126.

Lazear, E.P., and R.T. Michael (1980) "Family Size and the Distribution of Real Per Capita Income," *American Economic Review*, Vol. 70, No. 1, March, pp. 91–107.

———and———(1988) *Allocation of Income within the Household*, Chicago: Chicago University Press.

Levy, F. (1987) *Dollars and Dreams: The Changing American Income Distribution*, New York: Norton.

———and R.J. Murnane (1992) "U.S. Earnings Levels and Earnings Inequality: A Review of Recent Trends and Proposed Explanations," *Journal of Economic Literature*, Vol. 30, No. 3, September, pp. 1333–1381.

Lewbel, A. (1989) "Household Equivalence Scales and Welfare Comparisons," *Journal of Public Economics*, Vol. 39, No. 3, August, pp. 377–391.

———(1997) "Consumer Demand Systems and Household Equivalence Scales," in M.H. Pesaran and P. Schmidt (eds.), *Handbook of Applied Econometrics: Microeconomics*, Vol. 2, Oxford: Blackwell.

———and R. Weckstein (1995) "Equivalence Scales, Cost of Children and Wrongful Death Laws," *Journal of Income Distribution*, Vol. 4, No. 2.

Liegey, P. (1993) "Adjusting Apparel Differences in the CPI for Quality Differences," in M. Foss, M. Manser, and A. Young (eds.), *Price Measurements and Their Uses*, Chicago: Chicago University Press, pp. 209–226.

Lundberg, S. (1988) "Labor Supply of Husbands and Wives: A Simultaneous Equations Approach," *Review of Economics and Statistics*, Vol. 70, May, pp. 224–235.

Lundberg, S., and R.A. Pollak (1993) "Separate Spheres Bargaining and the Marriage Market," *Journal of Political Economy*, Volume 101, No. 6, December, pp. 988–1010.

———and———(1996) "Bargaining and Distribution in Marriage," *Journal of Economic Perspectives*, Vol. 10, No. 4, Fall, pp. 139–158.

Maasoumi, E. (1986) "The Measurement and Decomposition of Multi-Dimensional Inequality," *Econometrica*, Vol. 54, No. 4, July, pp. 991–997.

McElroy, M.B., and M.J. Horney (1981) "Nash-Bargained Household Decisions: Toward a Generalization of the Theory of Demand," *International Economic Review*, Vol. 22, June, pp. 333–349.

McKenzie, G.W. (1979) "Consumer's Surplus without Apology: Comment," *American Economic Review*, Vol. 69, No. 3, June, pp. 465–468.

———and I. Pearce (1976) "Exact Measures of Welfare and the Cost of Living," *Review of Economic Studies*, Vol. 43, No. 3, October, pp. 465–468.

McKenzie, L.W. (1956–57) "Demand Theory without a Utility Index," *Review of Economic Studies*, Vol. 24, pp. 185–189.

Mace, B. (1991) "Consumption Volatility: Borrowing Constraints or Full Insurance," *Journal of Political Economy*, Vol. 99, pp. 928–956.

Manser, M.E. (1987) "Cash-Equivalent Values from In-Kind Benefits: Estimates from a Complete Demand System Using Household Data," BLS Working Paper No. 173, December.

———and M. Brown (1980) "Marriage and Household Decision-Making: A Bargaining Analysis," *International Economic Review*, Vol. 21, February, pp. 333–349.

Manser, M.E., and R.J. McDonald (1988) "An Analysis of Substitution Bias in Measuring Inflation, 1959–1985," *Econometrica*, Vol. 56, No. 4, July, pp. 909–930.

Mariger, R.P. (1987) "A Life-cycle Consumption Model with Liquidity Constraints: Theory and Empirical Results," *Econometrica*, Vol. 55, No. 3, May, pp. 533–557.

Marshall, A. (1920) *Principles of Economics*, London: Macmillan.

Maskin, E. (1978) "A Theorem on Utilitarianism," *Review of Economic Studies*, Vol. 45, pp. 93–96.

Mayer, S.E., and C. Jencks (1989) "Poverty and the Distribution of Material Hardship," *Journal of Human Resources*, Vol. 24, No. 1, Winter, pp. 88–114.

———and——— (1992) "Recent Trends in Economic Inequality in the United States: Income vs. Expenditures vs. Material Well-Being," unpublished manuscript.

Michael, R.T. (1979) "Variation across Households in the Rate of Inflation," *Journal of Money, Credit and Banking*, Vol. 11, No. 1, February, pp. 32–46.

Moffitt, R. (1989) "Estimating the Value of an In-Kind Transfer: The Case of Food Stamps," *Econometrica*, Vol. 57, No. 2, March, pp. 385–410.

Morris, M.D. (1979) *Measuring the Condition of the World's Poor: The Physical Quality of Life Index*, New York: Pergamon Press.

Moulton, B.R. (1993) "Basic Components of the CPI: Estimation of Price Changes," *Monthly Labor Review*, Vol. 116, No. 12, December, pp. 13–24.

——— (1996) "Bias in the Consumer Price Index: What Is the Evidence?" *Journal of Economic Perspectives*, Vol. 10, No. 4, Fall, pp. 159–177.

———and K.E. Moses (1997) "Addressing the Quality Change Issue in the Consumer Price Index," *Brookings Papers on Economic Activity*, No. 1, pp. 305–349.

Muellbauer, J. (1974) "Prices and Inequality: The United Kingdom Experience," *Economic Journal*, Vol. 84, No. 333, March, pp. 32–55.

——— (1977) "Testing the Barten Model of Household Composition Effects and the Cost of Children," *Economic Journal*, Vol. 87, No. 347, September, pp. 460–487.

——— (1980) "The Estimation of the Prais-Houthakker Model of Equivalence Scales," *Econometrica*, Vol. 48, No. 1, January, pp. 153–176.

Murray, C.A. (1984) *Losing Ground: American Social Policy, 1950–1980*, New York: Basic Books.

Murray, M. (1994) "How Efficient Are Multiple In-Kind Transfers?" *Economic Inquiry*, Vol. 32, April, pp. 209–227.

Musgrave, J. (1979) "Durable Goods Owned by Consumers in the United States, 1925–77," *Survey of Current Business*, Vol. 59, No. 3, March, pp. 17–25.

Musgrave, R.A., and T. Thin (1948) "Income Tax Progression, 1929–48," *Journal of Political Economy*, Vol. 56, No. 4, December, pp. 498–514.

Nelson, J.A. (1988) "Household Economies of Scale in Consumption: Theory and Evidence," *Econometrica*, Vol. 56, No. 6, November, pp. 1301–1314.

—— (1989) "Individual Consumption within the Household: A Study of Expenditures on Clothing," *Journal of Consumer Affairs*, Vol. 23, Summer, pp. 21–44.

—— (1993) "Household Equivalence Scales: Theory versus Policy," *Journal of Labor Economics*, Vol. 11, No. 3, pp. 471–493.

—— (1994) "On Testing Full Insurance Using Consumer Expenditure Survey Data," *Journal of Political Economy*, Vol. 102, pp. 384–394.

Newbery, D.M. (1995) "The Distributional Impact of Price Changes in Hungary and the United Kingdom," *Economic Journal*, Vol. 105, No. 431, July, pp. 847–863.

Nicholson, J.L. (1976) "Appraisal of Different Methods of Estimating Equivalence Scales and Their Results," *Review of Income and Wealth*, Vol. 22, March, pp. 1–11.

Nordhaus, W., and J. Tobin (1972) "Is Growth Obsolete?" in *Measuring Growth: Fiftieth Anniversary Colloquium*, Vol. 5, New York: National Bureau of Economic Research.

Orshansky, M. (1965) "Counting the Poor: Another Look at the Poverty Profile," *Social Security Bulletin*, Vol. 28, No. 1, January, pp. 3–29.

—— (1966) "Recounting the Poor: A Five Year Review," *Social Security Bulletin*, Vol. 29, No. 4, April, pp. 20–37.

Paglin, M. (1975) "On the Measurement and Trend of Inequality: A Basic Revision," *American Economic Review*, Vol. 65, No. 4, September, pp. 598–609.

Pashardes, P. (1991) "Contemporaneous and Intertemporal Child Costs," *Journal of Public Economics*, Vol. 45, No. 2, July, pp. 191–213.

—— (1995) "Equivalence Scales in a Rank-3 Demand System," *Journal of Public Economics*, Vol. 58, pp. 143–158.

Pauly, M.V. (1986) "Taxation, Health Insurance and Market Failure in the Medical Economy," *Journal of Economic Literature*, Vol. 24, No. 2, June, pp. 629–675.

Pechman, J.A. (1985) *Who Paid the Taxes, 1966–1985*, Washington, D.C.: Brookings Institution.

Pollak, R.A. (1981) "The Social Cost of Living Index," *Journal of Public Economics*, Vol. 15, No. 3, June, pp. 311–336.

—— (1983a) "The Theory of the Cost-of-Living Index," in W.E. Diewert and C. Montmarquette (eds.), *Price Level Measurement*, Ottawa: Statistics Canada, pp. 241–323.

—— (1983b) "The Treatment of 'Quality' in the Cost-of-Living Index," *Journal of Public Economics*, Vol. 20, No. 1, February, pp. 25–53.

—— (1991) "Welfare Comparisons and Situation Comparisons," *Journal of Econometrics*, Vol. 50, No. 1/2, October/November, pp. 31–48.

—— and T.J. Wales (1979) "Welfare Comparisons and Equivalent Scales," *American Economic Review*, Vol. 69, No. 2, May, pp. 216–221.

—— and —— (1981) "Demographic Variables in Demand Analysis," *Econometrica*, Vol. 49, No. 6, November, pp. 1533–1552.

Poterba, J.M. (1989) "Lifetime Incidence and the Distributional Burden of Excise Taxes," *American Economic Review*, Vol. 79, No. 2, May, pp. 325–330.

—— (1991) "Is the Gasoline Tax Regressive?" in D. Bradford (ed.), *Tax Policy and the Economy*, Vol. 5, Cambridge, MA: MIT Press.

van Praag, B. (1971) "The Welfare Function of Income in Belgium: An Empirical Investigation," *European Economic Review*, Vol. 2, pp. 337–369.

—— (1994) "Ordinal and Cardinal Utility: An Integration of the Two Dimensions of the Welfare Concept," in R. Blundell, I. Preston, and I. Walker (eds.), *The Measurement of Household Welfare*, Cambridge: Cambridge University Press, pp. 86–110.

van Praag, B., T. Goedhart, and A. Kapteyn (1980) "The Poverty Line: A Pilot Survey in Europe," *Review of Economics and Statistics*, Vol. 62, No. 3, August, pp. 461–465.

van Praag, B., J. Spit, and H. van der Stadt (1982) "A Comparison between the Food Poverty Line and the Leyden Poverty Line," *Review of Economics and Statistics*, Vol. 64, No. 4, November, pp. 691–694.

Prais, S.J. (1959) "Whose Cost of Living?" *Review of Economic Studies*, Vol. 26, pp. 126–134.

—— and H.S. Houthakker (1955) *The Analysis of Family Budgets*, Cambridge: Cambridge University Press.

Pyatt, G. (1987) "Measuring Welfare, Poverty and Inequality," *Economic Journal*, Vol. 97, June, pp. 459–467.

Ravallion, M. (1994) *Poverty Comparisons: Fundamentals in Pure and Applied Economics*, Vol. 56, New York: Harwood Academic Press.

—— and S. Chaudhuri (1997) "Risk and Insurance in Village India: Comment," *Econometrica*, Vol. 65, No. 1, January, pp. 171–184.

Rawls, J. (1971) *A Theory of Justice*, Cambridge, MA: Harvard University Press.

Ray, R. (1983) "Measuring the Costs of Children: An Alternative Approach," *Journal of Public Economics*, Vol. 22, pp. 89–102.

Reinsdorf, M. (1993) "The Effect of Outlet Price Differentials on the U.S. Consumer Price Index," in M. Foss, M. Manser, and A. Young (eds.), *Price Measurements and Their Uses*, Chicago: Chicago University Press, pp. 227–254.

Robbins, L. (1932) *An Essay on the Nature and Significance of Economic Science*, London: Macmillan.

—— (1938) "Interpersonal Comparisons of Utility: A Comment," *Economic Journal*, Vol. 43, December, pp. 635–641.

Roberts, K.W.S. (1980a) "Price Independent Welfare Prescriptions," *Journal of Public Economics*, Vol. 13, June, pp. 277–298.

—— (1980b) "Possibility Theorems with Interpersonally Comparable Welfare Levels," *Review of Economic Studies*, Vol. 47, No. 147, January, pp. 409–420.

—— (1980c) "Interpersonal Comparability and Social Choice Theory," *Review of Economic Studies*, Vol. 47, No. 147, January, pp. 421–439.

——(1980d) "Social Choice Theory: The Single-profile and Multi-profile Approaches," *Review of Economic Studies*, Vol. 47, No. 147, January, pp. 441–450.

Rosen, H. (1978) "The Measurement of Excess Burden with Explicit Utility Functions," *Journal of Political Economy*, Vol. 86, No. 2, April, pp. S121–S136.

Rothbarth, E. (1943) "Note on a Method of Determining Equivalent Income for Families of Different Composition," in C. Madge (ed.), *War-time Pattern of Saving and Spending*, Cambridge: Cambridge University Press, Appendix 4, pp. 123–130.

Ruggles, P. (1990) *Drawing the Line: Alternative Poverty Measures and their Implications for Public Policy*, Washington: Urban Institute Press.

Samuelson, P.A. (1947) *Foundations of Economic Analysis*, Cambridge, MA: Harvard University Press.

——(1956) "Social Indifference Curves," *Quarterly Journal of Economics*, Vol. 70, No. 1, February, pp. 1–22.

——(1974) "Complementarity – An Essay on the 40th Anniversary of the Hicks-Allen Revolution in Demand Theory," *Journal of Economic Literature*, Vol. 12, pp. 1255–1289.

Sawhill, I.V. (1988) "Poverty in the U.S.: Why Is It So Persistent?" *Journal of Economic Literature*, Vol. 26, No. 3, September, pp. 1073–1119.

Schwab, R. (1985) "The Benefits of In-Kind Government Programs," *Journal of Public Economics*, Vol. 27, pp. 195–210.

Sen, A.K. (1970) *Collective Choice and Social Welfare*, Edinburgh: Oliver and Boyd; San Francisco, Holden Day.

——(1973) *On Economic Inequality*, Oxford: Clarendon Press.

——(1976) "Poverty: An Ordinal Approach to Measurement," *Econometrica*, Vol. 46, pp. 437–446.

——(1977) "On Weights and Measures: Informational Constraints in Social Welfare Analysis," *Econometrica*, Vol. 45, No. 7, October, pp. 219–231.

——(1983) "Poor, Relatively Speaking," *Oxford Economic Papers*, Vol. 35, pp. 153–169.

——(1984a) "The Living Standard," *Oxford Economic Papers*, Vol. 36, Supplement, pp. 74–90.

——(1984b) "Family and Food: Sex Bias in Poverty," in *Resources, Values and Development*, Oxford: Basil Blackwell, pp. 346–368.

——(1985) *Commodities and Capabilities*, Amsterdam: North Holland.

——(1987) *The Standard of Living*, Cambridge: Cambridge University Press.

——(1992) *Inequality Reexamined*, Cambridge, MA: Harvard University Press.

——(1995) "Rationality and Social Choice," *American Economic Review*, Vol. 85, No. 1, March, pp. 1–24.

Shorrocks, A.F. (1980) "The Class of Additively Decomposable Inequality Measures," *Econometrica*, Vol. 48, pp. 613–625.

——(1983) "Ranking Income Distributions," *Economica*, Vol. 50, No. 197, February, pp. 3–17.

———(1984) "Inequality Decomposition by Population Subgroup," *Econometrica*, Vol. 52, pp. 1369–1385.

———and J. Foster (1987) "Transfer Sensitive Inequality Measures," *Review of Economic Studies*, Vol. 54, pp. 485–497.

Slesnick, D.T. (1991a) "Aggregate Deadweight Loss and Money Metric Social Welfare," *International Economic Review*, Vol. 32, No. 1, February, pp. 123–146.

———(1991b) "Normative Index Numbers," *Journal of Econometrics*, Vol. 50, Nos. 1/2, October/November, pp. 107–130.

———(1991c) "The Standard of Living in the United States," *Review of Income and Wealth*, Series 37, No. 4, December, pp. 363–386.

———(1992) "Aggregate Consumption and Saving in the Postwar United States," *Review of Economics and Statistics*, Vol. 74, No. 4, November, pp. 585–597.

———(1993) "Gaining Ground: Poverty in the Postwar United States," *Journal of Political Economy*, Vol. 101, No. 1, February, pp. 1–38.

———(1994) "Consumption, Needs and Inequality," *International Economic Review*, Vol. 35, No. 3. August, pp. 677–703.

———(1996) "Consumption and Poverty: How Effective Are In-Kind Transfers?" *Economic Journal*, Vol. 106, No. 439, November, pp. 1527–1545.

———(1998a) "Are Our Data Relevant to the Theory? The Case of Aggregate Consumption," *Journal of Business and Economic Statistics*, Vol. 16, No. 1, January, pp. 52–61.

———(1998b) "Empirical Approaches to the Measurement of Welfare," *Journal of Economic Literature*, Vol. 36, No. 4, December, pp. 2108–2165.

Smeeding, T. (1982) *Alternative Methods for Valuing Selected In-Kind Transfer Benefits and Measuring Their Effect on Poverty*, Technical Paper No. 50, Washington, D.C.: Bureau of the Census.

Stoker, T. (1993) "Empirical Approaches to the Problem of Aggregation over Individuals," *Journal of Economic Literature*, Vol. 31, No. 4, December, pp. 1827–1874.

Stone, J.R.N. (1954) *The Measurement of Consumers' Expenditures and Behaviour in the United Kingdom*, Cambridge: Cambridge University Press.

Theil, H. (1967) *Economics and Information Theory*, Amsterdam: North Holland.

Thomas, D. (1990) "Intra-Household Resource Allocation: An Inferential Approach," *Journal of Human Resources*, Vol. 25, No. 4, Fall, pp. 635–664.

———(1994) "Like Father, Like Son: Like Mother, Like Daughter: Parental Resources and Child Height," *Journal of Human Resources*, Vol. 29, No. 4, Fall, pp. 950–988.

Tornqvist, L. (1936) "The Bank of Finland's Consumption Price Index," *Bank of Finland Monthly Review*, Vol. 10, pp. 1–8.

Townsend, P. (1985) "A Sociological Approach to the Measurement of Poverty: A Rejoinder to Professor Amartya Sen," *Oxford Economic Papers*, Vol. 37, No. 4, December, pp. 659–668.

Townsend, R.M. (1994) "Risk and Insurance in Village India," *Econometrica*, Vol. 62, No. 3, May, pp. 539–591.

Varian, H.R. (1982) "The Nonparametric Approach to Demand Analysis," *Econometrica*, Vol. 50, pp. 945–973.

————(1992) *Microeconomic Analysis* (3rd ed.), New York: W.W. Norton.

Vartia, Y. (1983) "Efficient Methods of Measuring Welfare Changes and Compensated Income in Terms of Ordinary Demand Functions," *Econometrica*, Vol. 51, pp. 79–88.

Vaughn, R.N. (1987) "Welfare Approaches to the Measurement of Poverty," *Economic Journal*, Vol. 97, pp. 160–170.

Watts, H. (1967) "The Iso-Prop Index: An Approach to the Determination of Differential Poverty Income Thresholds," *Journal of Human Resources*, Vol. 2, No. 1, pp. 3–18.

Wilcox, D.W. (1992) "The Construction of U.S. Consumption Data: Some Facts and Their Implications for Empirical Work," *American Economic Review*, Vol. 82, No. 4, September, pp. 922–941.

Willig, R.E. (1976) "Consumer's Surplus without Apology," *American Economic Review*, Vol. 66, pp. 589–597.

Wilson, J.F., J.L. Freund, F.O. Yohn, and W. Lederer (1989) "Measuring Household Saving: Recent Experience from the Flow-of-Funds Perspective," in R.E. Lipsey and H.S. Tice (eds.), *The Measurement of Saving, Investment and Wealth*, Chicago: University of Chicago Press, pp. 101–145.

Wolff, E.N. (1994) "Trends in Household Wealth in the United States, 1962–83, 1983–89," *Review of Income and Wealth*, Series 40, No. 2, June, pp. 143–174.

Zeldes, S.P. (1989) "Consumption and Liquidity Constraints: An Empirical Investigation," *Journal of Political Economy*, Vol. 97, No. 2, pp. 305–346.

Index

Afriat, S. N., 75
Aizcorbe, A. M., 69
Apps, P. F., 33
Arrow, K. J., 25, 39
Atkinson, A. B., 125–6, 160n7, 208
Auersberg, M., 146n25

Balk, B. M., 76, 80
Banks, J., 135n16
Barro, R. J., 12n10
Barten, A. P., 95, 120, 202
Barten equivalence scale, 95–9, 202
Becker, G. S., 32
Bishop, Y. M., 211
Blackorby, C., 22n28,n29, 24, 38, 127,
    146n25, 160, 202
Blundell, R., 13n15, 121n25
Boskin, M., 68n2, 69, 71, 74n13
Boskin Commission report, 67–8,
    191
Bosworth, B., 58n28, 142n20
Bourguignon, F., 33
Braithwait, S. D., 69
Branch, E. R., 52n21
Browning, M., 33, 119
Buhmann, B., 134, 135n16
Burtless, G., 58n28, 142n20

Census Bureau
    definition of poverty, 160–2
    equivalence scale, 90–1
    poverty statistics of, 3, 156, 196

reports of family income
    inequality, 2, 194–5
CEX. *See* Consumer Expenditure
    Survey (CEX)
Chaudhuri, S., 13n15
Chiappori, P. A., 33
Chipman, J. S., 25
Christensen, L. R., 65
compensation principles
    Kaldor-Hicks-Samuelson criterion,
    24–5
    Scitovsky criterion, 24
consumer durables
    aggregate expenditure share of
    PCE, 55–6
    average expenditure share in 1995
    CEX, 57–8
    service flows, 66
    share of expenditure of
    consumption poor, 173–4
    share of expenditure of income
    poor, 171–2
    treatment in CPI, 69–70
Consumer Expenditure Survey
    (CEX), 45, 48–52
    consumer units in, 140
    durables service flows, 66
    expenditure shares in 1995, 56–
    8
    income data of, 139–42
    in measurement of inequality,
    127–30

231

poverty indexes
axiomatic basis for (Sen), 158–9
Foster-Greer-Thorbeck, 159, 164–5
head count ratio, 159
as measures of loss in social
welfare, 160
poverty line
Census Bureau adjustment of,
161–6
consumption-to income ratio at,
168–9
cost-of-living indexes to adjust, 67
relative, 157–8
Ruggles proposal to adjust, 176
sensitivity of poverty to, 176–7
subjective thresholds, 158
poverty rate
using CEX and PCE-calibrated
CEX, 177–9
Census Bureau estimates, 166–8,
196
consumption-based estimates, 7,
157, 164, 170–5, 196
estimation of official, 160–6
female-headed households, 186–8
income- and consumption-based
measures compared, 166–75
regional, 183–5
sensitivity to different equivalence
scales, 180–2
sensitivity to price changes, 179–
80
tabulation using per equivalent
consumption, 182–8
Prais, S. J., 76–7, 120
Prais-Houthakker equivalence scale,
96n13, 120
Preston, I., 13n15
price changes
cost-of-living indexes to measure
effect of, 16–18, 21
group cost-of-living indexes, 75–8
in national price indexes, 72–85
resulting from quality changes,
70–4
in subgroups of population, 78–9
price indexes
defined for groups, 41, 87
defined for households, 16–18
Laspeyres, 86

PCE price index, 72, 77–80, 166–7
Tornqvist, 72, 80–1, 86
See also Consumer Price Index
(CPI)
prices
effect of changes on level of
inequality, 132–3
poverty rate sensitivity to, 179–
80
real prices (1946–95), 79–80
Pyatt, G., 160

Rainwater, L., 134, 135n16
Ravallion, M., 13n15, 160n7
Rawls, John, 26, 39–40
Reinsdorf, M., 69
Roberts, K. W. S., 27, 38, 40
Ruggles, P., 163n11, 176

Sabelhaus, J., 58n28, 142n20
Samuelson, P. A., 32
Savage, E. J., 33
saving
CEX data (1961, 1995), 58–9
as consumption smoothing, 145–6
saving/dissaving
among consumption poor, 174–5
distribution (1961–95), 144–6, 170–
5
among income poor, 171–3
Schmaus, G., 134, 135n16
Schwab, R., 44
Sen, A., 26, 29, 33, 157n2, 158–60
Shorrocks, A. F., 124n3, 160n7
Slesnick, D. T., 38, 76, 80, 96, 107,
128n11, 160, 163n11, 179n19,
202n2
Smeeding, T., 44n5, 134, 135n16,
179n19
Smolensky, E., 188n21
social choice theory
in welfare analysis, 24–8, 35–41
social cost-of-living index. *See* cost-of-
living indexes
social welfare
converted to monetary
equivalents, 40, 206
cost-of-living indexes in
measurement of, 6, 67
income-based statistics, 4